Magnanimity and Statesmanship

Magnanimity and Statesmanship

Edited by Carson Holloway

LEXINGTON BOOKS

A division of
ROWMAN & LITTLEFIELD PUBLISHERS, INC.
Lanham • Boulder • New York • Toronto • Plymouth, UK

LEXINGTON BOOKS

A division of Rowman & Littlefield Publishers, Inc.
A wholly owned subsidary of The Rowman & Littlefield Publishing Group, Inc.
4501 Forbes Boulevard, Suite 200
Lanham, MD 20706

Estover Road
Plymouth PL6 7PY
United Kingdom

British Library Cataloguing in Publication Information Available

Library of Congress Cataloging-in-Publication Data

Magnanimity and statesmanship / edited by Carson Holloway.
    p. cm.
 Includes index.
 ISBN-13: 978-0-7391-1741-5 (cloth : alk. paper)
 ISBN-10: 0-7391-1741-6 (cloth : alk. paper)
 1. Political leadership. 2. Political science—Philosophy. I. Holloway, Carson, 1969–
JC330.3.M24 2008
 320.01—dc22
                                          2007040137

Printed in the United States of America

♾™ The paper used in this publication meets the minimum requirements of American
National Standard for Information Sciences—Permanence of Paper for Printed Library
Materials, ANSI/NISO Z39.48-1992.

For Thomas K. Lindsay, teacher and friend

Contents

Acknowledgments

This book could not have been produced without the help of a number of people and institutions to whom I am deeply grateful.

First, I would like to thank the contributors for their willingness to participate and for producing such fine and thoughtful essays. I am also grateful to Lexington Books for publishing our work, and especially to Lexington's Joseph Parry for his part in helping to bring the project to completion. In addition, I owe a debt of thanks to Mary Dunn, UNO's Political Science Department secretary, for her help in preparing the manuscript.

The idea for this book was first conceived in the spring of 2005. I am thankful to Matthew Franck and Kenneth Deutsch for listening to me pitch the idea and giving me some advice on where to begin. I was able to move the project forward while I was a fellow in the James Madison Program in American Ideals and Institutions at Princeton University during the 2005–2006 academic year. I am grateful to the Madison Program and especially to its director, Professor Robert P. George, for supporting my work. In addition, the Association for the Study of Free Institutions provided generous support for the production of the book, for which I am deeply grateful to its president, Bradford P. Wilson, and its board.

Many thanks are also due to my family—and especially my wife, Shari—for their constant encouragement. Finally, I wish to express my gratitude to Thomas K. Lindsay, to whom this volume is dedicated, for being my first and finest teacher of Aristotelian magnanimity, by both precept and example.

1

Introduction

Carson Holloway

According to Aristotle's canonical account in the *Nicomachean Ethics*, the virtue of magnanimity, or greatness of soul, manifests itself in thinking oneself worthy of the greatest honors while in truth being worthy of them. Thus understood, magnanimity is intimately related to political leadership at the highest level, that is, to statesmanship. The greatest honor a community can bestow is surely its highest political office, for by investing a citizen with its supreme authority, the community also entrusts him with its most precious interests. It judges him to possess the virtues of mind and character necessary to be the guardian of the whole community's well-being. The community thus affirms his goodness, and even his extraordinary goodness. It honors him. Magnanimity, then, is the noble self-confidence of the man who knows that he has the moral and intellectual qualities required to execute the duties of the highest political office in an excellent manner. Put another way, the magnanimous man is capable of, and knows he is capable of, statesmanship.

The purpose of this volume is to deepen our understanding of magnanimity and statesmanship by exploring these themes in the thought and careers of a number of political philosophers and philosophic statesmen from various periods in the history of political thought. Such an undertaking, however, is subject to the following objection: how can magnanimity be relevant to the world of modern politics? Indeed, magnanimity would appear to be incompatible with modernity, for two reasons. In the first place, modernity is committed to an egalitarianism with which the idea of magnanimity seems to be at odds. The democratic societies of the modern world are largely predicated on a belief in the fundamental equality of all human beings. In contrast, the very idea of magnanimity seems to be inseparable from an aristocratic affirmation of inequality: the magnanimous man is better than his fellow citizens and knows it. Thus Aristotle even speaks openly of the magnanimous man's contempt for others. One might seek to reconcile magnanimity with modernity by noting that the latter, at least in its more moderate and therefore more enduring forms, does not affirm the absolute equality of men and therefore may be compatible with the recognition of superiority inherent in magnanimity. Even this qualification, however, seems to leave a fundamental tension. After all, the fundamental equality to which the more moderate strains of modernity limit themselves is a political equality: all men are created equal at least in the sense that no one can claim a right to rule another without the latter's consent. Yet magnanimity seems to flout even this limited claim of equality, for the magnanimous man claims to be more worthy to rule than others, claims to *deserve* to rule, regardless of whether his inferiors concede his worthiness or not.

In the second place, modern political life is informed by a limited conception of the aims of politics that seems to leave no place for the magnanimous man. For Aristotle, the ultimate aim of the *polis* was nothing less than human excellence. The political community, he claims, is ultimately a partnership in noble actions, and hence its highest concern is the cultivation of the virtues through which human nobility is manifested. It is in light of this elevated understanding of politics that the magnanimous man's claim to leadership makes sense. The great-souled man, Aristotle contends, is worthy of great honor only because he achieves greatness in all the virtues. It is reasonable that an association the purpose of which is to cultivate virtue will be led by the most virtuous member. Modern politics, however, has been influenced by modern political philosophy, which sought to make a break from the Aristotelian understanding of political life. Specifically, the modern political philosophers sought to lower the aims, or perhaps narrow the scope, of politics. For them, the political community should strive not so much to cultivate noble virtue as to secure the conditions of comfortable self-preservation. Government should not presume to direct man to his highest end, but merely protect his rights, leaving each to pursue such ends as seem good to him, so long as he does not threaten the rights of others. Such a politics seems to require less the noble and virtuous statesman than the competent and even-handed administrator. Of course, to the extent that we admire the magnanimous man's greatness, we might be tempted to regret or even disdain the modern diminution of politics that tends to exclude him. We might think that he could properly react to modernity in the olympian spirit of the fictional silent movie actress Norma Desmond of Billy Wilder's *Sunset Boulevard*: When someone remarks that she "used to be big," she responds: "I *am* big; it's the *pictures* that got small." Similarly, to those who suggest that modern politics has rendered his supposed greatness outmoded, the magnanimous man might say, "I *am* great; it's the *regimes* that have become petty." Regardless of whether we approve or disapprove of the modern shrinking of politics, however, we must admit that it has occurred and that the magnanimous man's greatness accordingly no longer seems to fit.

Despite these tensions, however, a case can be made for magnanimity's relevance even to modern politics, and hence that this book is worthy of the modern reader's attention. While modernity is no doubt committed to a kind of egalitarianism, a thirst for greatness nevertheless continues to influence our politics. This is certainly true on the part of ordinary citizens, who seem to long for political leaders who are a cut above the ordinary, a longing that is revealed in the reliable popularity of respectful, and sometimes even reverential, biographies of past statesmen, and particularly of the leading figures of the Founding generation. Indeed, voters often betray an implicit respect even for one of the magnanimous man's least democratic traits: his serene confidence in the rightness of his moral and political judgments, even when these fly in the face of common opinion. For while it may succeed in winning subsequent elections, poll-driven governance, when revealed as such, invariably provokes the contempt of voters themselves. But by disdaining pandering, citizens reveal a secret admiration for the statesman who leads according to his own convictions, regardless of public opinion. For their part, our officeholders, and especially those who hold or seek the highest offices, clearly aspire to a kind of greatness. They seek not merely to be administrators but statesmen. Hence their presentation of themselves as possessing some "vision" by which they will be able to lead the people to a more comprehensive and just understanding of the common good.

Moreover, magnanimity remains relevant to modern politics not only subjectively, in terms of the desires of citizens and statesmen, but also objectively, in terms of the real needs of modern societies. For despite the effort to limit politics to prosaic ends that seem not to require virtuous statesmanship, our political communities continue to encounter challenges that can only be addressed through a leadership that displays more than merely ordinary moral and intellectual capacities. This is most evident in the realm of foreign policy. The attacks of September 11, 2001, and the ensuing American war on terror, including the war in Iraq, have reminded us that, regardless of the hopes or expectations dominant at the end of the twentieth century, international politics has not yet evolved into the peaceful administration of global commerce. It to some extent remains a zone of deadly conflict among actors driven by differences of ethnicity, national interest, religious ideals, and political ideology. The successful navigation of these dangerous waters requires governments to balance various goods, all undeniably important yet in tension with each other. Thus our political leaders must seek to protect domestic security while also respecting civil liberties, to use force in defense of the nation while also according humane treatment to enemy combatants, and to articulate and act upon our political and moral principles yet without letting our foreign policy turn into an ideological crusade that might harm the nation's material interests. The prudent pursuit of these diverse goods calls for an uncommon intellectual subtlety and moral firmness, calls, in fact, for what Aristotle would call virtue or excellence: the excellence of the magnanimous statesman who wisely discerns, and courageously safeguards, the community's enduring interests despite the gusts of an impassioned public opinion.

Furthermore, even the domestic politics of modern societies continue to demand magnanimous statesmanship. As we suggested earlier, modern societies have tried to insulate politics from moral controversy by organizing political communities around the pursuit of noncontroversial goals like the security of equal rights and the fostering of comfortable self-preservation. Despite such intentions, however, the development of societies so constructed produces moral challenges that call for magnanimous statesmanship. Modernity liberates, and seeks to harness with a view to the common good, an individual acquisitiveness that pursues satisfaction in part through technological innovation. Thus the progress of technology is characteristic of modern societies. Technological development, however, though well-intentioned and often to the good, may, by generating unprecedented capacities, confront society with grave moral challenges. This arguably has been the result of advanced biomedical techniques, which sometimes call into question our accustomed understanding of how human beings are born, live, and die, and by extension perhaps render us uncertain of what it means to live a human life. Such technologies create moral dilemmas by juxtaposing the promise of great goods with the possibility of grave evils. And these dilemmas cannot be negotiated reasonably and fittingly only on the basis of the spontaneous surges of popular hope and fear that such technologies foster. Rather, the moral challenges created by technology seem to call for a public opinion informed by the arguments and leadership of citizens of rare moral refinement and fortitude.

Modern societies are also characterized by another kind of progress, the progress of equality. This progress arises, as Tocqueville observes, from the democratic man's appetite for greater and greater equality of conditions. In an aristocracy, he contends, the most extreme inequalities pass unremarked, because the society itself is organized on inegalitarian principles, and accordingly great differences in power, wealth, and status are taken to be the norm. Once democracy arises and conditions are generally equalized, however, every remaining inequality begins to catch the eye and offend the spirit. As Tocqueville also notes, however, the continual and unchecked advance of equality is by no means always consistent with justice or with a society's greatness. Every new demand for greater equality is supported by a powerful democratic desire, yet is possibly dangerous to other values, less cherished by democratic citizens yet equally necessary to a decent and stable society. Thus modern democracy needs statesmen with the magnanimous man's ability to transcend the common passions of common citizens, who can lead public opinion prudently by subjecting it to critical examination and, when appropriate, even resisting it.

If magnanimity remains relevant to modern politics, then it is the task of contemporary political science to explore it and seek to understand it. If modern societies continue to need magnanimous statesmanship, then it is the duty of a public spirited scholarship of politics to help the patriotic citizen to recognize and reward, and the potential statesman to understand and aspire to, true magnanimity. The present volume seeks to advance these aims.

The remaining chapters—each authored by a different scholar or pair of scholars, and each addressed to a particular political philosopher or statesman—are grouped into three parts. Part I examines the role of magnanimity and statesmanship in the thought of three important representatives of classical and Christian political philosophy. In chapter 2, I take up a paradox contained in the first—and still the most celebrated—account of magnanimity or greatness of soul, that found in Book IV of Aristotle's *Nicomachean Ethics*. On the one hand, Aristotle's account suggests that the magnanimous man will be the statesman *par excellence*. After all, his greatness in all the virtues generally renders him excellent precisely in those things for which the political community exists, and more specifically implies the possession of prudence, which Aristotle indicates is the virtue of the statesman. On the other hand, Aristotle identifies two traits of the magnanimous man that seem incompatible with excellent statesmanship. The magnanimous man is said to have contempt for ordinary people, an attitude that seems troubling in one who is to be the guardian of their well-being. In addition, Aristotle indicates that the great-souled man finds nothing great, which makes us wonder what can motivate him to political service. The chapter concludes by indicating how such traits might, contrary to our initial expectations, lend support to the magnanimous man's capacity for great statesmanship.

In chapter 3, James Fetter and Walter Nicgorski examine Cicero's treatment of magnanimity, noting how it both echoes Aristotle's account while also modifying it and carrying it into realms that Aristotle did not explicitly explore. In particular, they point out that, unlike Aristotle, Cicero gives sustained attention to the problem posed by a false magnanimity. Cicero suggests that popular opinion tends mistakenly to equate magnanimity with military glory, or with the spirit that wins honor by courageously confronting and surmounting the dangers of war. Such an imperfect magnanimity—one that is preoccupied merely with the honor to be won through impressive achievements and that is therefore indifferent to justice—is not only not a virtue but in fact a grave danger to the political community. For men driven by an unprincipled thirst for glory will use foul means to win absolute power within the city and will actively seek war, regardless of justice, in order to create a theater in which they can win fame. As a contemporary of Julius Caesar, Cicero knew all too well that the perils of a longing for greatness untempered by justice were more than merely theoretical. Cicero therefore undertakes to refine the desire for glory with a concern for justice and the common good. At the same time, however, as Fetter and Nicgorski note, Cicero remained sensitive to a very different threat to magnanimity and to the common good. While some men may be too enamored of the self-sufficiency to be won through astonishing public deeds, others may turn from political activity altogether in the pursuit of the self-sufficiency of philosophic leisure, thus depriving the city of the services of able and good men. Cicero's teaching therefore tries to strike a delicate balance, emphasizing both magnanimity's necessary connection to justice as well as its dedication to large or arduous public actions.

Chapter 4 concludes part I with Kenneth Deutsch's examination of Thomas Aquinas' effort to open a place for magnanimity within Christian ethics. It is sometimes held, Deutsch notes, that the apparent lack of great statesmanship in the modern world is due to the moral influence of Christianity. Christianity's emphasis on humility, it would seem, is at odds with magnanimity's open claims to greatness. For Aquinas, however, these two different and seemingly incompatible virtues can be harmonized when they are seen as manifestations of one quality, truthfulness, directed at different objects. That is, for Thomas a man can magnanimously recognize his superiority to others, because of the gifts that he possesses from God, while also humbly recognizing his inferiority to God, because of his own deficiencies. Indeed, Deutsch contends, the true magnanimous man will display not only Christian humility but also Christian charity, doing great deeds out of a desire to serve others. Moreover, the magnanimous statesman's charity sustains in him a principled prudence, for it makes him want to lead his fellow citizens to the good, yet also gives him a sympathy for human weakness and hence a mature tolerance for the limits it imposes on politics.

Part II takes up the role of magnanimity in modern political philosophy. In chapter 5, Geoffrey Vaughan considers the place of magnanimity and statesmanship in the thought of Thomas Hobbes. As we noted before, magnanimity seems to be in tension with the modern world. Not surprisingly, then, it does not occupy a prominent place in the thought of this leading intellectual architect of modernity. As Vaughan notes, Hobbes scarcely uses the terms magnanimity or statesmanship in the *Leviathan* or his other important writings. Nevertheless, Hobbes was not, Vaughan contends, indifferent to the virtues of great men or the good that they might do for society. Hobbes rather concluded that such virtues, whatever their splendor, were too rare, as well as too easily counterfeited, to be relied upon as the basis for civil society. He accordingly seeks to replace the classical and medieval reliance on virtuous statesmanship with a science of politics that assumes that most men are animated by individual self-interest and can therefore only be broken to the demands of civil society by fear of the visible power of an absolute sovereign. Magnanimity, moreover, turns out to be not only not essential to Hobbes's project but in fact problematic for it. As Vaughan notes, for Hobbes peace can only be maintained by the sovereign's monopoly on absolute power. Magnanimity's indifference to power, therefore, is no useful trait in a sovereign, who must jealously guard his power. Nor is magnanimity useful in subjects. For the magnanimous man's unusual detachment from external goods, manifested in his disdain for "little helps and hindrances," will likely be taken as a sign of his power. Yet, for Hobbes, a reputation for power is power, because it attracts the allegiance of those who need protection. But this in turn threatens the sovereign's monopoly on power and thus endangers the peace. For Hobbes, then, magnanimity is neither to be expected nor desired in either sovereigns or subjects.

The uncertain status of magnanimity within the modern world was a matter of intense interest to Alexis de Tocqueville, who, Peter Augustine Lawler suggests in chapter 6, was in fact preoccupied by magnanimity almost to the point of being a partisan of greatness. Lawler contends, however, that such a preoccupation is not unproblematic, for magnanimity itself is problematic, and not only in relation to modern egalitarian sensibilities. On Lawler's reading, Aristotle's account of magnanimity reveals that, in his quest for greatness, the magnanimous man falls short in relation to truth and justice. Seeking to gratify a spirited longing for self-sufficiency and individual significance, the magnanimous man is led to neglect a part of himself, *eros*, that points relentlessly to his contingency and dependence on others. He is thus closed to an important part of the truth about himself, and unjustly indifferent to, or unwilling to acknowledge, the goods that emerge from other sources than himself. In his *Souvenirs*— his recollections of his part in the events surrounding the Revolution of 1848— Tocqueville undertakes a critical self-examination of his own magnanimous desires. Here, Lawler observes, he rises above a mere partisanship of greatness and recognizes the uncomfortable (to the magnanimous man) truth: that his longing for greatness is inextricably bound up with his weakness, that his desire to do great deeds in the public arena emerges in large part not from a self-sufficient and disinterested benevolence but from a deep anxiety about his personal significance. Similarly, in *Democracy in America* Tocqueville resists the inclination to attend to greatness at the expense of justice. Tocqueville's own tendency, Lawler notes, is to examine modern democracy from the perspective of individual greatness, the conditions of which it tends to undermine. In the end, however, Tocqueville subordinates his own perspective to that of God, for whom democracy is more just than aristocracy because it elevates the condition of all, if only at the expense of the extraordinary grandeur of the few. This is not to say, however, that for Tocqueville magnanimity has no place within modern democracy. Rather, Lawler contends, a chastened magnanimity, one mindful of the greatness characteristic of *all* human beings, still has a role to play in democratic modernity: opposing the influence of materialism and pantheism, two democratic intellectual tendencies that undermine greatness by obscuring the truth about man, that he is a creature situated uniquely between the other animals and God.

Part II concludes with chapter 7, Jeffrey Church and Catherine Zuckert's account of Nietzsche's effort to revive magnanimity in order to remedy the ills of modernity. For Nietzsche, the coherence and vitality of a community depends on extraordinary individuals who do great deeds that affirm and exemplify the community's understanding of the noble and the base. Nietzsche finds, however, that modernity is, in part because of its egalitarianism, an impediment to the emergence of superior human beings who can define the community through noble deeds. Hence modernity's descent into nihilism. Nietzsche therefore brings forward as a remedy the overman, the conception of which, Church and Zuckert contend, is indebted to Nietzsche's appreciation of Aristotle's account of greatness of soul. Nietzsche's task, however, is greater than merely to rearticulate Aristotelian magnanimity. He must rather transform it for a world that has itself been transformed by Christianity and modernity. Similarly, the overman's task is perhaps greater than that of Aristotle's magnanimous man. For while the latter had only to exemplify a community's understanding of nobility, the former is called to create a new understanding of greatness for the human race itself.

The third and final part of the book turns to an examination of the thought and action of several leaders who might well be regarded as exemplars of magnanimous statesmanship. In chapter 8 James R. Stoner considers the example of Thomas More. At first glance, magnanimity seems to have little place in More's most famous writing, *Utopia*. The dialogue's primary interlocutor, Raphael Hythloday, disclaims all interest in public office, and the egalitarianism of the Utopian institutions he describes seems to leave little scope for honor. Nevertheless, as Stoner points out, the importance of magnanimity remains subtly present in *Utopia*. For More, the author takes care to present More the character as disputing Raphael's disdain for political service and questioning Utopia's communism on the grounds that it would deprive rulers of the outward manifestations of honor that they ought to have. Thomas More, however, is even more famous for his actions than his writings, and in particular for his unwillingness to support Henry VIII's efforts to secure a divorce and make himself head of the Church in England, which refusal led ultimately to More's execution. More's example thus raises the question of the relationship among magnanimity, statesmanship, and martyrdom. As Stoner notes, the compatibility of magnanimity and martyrdom seems evident, insofar as both the magnanimous man and martyr rise above the mundane considerations that animate most human beings. The relationship of martyrdom to statesmanship seems more problematic, however; for surely the martyred statesman has failed decisively and indeed been removed from office. Nevertheless, Stoner suggests, even a man who has resigned or been removed from high office may still engage in a kind of statesmanship by his moral example and influence. This was the case with More. Hence Henry's efforts to gain his public support for the king's supremacy despite the fact that More was no longer a public officer.

In chapter 9, Paul Carrese observes that while modern democratic theory tends to neglect greatness of soul, the career of George Washington demonstrates that Aristotelian magnanimity is essential to at least the coming into being of the most successful of modern democracies. In his role as Washington's biographer, John Marshall singled out Washington's magnanimity, his ability to rise above public passions in safeguarding the public interest, as one of his most important virtues. Taking his cue from Marshall, Carrese shows how the successful establishment of the American republic depended decisively and repeatedly on Washington's greatness of soul. American democracy originated in war, which meant that at its birth the public scene was necessarily dominated by the infant nation's victorious commanding general. It took a magnanimous detachment from power and glory for Washington to refuse the chance to become a king, thus allowing republicanism to take root. Indeed, Washington's magnanimity was displayed not only in his refusal to cooperate in schemes of military dictatorship, but also in his ability to dissuade other officers from pursuing them—an ability that depended in large part on the grandeur of his character, which inspired such admiration and devotion in his men. Later, Washington again showed magnanimity by entering the political realm and involving himself in controversial measures, such as the drafting of the Constitution. By his willingness to attach his name to unpopular but necessary measures, he showed that he regarded his popularity more as a kind of tool to be used in the service of his country than as an essential component of his happiness as a man. In view of these and other contributions examined by Carrese, it perhaps does not go too far to say that the American republic, though dedicated to a kind of equality, nevertheless owes its establishment to a single man's superiority of soul.

Magnanimity may be essential not only to the establishment of democratic institutions but also to their preservation under conditions of crisis. We are reminded of this truth by Joseph Fornieri's account, in chapter 10, of the American statesman who set out deliberately to imitate Washington's magnanimous desire to win his fellow citizens' esteem by deserving it: Abraham Lincoln. Fornieri takes up Kenneth Deutsch's suggestion in chapter 4 that we might look to Lincoln as a living example of the Christian magnanimity that combines grand ambition with genuine humility. Lincoln was undoubtedly ambitious, yet, as his *Lyceum Address* reveals, he was keenly aware of the dangers of an untamed longing for greatness, the unprincipled thirst for glory of an Alexander or Caesar, willing to win distinction equally by freeing the enslaved or enslaving the free. Lincoln, however, consistently united his grand ambitions to considerations higher than his own desires: he sought to make his ambition serve the preservation of the Union and the principles of justice he believed it sustained. According to Fornieri, Lincoln's desire for greatness was kept within moral bounds by his biblical humility, especially his humble awareness that the Divine Will might differ from his own, and even his country's, purposes. It was precisely this submissiveness to God's purposes that allowed Lincoln magnanimously to hold to just, prudent, and charitable policies even when they were temporarily unpopular: sustaining the Emancipation Proclamation despite the near certainty that it would lead to a loss in the 1864 election, and insisting on a policy of reconciliation with the defeated south despite a mighty current of northern vengefulness.

The magnanimous treatment of a vanquished enemy is the central concern of Will Morrisey's account of Winston Churchill in chapter 11, which brings this volume to a close. Morrisey takes as his point of departure the third injunction of Churchill's famous aphorism: "In defeat, defiance; in war, resolution; in victory, magnanimity; in peace, goodwill." Drawing especially on Churchill's histories of the two World Wars, he finds that for Churchill critical failures of magnanimity characterized the democratic statesmanship at the conclusion of World War I. Failing to be magnanimous in victory, the western leaders instead insisted upon terms that humiliated the Germans, made for a poisonous peace, and hence paved the way for a second war. These failures, Morrisey notes, raise the question of the relationship of magnanimous statesmanship to the regime. Earlier European peacemakers, he notes, could more easily display magnanimity. As aristocrats representing aristocratic regimes, they could ignore—if indeed they even felt—currents of popular opinion and concentrate on establishing the lasting peace that would be in each nation's long-term interests. In contrast, the statesmen of 1919 were the elected leaders of democratic regimes. As such they had to confront, and proved unable to resist, the vengeful passions of publics traumatized by war. Morrisey's reflections thus provide a fitting conclusion to this volume, for they sound one of its recurring themes: modern democracy's simultaneous ambivalence toward and need for magnanimous statesmanship. Thus the final chapter reminds us again of modern society's need to reflect on magnanimity, a project to which we hope the present volume will make a worthy contribution.

1

MAGNANIMITY IN CLASSICAL AND CHRISTIAN POLITICAL THOUGHT

2

Aristotle's Magnanimous Man

Carson Holloway

Aristotle's account in the *Nicomachean Ethics* of the virtue he calls *megalopsuchia*—commonly translated as magnanimity or greatness of soul—surely provides one of the most engaging and memorable discussions to be found in the corpus of his ethical-political works. Perhaps the arresting quality of these passages arises from the combination of magnanimity's undoubted importance and apparent mysteriousness. On the one hand, the great-souled man must be understood to occupy a central place in Aristotle's science of politics. After all, Aristotle indicates that science is concerned primarily with the just and the noble, that political life, properly understood and undertaken, aims to foster virtue and make men good. Yet the great-souled man is said to be the best or most virtuous of men, and hence the summit of the political community's achievement. On the other hand, the magnanimous man is something of an enigma. Concerned principally with honor, he is also aloof from it. Eager to serve his fellow citizens, he is also disdainful of them. Committed to greatness, he is said to find nothing great.

This chapter seeks to clarify our understanding of Aristotle's magnanimous man by recounting Aristotle's treatment of magnanimity, by indicating this virtue's relationship to statesmanship, and by offering reflections intended to suggest possible solutions to some apparent problems with Aristotelian magnanimity.

I. MAGNANIMITY IN THE *NICOMACHEAN ETHICS*

Aristotle begins his account of magnanimity by considering the things in relation to which magnanimity displays itself. Each virtue, Aristotle has suggested

13

and will continue to suggest throughout the *Ethics*, has some "object," some thing with which it is particularly concerned, some aspect of the human condition in relation to which it is exercised. We may also understand this object as some human good of which the virtue in question makes proper use. Thus, for example, moderation makes good use of food and drink, liberality of money, and wit of amusing conversation. What, then, is the good thing that the great-souled man uses well?

Aristotle begins to answer this question by considering the name itself: greatness of soul, or *megalopsuchia*, he notes, would seem to be related somehow to great things, or *megala*. Taking common opinion as his point of departure, as is his usual method of addressing moral and political questions, Aristotle holds more specifically that greatness of soul is shown in a certain accurate assessment of one's relationship to great things. A man is "thought to be great-souled" if he deems himself worthy of great things and is in fact worthy of them. Magnanimity is thus opposed to a foolish lack of self-knowledge, thinking oneself worthy of great things while in fact being unworthy of them. Magnanimity, however, is more than mere self-knowledge: it is knowledge of one's greatness. That is, it involves a self-assessment that is both accurate and lofty. Accordingly, a man who correctly believes himself to be worthy of little is moderate but not magnanimous (1123b1–5).[1]

One might suspect, at least on a superficial glance, that Aristotle's emphasis on greatness in the context of magnanimity is in tension with his more general presentation of the ethical virtues. After all, he repeatedly recurs to the notion that each excellence of character strikes a mean between two vicious extremes; yet here he holds that this particular virtue—and, as we will see, in some ways the master–virtue—itself possesses an element of the extreme: the great-souled man claims for himself the greatest things. Aristotle dispels this apparent contradiction by noting that the magnanimous man strikes the mean by virtue of the accuracy of his self-assessment. While he stands at an extreme point because of the greatness of the things he claims for himself, "by reason" of the "rightness" of his claim he achieves the mean; "for he claims what he deserves," in contrast to the vices corresponding to this virtue, which err through excess and defect (1123b12–16).

These vices Aristotle identifies as vanity and smallness of soul. On the one hand, the vain man thinks himself worthy of great things which he does not in fact merit. Aristotle adds, however, that the term vanity is not applied to everyone who thinks too highly of himself, thus hinting at, without developing, a more detailed account of the ways in which one might go wrong in evaluating one's worthiness. H. Rackham, one of Aristotle's translators, ventures the following explanation of this remark: vanity "does not apply to a man who deserves much but claims even more, nor to one who claims little but deserves even less." Following up this suggestion, we might suppose, as an example, a great general who thinks that his strategic genius renders him fit for the highest political offices. We might regard such a man as mistaken or misguided, but surely not as vain. The term does not seem to fit, because while this man thinks more highly of his capacities than is fitting, those capacities are nonetheless very considerable. Indeed, the term Aristotle uses for the vain man—*ho chaunos*—can also suggest emptiness or insubstantiality, just as the English word "vanity" tends to communicate a mere pretence of merit with little to support it. Nevertheless, we may note, following up the second half of Rackham's remark, that vanity implies not mere pretense to unmerited consideration, but more specifically pretense to unmerited *extraordinary* consideration. Thus, as Rackham indicates, a man who "claims little but deserves even less" is not usually called vain. We would not, for example, apply the term to a criminal who thinks himself worthy of the respect given to an ordinary citizen.[2]

The erroneous extreme in opposition to vanity is, Aristotle continues, smallness of soul (*micropsuchia*). Interestingly, however, there is a certain asymmetry between these opposed vices. While vanity, as we have seen, depends on both the inaccuracy and the size of one's claims, smallness of soul does not. Thus Aristotle contends that a man is small-souled if his self-assessment falls short of his actual worthiness, regardless of whether he is worthy of great, moderate, or small things. Indeed, Aristotle indicates that the most small-souled man of all would seem to be the one who underestimates his worthiness when it is in fact great, "for what would he have done had he not deserved so much" (1123b10–12)?

Aristotle proceeds to reveal more specifically the "great thing" in relation to which magnanimity is displayed. This turns out to be honor, and especially the greatest honors. The idea of magnanimity, Aristotle reminds us, is bound up with notions of "worthiness" and "greatness": the magnanimous man thinks himself worthy of, and is worthy of, great things, and in fact the greatest things. "Worthiness," Aristotle reasons, signifies the possession of a claim to some external good. Hence the "great thing" of which the magnanimous man rightly thinks himself worthy must be the greatest of external goods. This, he concludes, "we should assume to be the thing which we offer as a tribute to the gods, and which is most coveted by men of high station, and is the prize awarded for the noblest deeds" (1123b16–20). This is honor. Honor, then, is the greatest of external goods, and the magnanimous man is the one who is rightly disposed to honors and dishonors.

While focused on the one particular good of which magnanimity makes proper use, this definition nevertheless opens upon a more comprehensive excellence; for Aristotle contends that magnanimity implies the possession of all the virtues to an excellent degree. This understanding is already implied, Aristotle suggests, by the more general notion that the great-souled man is worthy of great things. Better men, we think, deserve better things, and so only the best of men can be worthy of the greatest things. Hence the "truly" magnanimous man must also be a good man (1123b29). The relationship between magnanimity and all virtue is confirmed by the view that the magnanimous man is worthy specifically of great honors. Honor, Aristotle notes, is the prize of virtue and is accorded to the good. Hence the man deserving of the greatest honors can only be the best of men. Magnanimity, he concludes, comes to light as a kind of *kosmos*, or ordered arrangement, of the virtues, for it "enhances their greatness, and it cannot exist without them." Thus it is difficult to be truly magnanimous, for this is impossible without also being noble and good (1124a2–5).

The magnanimous man's proper disposition toward great honors is characterized by a kind of moderation, a measured attraction that avoids the extremes of indifference and obsession. He will, Aristotle suggests, derive moderate pleasure from great honors bestowed by serious persons. In contrast, he will disdain both dishonor as well as honors given by ordinary men for some petty reason, for he is unworthy of such things. Moreover, Aristotle continues, while the magnanimous man's virtue is displayed especially in relation to honor, he will demonstrate a similar moderation with regard to wealth, power, and good and bad fortune, which will not leave him excessively pleased or grieved. A man who takes even honor as a small thing, Aristotle argues, will surely also regard the lesser external goods as small.

Having raised the issue of the great-souled man's disposition toward good and bad fortune, Aristotle takes the opportunity to address an erroneous understanding of the relationship between magnanimity and fortune. It is thought, he notes, that good fortune also conduces to magnanimity. After all, the wellborn, the powerful, and the wealthy are thought to be worthy of honor, since they are superior to others in certain things, and those who are superior in some good are honored more. Thus, one might conclude, such goods, by attracting honors to their possessors, make them more magnanimous. Nevertheless, Aristotle contends that in truth only the good man is honorable, and those who possess the goods of fortune without virtue cannot justly claim to be worthy of great things and cannot rightly be called magnanimous, for, again, magnanimity requires complete virtue.

Those who possess only the goods of fortune may, Aristotle concedes, bear some superficial resemblance to the magnanimous man. Because in the absence of virtue it is difficult to carry one's good fortune becomingly, those who excel in the gifts of fortune tend to become disdainful and hubristic, traits that may appear similar to the great-souled man's proclivity to look down on others. In contrast to modern egalitarian sensibilities, then, Aristotle does not find contempt for others necessarily inappropriate. To him, its propriety depends on its basis. Those who look down on others without themselves excelling in virtue are simply self-deceived, he suggests, since their worth is no greater by any serious standard; but the magnanimous man justly looks down on others because his self-estimate is correct.

We may note that Aristotle's correction of common opinion in this passage is in fact twofold. Common opinion tends to overestimate *its own* contribution to magnanimity, as well as the contribution made by power and wealth. That is, here Aristotle corrects a view that implies that the magnanimous man is merely the one who thinks himself worthy of great things and whose self-assessment is confirmed by the opinion of others. In fact, Aristotle teaches, one is not made magnanimous by being superior in goods honored by others, but by being superior in the goods that are in truth honorable. There is a difference between what is honored and what truly should be honored, and hence between the truly magnanimous man, on the one hand, and the one who is both thought magnanimous and thinks himself magnanimous, on the other. Thus Aristotle's account of magnanimity—like his account of ethical virtue itself—takes its point of departure from common opinion but ultimately transcends common opinion. It implies a natural standard of human excellence that exists independent of the opinions of men, although the quest for that standard may necessarily take those opinions as its starting point.

II. MAGNANIMITY AND STATESMANSHIP

What has magnanimity to do with statesmanship? We might be tempted to say, though perhaps this would go too far, that they are identical. For Aristotle, it seems, magnanimity implies statesmanship, understood not only as the wielding of political power but as doing so excellently. It at least implies the capacity to do so excellently. The magnanimous man is, at least in principle, the statesman *par excellence*. A number of considerations point in this direction.

The connection between magnanimity and statesmanship is not made explicit in the *Nicomachean Ethics* discussion of greatness of soul, but it is at least implied in the subsequent treatment of the vices opposed to this virtue. There we find that the great honors with which magnanimity is concerned are not so much the commendations of one's fellow citizens, however high they may be, but instead important works or duties with which one is entrusted. Thus Aristotle indicates that the small-souled err because they "hold aloof from noble enterprises and pursuits" (1125a27). The vain err similarly, though in the opposite direction, by undertaking "honorable responsibilities of which they are not worthy," and are subsequently revealed as unworthy due to their lack of capacity (1125a29–30). The honors with which magnanimity is concerned, it seems, are opportunities to serve one's fellow citizens. This understanding is made explicit in the treatment of magnanimity found in the *Eudemian Ethics*, where Aristotle indicates that greatness of soul is concerned with great "offices" (*EE* 1232b20–25).[3]

Other aspects of Aristotle's account of magnanimity in the *Nicomachean Ethics*, taken in conjunction with passages in the *Eudemian Ethics* and the *Politics*, also suggest a connection between the magnanimous man and the statesman. Once again, the magnanimous man is worthy of the greatest honors because he is great in all the virtues. Such excellence, however, implies the possession of prudence. A good and happy life, Aristotle is careful to emphasize in Book I of the *Nicomachean Ethics*, is not the result of mere possession of virtue, understood as a disposition, but of its active exercise. The active exercise of virtue in concrete circumstances requires, however, a knowledge of particulars in addition to an appreciation of the virtues themselves as general principles of action. This knowledge of particulars is provided by prudence, which Aristotle presents as a kind of cleverness about how to act in pursuit of virtue (1141b15–18, 1144a24–37). Hence the excellence attributed to the magnanimous man would be impossible if he lacked prudence. Indeed, Aristotle makes this clear in the *Eudemian Ethics*, where he notes that the great-souled man judges small and great things rightly, that is, in accordance with virtue and as the prudent man would (*EE* 1232a35–40). Prudence, however, is said by Aristotle to be the virtue "peculiar to the ruler" (*Pol.* 1277b26).[4] The magnanimous man could not be truly worthy of the highest honors understood as the highest offices if he did not possess prudence, and Aristotle's account suggests that his possession of prudence is not accidental but is essential to his magnanimity.

We may also note more broadly that the magnanimous man's general moral excellence is itself an indication that he is most suited to rule in the city. The city, Aristotle contends, is properly understood as a partnership in just and noble actions. It would seem reasonable, then, that the man who excels in such actions would be the most fitting ruler of such a community, just as the expert moneymaker would be the natural choice to lead a business enterprise. Hence Aristotle's argument in Book III of the *Politics* that virtue is the most authoritative claim to rule.

On the basis of the preceding discussion, which has emphasized the magnanimous man's active exercise of virtue and his suitability to public service, we can begin to understand Aristotle's strange evaluation—strange, at least, to us—of the respective merits of the vices opposed to magnanimity. In his treatment of the various ethical virtues, Aristotle sometimes indicates that all vices are not created equal. That is, each virtue is accompanied by two vices, one of excess and one of defect, both of which are opposed to the virtuous mean. Nevertheless, Aristotle indicates that in some instances one of these vices is more opposed to the mean, and hence worse, than the other. This is true, he suggests, in the case of magnanimity as well. Thus Aristotle closes his discussion of the vices related to magnanimity as follows: "Smallness of soul is more opposed than Vanity to Greatness of Soul, being both more prevalent and worse" (1125a33–34).

The modern reader will probably find such a judgment perplexing. Our immediate reaction to Aristotle's claim would probably correspond to David Hume's: "Men have, in general, a much greater propensity to overvalue than undervalue themselves; notwithstanding the opinion of ARISTOTLE."[5] It seems contrary to our experience to hold that most men tend to claim for themselves less rather than more than they merit. Given the restless acquisitiveness with which we are surrounded and which we feel in our own souls—both hallmarks of the commercial society we inhabit—we tend to think that daily life demonstrates that most men are all too happy to claim more than they deserve. Moreover, it seems contrary to some of our deepest sentiments to hold that the man who claims less than he deserves is a worse sort of character than the one whose claim is excessive. Living in, and imbibing the principles of, a modern democracy, we are egalitarians. As such, we feel the vain man's pretensions to superiority irritating and thus judge them as reprehensible. The small-souled man, however, provokes no such feelings, and may even seem charmingly unassuming by contrast to the vain man.

Nevertheless, if we attend to Aristotle's account of the "great things" with which magnanimity is concerned, we begin to see that his judgment about smallness of soul and vanity is correct, surely in relation to both the men of his time and the men of ours. Those "great things" or "great honors," again, are not simply the praises of his fellow citizens, but opportunities to serve them through virtuous action. The magnanimous man thinks he is worthy of, and is in fact worthy of, opportunities to exercise the moral virtues, especially in the context of offices of high responsibility. Thus the small-souled man in some way renounces self-love to the extent that he refuses to claim "good things" of which he is worthy (1125a20); yet one cannot call his behavior virtuously selfless, since the good things he might have taken would have been good for others as well: he is capable of rendering noble service to his fellows, but he declines because he is "too retiring" (1125a25). In contrast, the vain man, though a fool, at least has something generous about his character, to the extent that he tries to perform some good, even though he cannot do it successfully. In his discussion of liberality, Aristotle notes that the "liberality of a gift does not depend on its amount, but on the disposition of the giver"

(1120b9–10). On this view the small-souled man is marked by a lack of generosity that we do not find in the vain man: the latter wants to give something good that he does not really have, while the former refuses, perhaps through a kind of sloth or fear, to bestow a good that he does in fact possess. In this light we can see how smallness of soul is both more common and worse than vanity, for it refers to the widespread failure to exert one's soul with a view to superior goods—such as the exercise of the moral virtues—which are nevertheless difficult to achieve, in preference for lesser goods that are easier to achieve—such as the enjoyments that flow from gratification of the body and an undemanding sociability. This is the phenomenon to which Aristotle refers at the beginning of the *Ethics*, in his discussion of the various opinions about happiness, when he notes that the many "show themselves to be utterly slavish, by preferring what is only a life for cattle" (1095b19–21).

III. PROBLEMS OF ARISTOTELIAN MAGNANIMITY

At first sight, Aristotelian magnanimity may well appear offensive to the modern reader. By claiming and deserving great honors, by thinking he is better than most and by actually being better, the magnanimous man stands as an affront to our egalitarian sensibilities. Nevertheless, as we have seen, a closer inspection reveals him as a kind of benefactor. The great things he is willing to claim for himself are, it turns out, opportunities for virtuous service to others, especially through the exercise of political rule. He claims a great good for himself, but that good is itself the ability to do good for others. Such a disposition we can understand as characteristic of the best of men.

Nevertheless, we cannot ignore certain passages in Aristotle's treatment of magnanimity that are disturbing because they seem to call into question his virtue. Some aspects of the great-souled man's character appear to indicate a certain selfishness that is incompatible not only with modern democratic principles, but even with moral excellence as Aristotle presents it. Specifically, a number of passages suggest that the magnanimous man is preoccupied with his own superiority, that his virtue is exercised not for its own sake but merely as a means to elevating himself, in his own mind at least, above others.

The possible consequences of such passages are grave indeed. Aristotle teaches throughout the *Nicomachean Ethics* that the active exercise of ethical virtue is a source of solid human happiness. He also insists, however, that to be truly virtuous such actions must be undertaken for the sake of their own nobility, and not for any ulterior motive. If the magnanimous man turns out to practice virtue not for its own sake but for the sake of maintaining a superior position—even if only in his own mind, through a kind of self-pride—then his virtue will be, on Aristotle's own principles, a sham. But if even the virtue of the best of men turns out to be a mere counterfeit, then we must conclude that moral virtue itself is of very questionable goodness. In what follows then, I examine some elements of Aristotle's account that seem to imply that the magnanimous man is unfittingly obsessed with his own position and tries to reconcile them with a genuine virtue and suitability for statesmanship.

At one point in his discussion, Aristotle presents disdain, or a tendency to despise others, as a trait associated with magnanimity. Such a characteristic would seem to undermine the great-souled man's virtue as well as his fitness for political rule. After all, the magnanimous man is said to be eager to serve, but how can one be eager to serve those one despises (1124b18)? And surely affection for one's fellow citizens is at least a necessary, if not a sufficient, qualification for the statesman. For how can one secure the common good if one disdains the people whose good it is?

Here everything depends, however, on Aristotle's precise formulation, which, if we attend carefully to it, suggests that these difficulties need not arise. The magnanimous man, Aristotle contends, is not prone to rejoice or grieve excessively at good or bad fortune. After all, since even honor, the greatest of external goods, is small to him, so will be lesser external goods, like power and wealth, that are subject to the vicissitudes of fortune. Therefore, Aristotle concludes, the great-souled are "thought [*dokousin*] to be haughty [*huperoptai*]" or disdainful (1124a20). The magnanimous man's disdain, then, is more a matter of appearance than reality. Aristotle refers here not to the magnanimous man's character but to how he seems to others, and especially to others who are not as virtuous as he. The man who finds serious and fully human happiness in the active exercise of virtue will take comparatively little interest in wealth and power. Hence he will hold aloof from activities organized around the pursuit of these goods—that is, from most of the action and conversation of most of his fellow citizens. It is perhaps natural, though mistaken, that these should perceive his commendable disinterest in their chief enthusiasms as a blameworthy disdain for themselves. Indeed, Aristotle suggests that such misunderstanding, and hence misplaced blame, is likely to be the lot of the virtuous man. Each virtue is a mean between two vicious extremes, but in each case the mean itself looks vicious to those at the extremes. Thus "a coward calls a brave man rash and a rash man calls him a coward, and correspondingly in other cases" (1108b23–26). Because most men are less than virtuous, the best men will look less than virtuous to most men. Such appearances, however, say nothing about the actual character of the truly good.

The following passage presents a similar problem, to which a similar solution is perhaps available:

> He is fond of conferring benefits, but ashamed to receive them, because the former is a mark of superiority and the latter of inferiority. He returns a service

done to him with interest, since this will put the original benefactor into his debt in turn, and make him the party benefited. The great-souled are thought to have a good memory for any benefit they have conferred, but a bad memory for those which they have received (since the recipient of a benefit is the inferior of his benefactor, whereas they desire to be superior); and to enjoy being reminded of the former but to dislike being reminded of the latter: this is why the poet makes Thetis not specify her services to Zeus; nor did the Spartans treating with the Athenians recall the occasions when Sparta had aided Athens, but those on which Athens had aided Sparta (1124b10–18).

This passage certainly appears to indicate that the magnanimous man is animated not so much by a desire for the nobility of virtuous action as for superiority of position. Thus he bestows goods on others because this is a mark of superiority, and he tends to forget, and to dislike being reminded of, good deeds done to him by others, for he desires to be in the superior position. The impurity of his motives for virtuous action seem to undermine his claim to true virtue, and to the extent that his concern with superiority drives him to a kind of ingratitude he appears to move even in the direction of outright vice. Can a belief in the magnanimous man's genuine moral earnestness be preserved in the face of such phenomena?

    In an effort to attain this end, I would propose the following rereading of this important passage. The passage can be broken into two parts. The first speaks of the magnanimous man in the singular, and in it Aristotle makes a positive assertion about what the magnanimous man "is." The second speaks of the magnanimous in the plural, and is presented as an account of what they are "thought" to be. The first part can be read as suggesting that the magnanimous man desires to confer benefits because this makes him superior. It is not clear, however, that this is the only possible reading. The sense could equally be that because the magnanimous man is a superior sort of character he desires to provide benefits to others rather than receive them from others. That is, it could be that the superiority to which the passage refers is the cause but not the motive of his beneficial actions. Similarly, his aim in repaying benefits with interest may be not that he wants to put the other in a dependent position, but simply that he wants his fellows to have gained rather than lost by their association with him.

    The second part of the passage—with its reference to a distaste for being reminded of benefits one has received—also suggests a selfish preoccupation with status. Nevertheless, this portion does not positively assert characteristics of the magnanimous man but instead refers to what is "thought" of magnanimous men or how they "seem." The suggestion that this part refers less to the reality of the magnanimous man than to the common view of him is furthered by Aristotle's reference to the actions of Zeus and the Athenians as examples of magnanimous behavior. We may justly wonder, after all, whether Aristotle—who elsewhere presents the Homeric heroes as examples of *false* courage—would seriously present Zeus as an instance of genuine magnanimity, and whether he would—after implying that magnanimity is rare because it is so difficult—offer up a whole people as an example of magnanimity.

Could this section then possibly be intended to provide insight not into the actual character and motivations of the magnanimous man, but instead into the perhaps cynical interpretations of him indulged by men who are his moral inferiors? After all, the notion that the great-souled man likes to be reminded of services he has performed would seem to run counter to Aristotle's later assertion that he does not care to be praised—a claim that Aristotle makes himself, without a qualifying reference to the "seeming" of the great-souled man (1125a6). Perhaps this appearance of a culpable forgetfulness and resentment of benefits received actually arises from a cruder sort of human being's (somewhat malicious) misperception of the magnanimous man's moral refinement. With regard to appearing to forget benefits received, it may well be that, precisely because he is admirably unattached to external goods, the good turns done to the magnanimous man by others will not appear as great to him as they do his benefactors. Thus they receive his placid self-sufficiency as a kind of lack of gratitude. With regard to a dislike of being reminded of benefits bestowed on him, it might be that the magnanimous man is pained less at the memory of his former neediness than at the undignified behavior of the person reminding him. Generally, reminding others of their former dependency is thought to be poor manners precisely because it bespeaks a desire to lord it over them. The person who does this *is* seeking precisely the superiority that the magnanimous man is commonly (but erroneously) thought to seek, and the vulgarity of such behavior would no doubt pain any person of moral sensitivity whether it was done to himself or to someone else.

If these considerations succeed in saving the magnanimous man from the charge that he is really more concerned with his superior status than with the nobility and beauty of virtuous activity, there is nevertheless no denying that the magnanimous do look down on other men. Aristotle puts this characteristic forward as a fact of the magnanimous man's character, without reference to how he is "thought" to be by others. Thus he claims that the great-souled man is inclined to be "outspoken" and "frank" because he looks down on other men (1124b30). We are apt to take this "looking down" on others as evincing a hostility to them and hence as incompatible with the benevolence we expect of the good man and demand of the statesman. We tend to understand "looking down" in such terms because we are committed to equality and hence inclined to view any denial of equality as implying some viciousness. Yet it need not be so. Looking down on another need not preclude affection for him and genuine commitment to his well-being. Any decent father looks down on his children, even as he loves them, because he cannot simply share their point of view. The same is true of the magnanimous statesman's relationship to his fellow citizens. In both cases, the ruler takes his charges' interests more seriously than their desires, and he is aware that their tendency to do the opposite is a real inferiority in them that renders him more suited to manage their affairs than they are themselves. And in both cases his ability to do good to them depends precisely on this ability to look down on them.

Another series of passages in Aristotle's account imply not a questionable thirst for superiority but a disturbing vacancy in the soul of the magnanimous man. Aristotle says on three separate occasions that to the magnanimous man nothing is great (1123b33, 1125a3, 1125a15). These passages, like the ones examined before, seem to carry the most dire implications. Aristotle begins the *Nicomachean Ethics* by assuring the reader that a stable natural happiness arises from the activity of the moral virtues. He reiterates this understanding throughout the work. Yet in his account of magnanimity, he reveals that for the best of men, the man who achieves greatness in all the virtues, nothing is great. A life in which nothing is great, however, does not seem an attractive prospect. We wonder, then, whether Aristotle intends his account of magnanimity to disclose an emptiness and incoherence at the heart of the moral life. After all, if he claims that the man to whom nothing is great will have no inducement to unjust actions, he would also seem to have no inducement to just or noble actions. Does the magnanimous man transcend honor in the pursuit of nobility only to find nothingness?

We might attempt to solve this difficulty, and preserve the genuine goodness of the moral and political life, by contending that Aristotle intends these passages to indicate only that no *external* goods are great to the magnanimous man. This is the suggestion of Thomas Aquinas.[6] This approach would seem to address the problem successfully, because a sense that external goods are small is certainly compatible with a sense that the actions of virtue are great. It also has a certain plausibility, insofar as the horizon of magnanimity in the precise sense is defined by external goods, and more specifically by the greatest of external goods, honor. As we have seen, magnanimity as such is a proper disposition to the greatest honors.

Nevertheless, Thomas's solution seems imperfect for the following reasons. First, although Aristotle begins by discussing magnanimity in this precise sense, he does not confine himself to this sense. Rather his discussion naturally extends to the other, non-external goods, such as virtue itself, with which the magnanimous man is concerned. Second, when Aristotle says that nothing is great to the magnanimous man, he does so in each case without any qualifying reference to external goods. We are thus led to wonder whether the goodness of the moral and political life can be harmonized with the magnanimous man's sense that even his own great virtue is not in the end a great thing.

I will venture to suggest that such a harmonization is possible in light of the following considerations. From the fact that nothing is great to the magnanimous man, it does not follow that nothing is good, or admirable, or desirable to him. Aristotle says that he honors few things, thus implying that he *does* honor some things, and that he thinks life at any cost is unworthy, thus implying that there *are* things that make life worthy to him (1124b5–10). Here is it worth remembering that "great" is a relative term. It begs the question: great compared to what? A thing cannot be great compared to itself, and accordingly the great-souled man's greatness will not appear great to him, although it may well be a source of natural satisfaction. An analogy from the arts might here prove illuminating. A virtuoso musician, one capable of executing the most difficult pieces with ease, will not find his virtuosity great in the same way that he would have found it in another performer (or speculatively in his future self) when he was a novice. His displays of technical brilliance are astonishing to others, but not to him. None of this is incompatible, however, with a genuine enjoyment of his abilities and, more important, of the music itself which they allow to come to life.

Moreover, this lack of a sense of greatness can be wholesome. By his virtuosity such a musician earns a certain dual freedom. This is, first, a freedom to appreciate the most difficult pieces of music for their musical beauty and not for the impressive technical mastery they demand. It is, second, a freedom to appreciate the equal beauty of music that does not demand such skill. Thus the greatest musicians are often happy to perform beautiful but simple pieces because they know that they do not need to prove their virtuosity to themselves or anyone else.

Something similar may come about in the case of the magnanimous man. Because he is so supremely confident of his worthiness, he is willing to take on the highest political responsibilities. Yet, also because of this same confidence, he does not feel the need to prove his worthiness, to himself or others, by the exercise of political power. Nor, for that matter, does he feel a need even for the noble activities themselves that are made possible by supreme political power. Because he already organizes his life around noble activities, he will not view statesmanship as a compelling opportunity to put his life on a fundamentally higher plane. This is not to say that for the magnanimous man political service is purely self-sacrifice. He may well recognize that high office will add to his happiness by providing an opportunity to exercise his virtues on a wider basis. He will not, however, view it as something that will make him happy, because he already is happy.

Once again, this detachment—this ability to see opportunities for the greatest displays of virtue as not great but merely worthwhile with a view to the common good—is wholesome. Presumably, everyone would admit that a man who hankers for power and honor as good in themselves is a potential political troublemaker. So, too, however, is the man who craves power and honor because he feels that his soul is somehow not complete without the chance to be a large-scale benefactor. Each sort is likely to introduce conflict into the city because each thinks it important that *he* hold the office, rather than that the office be nobly discharged. The magnanimous man is not of either sort, and he calls to mind Aristotle's remark in the *Politics* that the virtuous would engage in faction with most justification, but they in fact do so least of all (*Pol.* 1301a38–39).

IV. THE LIMITS OF MAGNANIMITY

Again, the point of the foregoing arguments is to try to preserve the goodness or worthiness of the magnanimous man's life, and hence the moral political life itself, in the face of Aristotle's repeated assertions that to the magnanimous man nothing is great. We must concede, however, that even if these arguments should prove persuasive as far as they go, there remains a *certain* emptiness in the magnanimous man's soul, if not an absolute vacancy. As we have seen, magnanimity is related to prudence, and in fact the possession of one of them seems to imply the possession of the other. In his discussion of prudence, however, Aristotle notes that prudence, which is concerned with the human good, cannot be the highest faculty, because there are things in the cosmos far higher than the human things. Presumably, such things would appear great to any human being, even the best of them. The magnanimous man, however, would seem to be unaware of these higher than human things, insofar as to him nothing is great. There is, then, an emptiness in his soul, or rather in a part of his soul. The great-souled man is not—or is not necessarily—a philosopher, and to that extent he is unaware of, or at least insufficiently acquainted with, the divine, and to this extent a part of his soul, and even the highest part, remains unsatisfied.

That the magnanimous man finds nothing great, then, is ultimately a sign of a certain deficiency or imperfection in him. We may conclude in his defense, however, that this deficiency, however serious, need not imply a denigration of his excellence such as it is. That is, he is deficient because of the virtue he lacks, but that lack does not imply the insubstantiality of the virtue he has. We would rightly conclude that a man who organizes his life around the pursuit of bodily pleasure and knows nothing of nobility and virtue has a certain emptiness in his soul. Such an observation takes nothing away, however, from the genuine, though limited, natural goodness of the bodily pleasures. Similarly, the deficiency stemming from the magnanimous man's unfamiliarity with philosophy shows not that moral and political virtue lacks a natural goodness, only that it alone is not complete.

NOTES

1. Unless otherwise indicated, parenthetical citations of the Bekker numbers refer to the *Nichmachean Ethics*. I have relied throughout this chapter on H. Rackham's translation (Cambridge, Massachusetts: Harvard University Press, 1999).

2. Aristotle, *Nicomachean Ethics*, trans. H. Rackham (Cambridge, Massachusetts: 1999), 214, note a.

3. Here and in all subsequent references I abbreviate the *Eudemian Ethics* as *EE*. I have used the translation of H. Rackham, *The Athenian Constitution, The Eudemian Ethics, On Virtues and Vices* (Cambridge, Massachusetts: Harvard University Press, 1981).

4. Here and in subsequent references I abbreviate the *Politics* as *Pol*. I have relied on Carnes Lord's translation of the *Politics* (Chicago: University of Chicago Press, 1984).

5. David Hume, *An Enquiry Concerning the Principles of Morals*, ed. Tom L. Beauchamp (Oxford: Oxford University Press, 1998), 69.

6. Thomas Aquinas, *Commentary on Aristotle's Nicomachean Ethics*, trans. C. I. Litzinger, O.P. (Notre Dame: Dumb Ox Books, 1993), 239.

3

Magnanimity and Statesmanship: The Ciceronian Difference

James Fetter and Walter Nicgorski

It is not surprising that Cicero, who was both a practitioner and philosopher of statesmanship, would discuss magnanimity, which, according to Aristotle, is one of the defining virtues of the great statesman.[1] What might be surprising is that, however indebted Cicero is to Aristotle and to the Peripatetic school which Aristotle founded, his discussion of magnanimity is no mere translation or rephrasing of Aristotle's consideration of this virtue in the *Nicomachean Ethics*. Although there is no evidence that Cicero directly knew and thus was able to engage the sections on magnanimity in the *Ethics,* Cicero's understanding of this quality shares much with that of Aristotle.[2]

Cicero's consideration further appears to have been influenced by developments in the Stoic school after Aristotle and in the interaction between the Stoic and Peripatetic schools in that same period. Cicero's immediate source for his explicit and extended treatment in his *On Duties* (*De Officiis*) appears to be the modified Stoic thinker Panaetius (185–109 BC). Thus, Cicero puts his stamp of approval on a conception of magnanimity that has already departed from Aristotle's and that seems to address some deficiencies of the great philosopher's foundational contribution. This is not to say that Cicero's conception is without its own tensions and enigmatic aspects.

In what follows, we seek to explicate Cicero's teaching about magnanimity, to highlight its overlap with and differences from Aristotle's understanding, and finally to draw attention to difficulties in that teaching even while appreciating its significance for our modern democratic age. Most of what follows is based on the systematic treatment of magnanimity in Books I and III of *On Duties*. In addition, we have inspected and, when appropriate, utilized all of Cicero's references to magnanimity (generally in some form of the Latin phrases, *magnitudo animi* or *magnus animus*) throughout his large corpus of writings, including speeches and letters. References to this concept beyond *On Duties* show a consistency with what comes to light immediately below. This is not to say that the various usages always have the precision found in his extended and systematic treatment. In the speeches and letters and even in other philosophical works colored by his self-consciously rhetorical mode, Cicero is often inclined to pleonasm as a way of emphasis; in those instances it is sometimes difficult to see just how magnanimity differs from courage or even from justice and overall virtue.[3] As in our own day, ordinary discourse and persuasive discourse do not always lend themselves to the sharp distinctions expected in dialectic and good philosophical conversation.

A further word about *On Duties* is appropriate here. This is a writing in the form of an extended letter to his son, Marcus, studying philosophy in Rome at the time and specifically studying under a Peripatetic teacher named Cratippus. That contrived setting leads Cicero to remark that "my philosophy is not very different from that of the Peripatetics (for both they and I claim to be followers of Socrates and Plato)" (1:2).[4] In these same early pages, Cicero affirms that his philosophical loyalty is to the school of Academic skepticism (the school that picks and chooses what seems most likely to be the truth) and that he is heavily reliant here, notably in Books I and II, on an earlier work on moral duty by the Stoic Panaetius (1.6–7, 9; 2.60; 3.7–8). *On Duties* is Cicero's last philosophical writing, done in the very last year and a half of his life, and it can be seen as a work where Cicero strives to resolve to some extent the various tensions in his life and earlier writings. Notable in this regard is his hovering between the Stoic and Peripatetic views on happiness in his earlier and other major moral writing, his work *On the Ultimate Good and Ultimate Evil* (*De Finibus*). That last year or so of his life was also the period immediately after the assassination of his sometime ally but oft-times nemesis, Julius Caesar. Caesar's shadow lingers over *On Duties*, no place more clearly than in the discussion of magnanimity. *On Duties* has been a major moral text in Western history, often seen as second only to the Bible in its formative power from the period of the Christian Church Fathers to the American Founders, peaking in its impact in the late Middle Ages and Renaissance. The conception of magnanimity offered in *On Duties* is clearly an important one to the Western understanding of this idea, and it appears that its differences from that of Aristotle have not been generally noted and appreciated.

I. CICERO'S MAGNANIMITY

Cicero sets the stage for his discussion of magnanimity with his first reference to this virtue in *On Duties*, drawing attention to the magnanimous man's self-sufficiency both with respect to other men and to the vicissitudes of fortune. Specifically laying the foundation of the virtues in certain inclinations, Cicero writes:

> Above all, the search after truth and its eager pursuit are peculiar to man. . . . To this passion for discovering truth there is added a hungering, as it were, for independence, so that a mind well-moulded by Nature is unwilling to be subject to anybody save one who gives rules of conduct or is a teacher of truth or who, for the general good, rules according to justice and law. From this attitude come greatness of soul [*magnitude animi*] and a sense of superiority to worldly conditions (1.13).

This passage indicates that the detachment of Cicero's magnanimous man from ordinary worldly considerations rests on, or is closely associated with, his desire for truth and for a life in accord with it, not on the knowledge of his own greatness or the desire for honor as can appear to be the case in Aristotle's conception. One would therefore expect Cicero's magnanimous man to be more open to philosophy than is Aristotle's. As the following discussion of Cicero's treatment of magnanimity will show, this is, in fact, the case.

The context for Cicero's discussion of magnanimity is his explanation of the four virtues that he considers to be the sources of "all that is morally right" (1.15). Magnanimity is the third of these four virtues, the other three being, respectively, the development and perception of the truth or wisdom, justice in dealings with others, and self-control or moderation. Although Cicero considers all four virtues to be related to one another, he discusses each separately and in the order in which he lists them. He also considers them all essential to moral action and does not provide a formal ranking of them.

What is immediately notable is that in Cicero's enumeration magnanimity has simply displaced courage; in other words, one might say that magnanimity has come to be the name both for an enlarged conception of courage and something more. Magnanimity in Cicero's formulation is now one of what will come to be later known as the four hinge or cardinal virtues. That is not to say that it has always held in later times the form of diminishment or preeminence that Cicero assigned it, but a different way of understanding magnanimity from that of Aristotle's is clearly at hand. No longer is magnanimity a fifth virtue, a kind of culminating virtue, a virtue with some strange characteristics that must have tempted people then, as we know it now does, to doubt whether it is truly a virtue. Aristotle himself, however, seems to have planted the seeds for developments that took place after him, likely both in the Stoic and Peripatetic traditions, and that find expression in the Ciceronian differences on magnanimity. Aristotle had not strictly limited courage to the battlefield of war; yet for him the virtue of courage was still primarily equated with steadfastness in the face of the prospect of a sudden and violent death in battle.[5] Though Aristotle's magnanimous man is wedded to the truth as an exemplar of all the virtues, there remains an ambivalence both about philosophy and the pursuit of truth and about any sense of rest in the larger or transcendent truth of the whole. The emphasis for Aristotle's magnanimous man is clearly on the truth about himself in relationship to others.

Though Cicero seems to withhold from magnanimity any sense that it is, independent of politics, the overall or culminating virtue, he does understand it as closely dependent on the other basic virtues for he holds the view of the unity and thus interdependence of all the virtues. Magnanimity then cannot exist without the other key virtues. After wisdom, it shares with justice and moderation

> the task of providing and maintaining those things on which the practical business of life depends so that . . . largeness and nobility of soul may be revealed not only in increasing one's resources and acquiring advantages for one's self and one's family but far more in rising superior to these very things (1.17).

Whatever differences Cicero has with an Aristotelian conception of magnanimity, he uses Aristotelian method in developing his explanation of this virtue—that is, he begins his more formal discussion of magnanimity by referring to common opinions about the magnanimous man and, as his discussion proceeds, by modifying them.[6] Specifically, he opens the section of Book I of *On Duties* devoted to magnanimity with reference to the high estimation in common opinion of the person marked by this quality and the widespread view that magnanimity is synonymous with military glory and manly endurance; the heroic ideal of courage is most in mind in the common view of magnanimity.

> We must realize, however [*autem*], that while we have set down four cardinal virtues from which as sources moral rectitude and moral duty emanate, that achievement is most glorious in the eyes of the world which is won with a spirit great, exalted and superior to the vicissitudes of earthly life (1.61).

The examples that follow this statement indicate that this popular admiration of "glorious achievement" is above all, if not exclusively, directed at military triumphs and heroism.

This introduction also sets up an implicit contrast between actual magnanimity and the common opinion of it. By using "*autem*" to set up the juxtaposition of the four virtues and the seeming glory of the actions of the magnanimous man, Cicero points to the possibility that the common understanding of magnanimity is somehow incorrect or superficial. By implication, his account of this virtue is intended to correct such misleading and perhaps even dangerous misunderstandings.

Cicero next directly addresses the most prominent element of this popular understanding, the conflation of magnanimity with military glory. In praising great-souled men, Cicero claims, both Greek and Roman orators exalt great military heroes and victors of major battles. Noteworthy Roman generals, who consider themselves to be great-souled, also wish for their statues to be in military uniform as a symbol of the importance they place on their martial exploits. In the face of this public opinion and such practices, Cicero exhorts great-souled men to refrain from seeking military authority and, at times, to resign it if they possess it or decline it, if others offer it to them (1.68).

This misunderstanding of magnanimity leads directly to the dangers that an imperfect great-souled man can pose to the political community (state).

> But if the exaltation of spirit seen in times of danger and toil is devoid of justice and fights for selfish ends instead of for the common good, it is a vice; for not only has it no element of virtue, but its nature is barbarous and revolting to all our finer feelings (1.62).

True magnanimity therefore depends for its very existence upon justice, Cicero's second cardinal virtue and one entrusted by him with care for the common good. A man who would otherwise be great-souled but who lacks this virtue as a guiding principle not only falls short of embodying perfect virtue but is even vicious and poses an imminent threat to the state because of his likely unquenchable thirst for power. The same sort of man, whose immunity to fear proves so useful to defend the state in troubled times, can also be its greatest enemy, if he be without justice.

Cicero pays considerable attention to this deviant form of magnanimity. He frequently repeats the warning that a man who has the potential to be magnanimous but who lacks the restraints of justice will seek absolute power at any price, tending to aspire to be sole ruler. In one of his more forceful statements about men of this type, he writes:

> such men do not allow themselves to be constrained either by argument or by any public and lawful authority; but they only too often prove to be bribers and agitators in public life, seeking to obtain supreme power and to be superiors through force rather than equals through justice (1.64).

Such a man is therefore a danger to any free state, because he is willing to employ any means to become a tyrant, and neither arguments nor considerations of justice are sufficient to restrain him.

Men of this type also are inclined to make war to attain glory for themselves, even when doing so would be altogether unjust. "This is notably," writes Cicero, "the case with men of great spirit and natural ability, and it is the more likely to happen, if they are adapted to a soldier's life and fond of warfare" (1.74). Like the men who strive after absolute power, those who desire war for the sake of glory possess great abilities, even a certain kind of magnanimity, along with their limitless ambition. The war-inclined also pay equally little heed to justice, since war is just only if it is undertaken "in such a way as to make it evident that it has no other object than to secure peace" (1.80). This further underscores Cicero's rejection of the uncritical adoption of the popular conception of magnanimity as essentially glory in war.

The case of Caesar is, of course, much on Cicero's mind, for Caesar's dictatorship is for Cicero the chief manifestation in his life of the boundless lust for power that he opposes with such vehemence in his discussion of magnanimity. Cicero wishes to ensure that his version of the magnanimous man would never succumb to the temptation to imitate Caesar and seek absolute power for himself. Cicero indicates that this consideration weighs heavily upon his mind when he writes about causes of injustice:

> For whenever a situation is of such a nature that not more than one can hold preeminence in it, competition for it usually becomes so keen that it is an extremely difficult matter to maintain a "fellowship inviolate." We saw this proved but now in the effrontery of Gaius Caesar, who, to gain that sovereign power which by a depraved imagination he had conceived in his fancy, trod underfoot all laws of gods and men. But the trouble about this matter is that it is in the greatest souls and in the most brilliant geniuses that we usually find ambitions for civil and military authority, for power, and for glory, springing up; and therefore we must be the more heedful not to go wrong in that direction (1.26).

The problem of Caesar is therefore the most pressing concern for Cicero as he explicates magnanimity. Although he grants the politically active magnanimous man an exalted position as the ideal embodiment of virtue, he does not wish to grant this man limitless power of the sort that Caesar took for himself. Furthermore, since the institutions of the Roman Republic were clearly unable to restrain Caesar's ambition, Cicero wishes to instill in the potentially magnanimous man the self-restraint necessary to prevent him from becoming an autocrat, even if he were presented with the opportunity to do so. He wants the magnanimous man to possess true magnanimity, one grounded in justice.

Caesar's case also helps to explain Cicero's rejection of the almost exclusive association of magnanimity with martial valor in the popular imagination. As Caesar demonstrated, a general who considers himself entitled to glory, honor, and absolute power is far more dangerous than an ambitious civilian politician, for the general can use his army to seize power by force, an option that may not be open to a civilian leader. If, therefore, the greatest honors are the exclusive domain of successful generals, the danger that a great-souled man would follow Caesar's example is magnified, unless he proves able to restrain his own ambition.

However much Caesar and his military route to power and then absolute power is on Cicero's mind and however much Cicero is interested in increasing among the public and the ambitious young an appreciation for courage and glorious achievement (such as he regarded his own) in the role of civilian statesmen, Cicero's honesty compels him to acknowledge that the talented and ambitious will ever be tempted to seek the false glory of public acclaim. His letters reveal a personal struggle with what he regards, in his clearest moments, an undue concern with fame and glory. Thus the problem of a disordered magnanimity is not limited to a handful of ambitious men who reject justice outright. Even those who would act justly under normal circumstances could pose a similar danger to the political community, especially if they do not think that they have been duly rewarded for their heroic acts on the state's behalf. "For scarcely can the man be found," writes Cicero in *On Duties*, "who has passed through trials and encountered dangers and does not then wish for glory as a reward for his achievements" (1.65). For Cicero it seems apparent that the possible conflict between the great-souled man and a society organized according to principles of justice, and thus with an appropriate regard for liberty, is the most daunting challenge he faces as he attempts to construct a viable conception of the virtue of magnanimity.

Nevertheless, Cicero is not oblivious to the importance of traditional courage and does not reject this virtue long associated, as it is primarily in Aristotle, with bravery on the battlefield. Instead, he envisions an enlarged conception of this virtue that, joined with wisdom, provides the great-souled man with the needed self-restraint to resist the temptation to become another Caesar. This courage, now to be called magnanimity, encompasses more than the mere absence of fear in the heat of battle; it also requires a devotion to justice and the good of the community.

Cicero could not be clearer on this point. Following the Stoics, he defines courage as "that virtue which champions the cause of right" (1.62). The courageous man must therefore also be a just one, thereby precluding him from engaging in the tyrannical excesses of a Caesar or rushing to war without justification. Earlier in his *Tusculan Disputations* Cicero gave a more extended definition of courage that clearly showed its enlargement to what he understands magnanimity to be in *On Duties*: after several definitions from Stoic thinkers, all removed from any narrow tie to battlefield courage, Cicero cites the renowned Stoic philosopher Chrysippus defining courage (*fortitudo*) as "knowledge of all that might need to be endured or the disposition of the soul, obedient to the supreme law, in suffering and forbearing without fear."[8]

The courageous man must also be public spirited. Citing Plato, Cicero says that "'even the courage that is prompt to face danger, if it is inspired not by public spirit, but by its own selfish purposes, should have the name of effrontery rather than of courage'" (1.63). Courage, while a virtue of the individual, is centered on the good of the community rather than the apparent good of the individual who possesses it. The courageous man must not only be just but must also serve the community in times of need, even if this requires personal sacrifices on his part.

Then in formally defining magnanimity, we see Cicero folding a true and genuine courage right into it. In fact the definition which follows here is presented as applicable to both courage and magnanimity; those are two different terms for the same virtue.

> The soul that is altogether courageous and great is marked above all by two characteristics: one of these is indifference to outward circumstances; for such a person cherishes the conviction that nothing but moral goodness and propriety deserves to be either admired or wished for or striven after, and that he ought not to be subject to any man or any passion or any accident of fortune. The second characteristic is that, when the soul is disciplined in the way above mentioned, one should do deeds not only great and in the highest degree useful, but extremely arduous and laborious and fraught with danger both to life and to many things that make life worth living (1.66).

Cicero's understanding of courage serves as the clear basis of the first part of his definition of magnanimity. Since true courage requires devotion to the right above all else, it follows that the great-souled man will give priority to right action over outward circumstances and will therefore be indifferent to them.[9]

The relation of the second part of Cicero's definition to courage is less clear. Although courage also requires the great-souled man to place the political community's interests ahead of his own and thus to perform useful actions, he would under ordinary circumstances have no reason to expose himself to danger that is associated with great things or deeds. To do so, without some necessary reason, would seem to be recklessness rather than courage which means, it seems, that magnanimity cannot be realized under ordinary circumstances. Cicero's courageous and magnanimous man would, of course, take risks for the defense of the state, but like Aristotle's magnanimous man, he would often seem to have no reason to do so.[10]

The truly magnanimous man would also see no need to demonstrate his courage to others, another possible reason for taking dangerous actions in the absence of necessity. The first part of Cicero's definition precludes this, since honor would be one of the many worldly cares from which the magnanimous man is detached. Cicero directly states that the magnanimous man should be unconcerned with popular acclaim.

> Moreover, true and philosophic greatness of spirit regards the moral goodness to which Nature most aspires as consisting in deeds, not in fame, and prefers to be first in reality rather than in name. And we must approve this view; for he who depends upon the caprice of the ignorant rabble cannot be numbered among the great (1.65).

Not only, then, would the magnanimous man refrain from taking actions for the purpose of appearing noble to the people, but anyone who did so would preclude himself from attaining magnanimity.

It would therefore seem more consistent with Cicero's definition of courage for the great-souled man to take dangerous and arduous actions only when the circumstances required it. However, Cicero omits any mention in his definition of the context in which the magnanimous man would take such actions, and he characterizes them as the mark of a great soul. In this regard, he does not match Aristotle, whose magnanimous man, as just mentioned, is not fond of taking risks or exposing himself to danger but will do so when necessary.[11]

Several complementary explanations account for this seeming inconsistency. First, *On Duties* is, above all, as its title suggests, a work on moral duties and, as such, is more oriented toward practical life than are most of his other philosophical writings. As Cicero states in his introduction, "Although philosophy offers many problems, both important and useful, . . . those teachings which have been handed down on the subject of moral duties seem to have the widest practical application" (1.4). Furthermore, since this text is addressed to Cicero's son and likely other young men, it appears to serve a didactic as well as a philosophical purpose. One may then expect Cicero to discuss the virtues in such a way as to provide his son, a representative of the choice young men of Rome, with clear examples of the best way to live his life in accordance with his duties to others and, most of all, to Rome itself. The magnanimous man is held up as a prime example for any talented young man to follow, and Cicero may in fact be taking great care to ensure a portrayal of him that conveys not a hesitating but an unambiguous endorsement of courageous service to Rome.

These two related attributes of the text imply one explanation for Cicero's omission of necessity in defining the magnanimous man as distinguished by his willingness to subject himself to danger on behalf of the state. Since the magnanimous man is in part a didactic example as well as a philosophical construction, Cicero uses the discussion of magnanimity as a platform for extolling exceptional devotion to the state and the courage necessary for such devotion. Furthermore, the magnanimous man will, in practice, be called upon to serve the state, and Cicero does not wish to leave any room for men with the potential to devote themselves to public life and the defense of the state to consider themselves free from such obligations. As he makes very clear in the opening of his *Republic* (*De Re Publica*) and in its closing Dream of Scipio, the usual condition of life in Rome is one that has great need and poses great challenges for both civilian and military leadership. In Cicero's view, talented young men must prepare and position themselves for arduous endeavors and dangers of leadership. There is little need then, in this practical context, to make clear that one embraces danger only when necessary.

In particular, Cicero is concerned about the attraction of both the retired life of contemplation and that satisfying retreat to the gardens of Epicurus; he is concerned about the possibility that good and talented men will turn away from the dangers of service to the political community in choosing such lives. This provides another explanation for the strength of his assertion that magnanimous men are marked by the performance of arduous tasks, tasks of the sort that philosophers are unlikely to find occasion to perform. By defining magnanimity in such a way as to preclude the quiet life, Cicero hopes to divert choice young men away from it and toward the public sphere.

Cicero does not, of course, intend to turn himself or others away from philosophy. It seems that a genuinely philosophical life captures at least a certain part of magnanimity and that philosophy often contributed to the magnanimity manifest in the models offered by Roman heroes.[12] Writing about this dimension of a philosophical life, he observes that among those, who seek the detachment from worldly cares he praises, "have been found the most famous and by far the foremost philosophers" (1.69). Although he does not mention any philosophers by name, it is reasonable to assume that he has in mind Socrates, Plato, Aristotle, and other thinkers to whom he acknowledges a substantial intellectual debt.[13]

Nevertheless, he ranks magnanimous statesmen higher than these foremost philosophers. While such statesmen share the desire of the philosophers to elevate themselves above the vicissitudes of fortune, their way of life "is more profitable to mankind and contributes more to their own greatness and renown" (1.70). This echoes Cicero's description of the second part of the definition of magnanimity, in which he claims that all the splendor and greatness[14] of magnanimity arises from this part (1.67). The life of a statesman would therefore seem to be the most befitting to the nature of a magnanimous man.

Here in *On Duties* Cicero makes even stronger and explicit statements about the compelling duty of political leadership, statements that recall one of the themes of his *Republic*, which appeared ten years earlier. There Cicero had emphasized, a concept not absent from Aristotle, that virtue is possessed when actualized in acts and practices and, in a more distinctively Ciceronian vein, that the founding and leading of states or political communities is the greatest of virtues. Here in *On Duties* Cicero ties the high need for and thus priority of statesmanship to magnanimity:

> Those whom Nature has endowed with the capacity for administering public affairs should put aside all hesitation, enter the race for public office and take a hand in directing the government; for in no other way can a government be administered or greatness of spirit be made manifest (1.72).

The assertion that magnanimity can be made manifest in no other way than through statesmanship might seem something of a rhetorical exaggeration, for he refers to the detachment of philosophers in the very next sentence. However, for Cicero the great and arduous and clearly dangerous tasks were those of political leadership. Magnanimity in its fullest sense comes to fruition in statesmanship more so than in philosophy.

This argument accentuates a tension within Cicero's account of magnanimity, a tension which arises from his definition of this virtue. If a magnanimous man must possess a quiet mind and be detached from worldly cares, then it would be highly counterproductive for him to engage in activities that threaten his life and endanger the things that make life worth living. Conversely, the life of a philosopher, which seems above all to directly lead to the attainment of equanimity and freedom from anxiety, does not afford a magnanimous man the necessary opportunities to perform useful and perilous actions. Cicero's own life and writings are testimony to the tension between the attraction to the life of philosopher and the constant disturbances and anxieties that are associated with commitment to the active political life.

Cicero acknowledges this tension within his conception of magnanimity. He recognizes the difficulty of reconciling the two parts of this virtue as embodied in its most complete manifestation, the great statesman.

> Not without reason, therefore, are stronger emotions aroused in those who engage in public life than in those who live in retirement, and greater is their ambition for success; the more, therefore, do they need to enjoy greatness of spirit and freedom from annoying cares (1.73).

However, whereas Aristotle was content to leave unresolved certain tensions within his account of magnanimity, Cicero strives to eliminate all inconsistency from his. He tries to overcome this tension by counseling any potential statesman to plan ahead, ensure that he is in a position to enter public life, and keep his composure even in the worst of times. While recognizing that this requires that the statesman possess both "great personal courage" and "great intellectual ability by reflection" (1.81), he seems to consider it a genuine human possibility or at least the kind of model, rarely if ever attained, represented in the tradition of the "Stoic Wiseman."

Cicero takes this argument a step further. Recognizing that even the most careful preparation and reflection may not always be sufficient to avoid disaster, he argues that a magnanimous man can maintain a quiet mind without regard to the circumstances in which he finds himself, including situations in which he is destined to suffer the worst possible fate, such as a prolonged and agonizing death by torture. If justice dictates that the magnanimous man endure such an unimaginable hardship, then he would be happier in doing so than if he remained safe in the comfort of his home with his family and fellow citizens.

Cicero uses the example of Regulus, Roman consul and military leader, who voluntarily returned to Carthage to face such a fate, to stake out this radical position. Regulus was taken prisoner by the Carthaginians and was then released after swearing to return to face torture and ultimately death, unless certain Carthaginian prisoners of war were released. However, instead of advocating for the release of these prisoners upon his return to Rome, he made the case that it was in the public interest to keep them in custody and then returned to Carthage, as promised. He was subsequently tortured to death through the forceful denial of sleep (3.99–100).

Cicero states that Regulus's reasons for ignoring apparent expediency and advocating a course of action that led to his own death by torture arose from courage and greatness of soul (3.99). Further, Cicero claims that, even while undergoing torture, "he enjoyed a happier lot than if he had remained at home an aged prisoner of war, a man of consular rank forsworn" (3.100). Because maintaining custody of the Carthaginian prisoners was in the best interests of Rome, and because the breaking of an oath sworn under the laws of war was unjust, Regulus preferred to follow the mandate of courage and embraced his painful end without reservation.

Although this example does not constitute a formal argument for the position that a magnanimous man must maintain a quiet mind even while undergoing the worst imaginable suffering, it is clear that Cicero holds this position.[15] This is also the position that Cicero must maintain in order to ensure the internal consistency of his conception of magnanimity. If the magnanimous man were unable to bear such suffering with detachment or even happiness, then it would be impossible for him to be distinguished simultaneously by both aloofness from worldly concerns and the performance of useful acts that may also result in an agonizing death.

This position is, in turn, premised upon a strong yet unproven claim. In order for Regulus, or any other magnanimous man, to accept such extreme discomfort with equanimity, it must be within the realm of human possibility to be happy while on the rack, as it were. Cicero asserts that it is, but he does not support this assertion with philosophical argument within his discussion of magnanimity in *On Duties*.[16]

II. CICERO'S MAGNANIMITY AND ARISTOTLE'S: RELATED AND COMPARED

Cicero's view in this context that virtue alone is sufficient for happiness and that the genuinely magnanimous man is therefore always happy is, perhaps, his most fundamental departure from Aristotle, for whom pleasure is an ingredient in happiness.[17] Although Cicero struggles with the differences between the Peripatetics and Stoics on this matter in other works, especially in *On the Ultimate Good and Ultimate Evil*, here in *On Duties* he clearly comes down on the Stoic side that virtue assures happiness. Since Regulus's experience was the antithesis of pleasure, Aristotle would not maintain that Regulus, or any other human being, could be happy under these conditions. He also states directly and forcefully in Book VII of the *Nicomachean Ethics* that one who suffers on the rack cannot possibly be happy.[18] He would therefore reject Cicero's claim to the contrary and, along with it, the attempt to reconcile equanimity with toil and danger. It is also worth noting that Aristotle never once refers to the magnanimous man as happy.[19]

Other differences on magnanimity between Cicero and Aristotle can best be summarized at this point against the important background of what they share, namely, a conception of magnanimity as the virtue that allows one to stand confidently aloof from and indifferent to the vicissitudes of fortune as well as to such ordinary concerns as wealth, status, power, and the praise of common people should they even receive it.[20] It is a virtue that disposes its possessor to great enterprises in which even life itself might be risked and surrendered. To be sure, Aristotle's magnanimous man is not easily moved by fortune but is not altogether unconcerned with it either.[21] Nor, of course, is he unconcerned with honor, as one whom virtue alone made happy should be and as Cicero's magnanimous man indeed is.[22]

Cicero departs from Aristotle in choosing to base his idea of magnanimity on courage rather than on the pursuit of highest and justly deserved honors, the defining concern of Aristotle's magnanimity. Furthermore, instead of claiming, as Aristotle does, that the magnanimous man is great in large part because he is aware of his own greatness through self-knowledge, Cicero shifts the focus to the magnanimous man's freedom from passion and attachment to the Stoic doctrine that virtue is the only—or, at least, the highest—good. The Stoic texts that we have from the period preceding Cicero do not contain any extensive or systematic consideration of magnanimity. However, there is evidence that the Stoic tradition stripped Aristotelian magnanimity of some of its more self-regarding aspects, linked magnanimity with courage and challenged a conception of courage that saw it exclusively or primarily as valor in war.[23] It appears then that some of Cicero's departures from Aristotle in explicating magnanimity are largely attributable to his appropriation of Stoic material in arriving at his own understanding of this virtue.

With one exception, Cicero's other differences from Aristotle regarding magnanimity appear to emerge from Cicero's emphatic concern with and practice of statesmanship and from his Roman patriotism and related attachment to republican liberty. The exception is the paradox that Aristotle, "the philosopher" of antiquity and the Western tradition, defines a magnanimous man who is not particularly philosophical while Cicero, "the statesman" of antiquity and beyond, clearly sees a philosophical dimension to magnanimity. Whereas Aristotle's magnanimous man, considering nothing great, is indifferent to philosophy and appears to lack the capacity to philosophize,[24] the greatness of soul of Cicero's model is nourished and sustained by philosophy, a point especially and dramatically made in his *Republic*'s concluding Dream of Scipio. It is important to recall here that Aristotle's magnanimous man, although a peak of human excellence as defined by the moral virtues, does not represent the highest human existence. The tensions within Aristotle's conception of magnanimity, specifically the conflict between the magnanimous man's search for honor and his desire for self-sufficiency, point the way toward the contemplative man as the ultimate pinnacle of human excellence.

Cicero's elevation of philosophy in relation to magnanimity is done in a way consistent with the higher rank he accords to statesmanship throughout his writings. Understandably Cicero places a greater emphasis than Aristotle does on the relationship between magnanimity and statesmanship.[25] Whereas Aristotle makes at most passing references to the political role of the magnanimous man and leaves it to his readers to reconstruct the idea of the great statesman from his discussion of magnanimity, Cicero, as shown above, refers numerous times to both the political aspects of this virtue and the political role of the man who most perfectly embodies it. For Cicero, magnanimity is best manifested and likely only capable of full realization in the life of the statesman. His teaching on magnanimity then merges with his conception of the model statesman. Magnanimity is an important dimension of the model statesman but not all that is needed.

Cicero's explicit political concern leads, it seems, to other differences with Aristotle on magnanimity. Although a sense of the tension within the character of the magnanimous man and between such a man and a just and free society can be found in Aristotle, Cicero goes to far greater lengths in describing the threat to the political community posed by the overweening ambition of men who are otherwise great-souled and supremely talented but who lack the restraint of justice. Whereas Aristotle does not once mention this threat within his discussion of magnanimity within the *Nicomachean Ethics* and addresses it only by implication in the *Politics*,[26] Cicero makes repeated and emphatic references to it throughout his discussion of this virtue in *On Duties*. He also does not adopt Aristotle's solution or dismissal of the problem: the idea that the magnanimous man does not hold power in high regard, is disinclined to act in an ignoble fashion, and would, as a result, be unlikely to seize power by devious or unlawful means.[27] Cicero's concern with the corruption of potential magnanimity was seen to be informed by his perception of the tyranny of Caesar, and this drew him to emphasize a conception of magnanimity that included inner restraints in favor of a just and good political leadership. He turned this way, it seems, because he found that no political institutions, however well-designed, are sufficient to check the power of a very talented and ingenious politician, let alone a general with numerous forces under his command.

Cicero's emphatic concern with a true and thus magnanimous statesmanship likely played a role in his finding no room for another feature of the Aristotelian magnanimous man, specifically his tendency to be idle except when pursuing great honors or performing great tasks.[28] As Cicero makes clear in the preface to his *Republic*, this represents an unworkable and therefore dangerous approach to our political duties. His criticism of philosophers who take such an approach clearly represents what he would also direct at this feature of the Aristotelian magnanimous man.[29] Instead of waiting in the wings during times of peace and taking control in the midst of a crisis, a statesman must ensure that he is in a position to take action. To that end, he must at all times prepare for political leadership and seek or hold political office, even if doing so may not result in the immediate bestowing of great honors upon him or if he does not yet have the opportunity to take great actions. Otherwise, he will not only be powerless to act in times of crisis but also will lack the necessary political skill to lead when such skill is most needed for the safety of the political community.[30]

Both of these departures from Aristotle make Cicero's conception of magnanimity a more workable model of the ideal statesman than its predecessor, not only for Cicero's own time but also for our own democratic age. Neither

Aristotle's nor Cicero's magnanimous man can be said to seek popular acclaim for its own sake or to regard popular approval alone as the ultimate authority in political matters. Neither then could be seen to offer a model of statesmanship in which pure democracy is the governing ideal. Nevertheless, because Cicero's magnanimous man possesses far stricter internal checks on his desire for power than does Aristotle's, he would seem less likely than the Aristotelian magnanimous man to encroach upon the people's just freedom, if elected to public office.

More importantly, perhaps, the Aristotelian magnanimous man may never attain public office in a democracy in the first place. As in Cicero's time, the process of election to public office would require the great statesman to suffer many indignities and take many actions that were, in themselves, far from great or noble. Cicero's magnanimous statesman, as already shown, would be willing to undergo such a process to place himself in a position to benefit the state, whereas Aristotle's may wait for an opportunity to take great actions to fall into his lap, an unlikely event in a large, modern, democratic state.

Overall and with a special focus on his work, *On Duties,* it can be said that Cicero considers the magnanimous statesman to be the pinnacle of human excellence, and he strives to reconcile the tensions that seem just beneath the surface in this model. In this effort he even takes the extreme position that the magnanimous man remains happy and aloof from worldly cares when subjected to the worst sort of torture.

If one is willing to accept that happiness remains possible under these conditions, then Cicero's magnanimous man is clearly a more perfect human being than Aristotle's. He, unlike Aristotle's magnanimous man, is free from all internal contradictions and enjoys perfect self-sufficiency. He is also able to engage in both philosophy and politics, the two pursuits which both thinkers consider superior to all others, in spite of their disagreement regarding the value of each relative to the other.

If, however, one follows Aristotle in considering pleasure an essential ingredient of happiness, then Cicero's magnanimous man, while an attractive ideal, is beyond the realm of human possibility. He, even more than Aristotle's magnanimous man, would be afflicted with tensions bordering on contradictions. While wishing to possess an unruffled quietude and also to risk all comfort in the defense of the state, he would find himself being forced to choose to follow one part of his nature and abandon the other. Either he leads the life of the philosopher, in which case he may never perform courageous actions, or he throws himself into public affairs, in which case he could never experience the detachment from worldly matters for which he is suited. Then too through the suffering he experiences, he would want to affirm his happiness as guaranteed by his virtue. Regardless of his choices, the happiness

which Cicero attributes to him would remain elusive, and Aristotle's magnanimous man would be a more realistic, if somewhat less elevated, arche-
type of the great man.

NOTES

1. Aristotle, *Eudemian Ethics* 1232b20–25 and associated discussion in chapter 2
of the present volume, 17–20.
2. One way or another Cicero seemed to know his Aristotle well. He had access to
as much, if not more, of the Aristotelian corpus than is now extant, and he appropri-
ates Aristotelian arguments at various points in his writings. Cicero lived at the very
juncture in time and even in place when and where the new Aristotelian corpus of Andronicus was put together and made available and the hitherto known popular or ex-
oteric writings (including dialogues) of Aristotle began their disappearance, which
has resulted in their all but complete loss. The story of both the puzzle of the disappearance of Aristotle's popular writings after the Andronicus edition of Cicero's lifetime and the development of that edition at Rome, with the hand of Cicero likely involved, is told succinctly in Roger Masters, "The Case of Aristotle's Missing
Dialogues," *Political Theory* 5 (February, 1977): 31–33. Cicero did not, it seems,
know with assurance that our *Nicomachean Ethics* and *Politics* were works of Aristotle. Cicero never cites these works directly, though he mentions the *Nicomachean
Ethics* and shows himself aware that this work is attributed to Aristotle; he himself is
inclined to think it was authored by Aristotle's son Nicomachus (*De Finibus* 5.12). As
early as 55 B.C., during a time when other letters indicate Cicero is reading Aristotle,
Cicero writes Atticus (*Ep. Att.* 4.10) that he "is being sustained by the library of Faus-
tus" at Cumae, a library thought to contain the esoteric writings of Aristotle and
Theophrastus. See Dorothea Frede, "Constitution and Citizenship: Peripatetic Influence on Cicero's Political Conceptions in the De re publica," in *Cicero's Knowledge
of The Peripatos*, ed. William Fortenbaugh and Peter Steinmetz, (New Brunswick,
N.J.: Transaction Publishers, 1989), 95, n. 18. While conceding that Cicero could
"have discovered all the Andronican Aristotle," Donald Earl raises doubts about the
presence of the Aristotle manuscripts in the library at Cumae and Cicero's knowledge
of the new Aristotle, "Prologue-form in Ancient Historiography," *Aufstieg Und
Niedergang Der Römischen Welt I. 2* (Berlin: Walter De Gruyter, 1972), 853, 850ff. A
similar conclusion regarding Cicero's knowledge of "the mature Aristotle" was
reached earlier, though without much argument, in W. W. How, "Cicero's Ideal In His
De Republica," *Journal of Roman Studies* 20 (1930): 27. Powell emphasizes the different views on the extent of Cicero's knowledge of the Andronican Aristotle, and
Long urges readers to keep an open mind on the question even as he inclines against
thinking Cicero knew much of our Aristotle. J. G. F. Powell, "Introduction: Cicero's
Philosophical Works and their Background," and A. A. Long, "Cicero's Plato and
Aristotle," in *Cicero the Philosopher*, ed. J. G. F. Powell (Oxford: Clarendon Press,
1995), 18, 42–43, and n.11.

3. For example, *Tusculanae Disputationes* (hereafter *Tusc. Disp.*), 2.53 and *De Finibus*, 2.95.

4. We use the following translation here and throughout the paper: Marcus Tullius Cicero, *De Officiis*, trans. Walter Miller. (Cambridge: Harvard University Press, 1913).

5. Aristotle, *Nicomachean Ethics*, 1115a30–34; 1117b12–14.

6. See chapter 2 of the present volume, 14ff.

7. *To Friends (Ep. fam.)* 9. 14. 2; *To Atticus (Ad Att.)* 2.17; *Pro Archia* 28. Plutarch in his *Lives* ("Demosthenes," "Cicero" and "Demosthenes and Cicero") pays considerable attention to Cicero's "love of distinction," a quality seen as good in some ways but overall thought to be carried to excess by Cicero. One of Cicero's lost works is *De Gloria*; he alludes to it and may well be summarizing it in *On Duties* 2.31.

8. *Tusc. Disp.*, 4.53 (translation is ours).

9. Other places in the writings of Cicero where courage is displaced by magnanimity or is seen as a part of it are *Tusc. Disp.*, 2.32, *De Partitione Oratoria*, 77, *De Oratore*, 1.56, 2.67.

10. *Nicomachean Ethics*, 1124b 6ff.

11. *Nicomachean Ethics*, 1124b25–26.

12. Larry Arnhart aptly observes that Cicero uses "philosophic magnanimity to moderate the restless ambition of the magnanimous statesman without weakening his motives for political activity." "Statesmanship as Magnanimity: Classical, Christian & Modern," *Polity* 16, no. 2. (Winter, 1983): 267.

13. Cicero praises Socrates' magnanimity in *Tusc. Disp*, 1.71.

14. Cicero uses the term *amplitudo* in both places.

15. Cicero does, in fact, state that he holds this position at *Tusc. Disp.*, 5.80, although he acknowledges at 76 that pain is the greatest enemy of magnanimity and the other virtues.

16. One must turn to Book V of the *Tusc. Disp.* for Cicero's argument that virtue alone is sufficient for happiness, a full evaluation of which is beyond the scope of this paper.

17. *Nicomachean Ethics*, 1177a 23ff.; also, 1153b 12ff.

18. *Nicomachean Ethics*, 1153b 18–20.

19. We wonder then whether Aristotle's magnanimous man is altogether happy, as is commonly thought and claimed above by Holloway in Chapter 2 of the present volume, 26.

20. *Nicomachean Ethics*, 1124a 4ff. and *On Duties* 1.65, quoted and discussed above.

21. *Nicomachean Ethics*, 1124a 14ff.

22. *On Duties* 1.66, quoted and discussed above.

23. A. A. Long and D. N. Sedley (eds.), *Hellenistic Philosophers: Translations of the Principal Sources with Philosophical Commentary*, Vol. 1 (Cambridge: Cambridge University Press, 1987), 377–78.

24. *Nicomachean Ethics*, 1125a2–3, where Aristotle writes: (oude *thaumastikos*: ouden gar mega autôi estin) "He (the magnanimous man) is not inclined to wonder, because nothing is great to him" (translation and emphasis ours). The term *thaumastikos*,

which appears only once in the extant Aristotelian corpus, is derived from the verb *thaumazein*, to wonder, which is also used by both Plato and Aristotle to signify the state of mind that serves as the precursor to philosophic investigation. Because the magnanimous man is not inclined to wonder, he lacks the most basic prerequisite for philosophy. See Holloway in chapter 2 of the present volume, 26–27, for a similar argument, as well as Harry Jaffa, *Thomism and Aristotelianism: A Study of the Commentary by Thomas Aquinas on the Nicomachean Ethics* (Chicago: University of Chicago Press, 1952), ch. vi. For arguments in favor of the opposite interpretation—that the magnanimous man is, in fact, capable of philosophy—see Arnhart, "Statesmanship as Magnanimity," 265ff. and Jacob Howland, "Aristotle's Great-Souled Man," *The Review of Politics* 64, no. 1 (Winter, 2002): 27–56, especially 47ff. A definitive attempt to settle this controversy is beyond the scope of this paper.

25. Arnhart, "Statesmanship as Magnanimity," 264.

26. Aristotle, *Politics*, 1325a 34ff.

27. See chapter 2 of the present volume, 21.

28. *Nicomachean Ethics*, 1124b25–27.

29. Cicero's only reference to magnanimity in *De Re Publica* is within this discussion. See Book I, 9, where he states that magnanimous men should be involved in politics to ensure that they are not ruled over by wicked men.

30. *De Re Publica* 1, 11.

4

Thomas Aquinas on Magnanimous and Prudent Statesmanship

Kenneth L. Deutsch[1]

The contemporary Western world has experienced very few statesmen. Some commentators have placed primary responsibility for this phenomenon on the influence of Christianity on our civilization. Leo Strauss mentions "the Christian mistrust of purely human virtue, for the sake of humiliating pride in its own virtues."[2] Christian moral teaching is seen to conflict with human excellence. Christianity, it has also been claimed, negates the heroic virtues of "magnanimity" or greatness of soul that are considered basic to statesmanship. Christian humility has restricted men and women of great ambitions. The critics of Christianity claim that revival of statesmanship would require a return to the Greek and Roman pagan virtues of magnanimity—the pursuit of great ambition that strives for fame and power, honor and glory, which will manifest itself in deeds surviving the vicissitudes of political life.[3] It is the purpose of this chapter to demonstrate, through a discussion of Thomas Aquinas' political thought, that a Christian notion of the magnanimous and prudent statesman is conceivable and consistent with Christian ethics. Before exploring Thomas Aquinas' approach to magnanimous statesmanship in some detail, we shall compare the meaning that Aristotle and Augustine gave to the virtue of magnanimity as a feature of political leadership.

ARISTOTLE AND GREEK MAGNANIMITY

Aristotle was a true representative of the ancient Greek position which expressed a supreme disdain for servile subjection. The Greeks contrasted human grandeur (*megalopsychia*) with servile subjection. The Romans would later refer to this grandeur as "greatness of soul" (which Cicero translated as *magnanimitas*). For Aristotle this grandeur was based on an ethically good attitude toward life.

The Greek notion of human grandeur took two forms, both founded on the same basic attitude—the disdain for servile subjection. One form was active and consisted of political grandeur. This disposition sought to make great plans and use one's talents to carry them out. The world of material interests was held in contempt for a great cause. The other form was contemplative ethical grandeur. Here human greatness must be founded in ethical excellence. Socrates is the prototype of this approach in which the wise person transcends all the outward vicissitudes of political life through inner integrity, self-awareness, and self-respect. For the person of ethical grandeur, the political actor is a dangerous fool who must be kept down.[4]

The Aristotelian man of grandeur is a variation on the two Greek forms. Magnanimity is the crown of all the virtues because it presupposes excellence in all of them. It is the virtue that concerns itself with the right attitude towards the most important of all external goods: honor, or the recognition of one's own excellence. Since the truly great souled man is preeminent in all the virtues, he deserves the highest honor. Any honor that he demands is only what is his due. Magnanimity is the only virtue that cannot lapse into vice. For Aristotle, no truly great-souled man can claim more honor than is his due. If he actually has the excellence of soul that deserves the highest recognition, failure to demand that recognition would be a mark of weakness, a sign of pusillanimity.

The magnanimous man does not set his heart on either political power or riches for themselves, but he esteems them for the honor that accrues to their possessor. He is conscious of the fact that, for the small-minded many, political power and/or wealth are more easily discernible than the virtue that is his true claim to respect. For Aristotle, the truly magnanimous man has contempt for his *merely* rich and powerful inferiors. That contempt is justified by the fact that he *is* superior, whereas that of the merely rich and powerful is not justified because they are only *apparently* superior. This magnanimous man should be a ruler. It is not the glory of the cause nor the help he might render to others that galvanizes him into political action but the fear of having his own reputation besmirched with the accusation of cowardice. In the absence of any extramundane immortality to look forward to, Aristotle affirmed the pagan Greek concern for the perdurance of his name and fame after death by the political and other deeds done while he still lived.

From the Christian perspective, Aristotle's magnanimous statesman is characterized by some self-centered qualities that are at the basis of statesmanship. Aristotle's magnanimous statesmanship betrays the "bad side" of Aristotle's ethics.

AUGUSTINE'S REACTION TO PAGAN HUMAN GRANDEUR

The teachings of Jesus emphasized that he was a king, but that his kingdom was not of this world. His kingdom was not a thing of political power but a reign in the souls of men who were meek and humble. To the Jews this would be a disappointment and a scandal—a "stumbling block." To the Greeks, his example of humility, charity, and universal forgiveness was mere foolishness. Jesus' claims to be divine and yet his refusal to accept the honors and acclaim demanded by even the mere earthly kings would have made Jesus, in pagan Greek eyes, a kind of apotheosis of the pusillanimous man. Jesus also emphasized that human beings had dignity as children of God and that there was the motive for loving and honoring each other. This emphasis on the great dignity and worth of every single human individual was seen by the Greek and Latin Church fathers as a corrective both to the Roman aberration of the total subordination of the individual to the state and the Greek pursuit of personal glory.

Such high-minded pagan figures as Epictetus, Marcus Aurelius, and Celsus could only view Christian humility and martyrdom as weak and cowardly pettiness that expressed perverse disgust for human grandeur and distrust of the autonomous power of men. Celsus viewed Christian humility as not only a plagiarism of Plato, but claimed that the Christians had interpreted Plato incorrectly. For Plato's *tapeinos* or humble man must always bear witness to a "well-ordered" humility. According to Celsus the Christians did not preach this reasonable ordering: Christians, after all, allowed thieves and prostitutes to enter first what they called the kingdom of God.[5]

For Augustine and many of the early Church fathers, humility or greatness of soul is an original Christian quality that was unknown among the pagans. Augustine was to express this general patristic conviction very clearly: To know your own humanity is true humility, for true humanity is God's creation that has been vitiated by human sin. Therefore knowing oneself in the light of God and sin should bring about humble obedience in faith—this should be called *magnanimitas*, human greatness. So over against pagan humanism and statesmanship, Augustine stressed the grandeur of God who has mercy on man in his insignificance. Members of the City of God may be recognized for their achievement, but they must transmit all the recognition they receive to the glory of God. True happiness cannot come to Christian statesmen from power, wealth, or adulation:

> But we say they are happy if they rule justly; if they are not lifted up amid the praises of those who pay them sublime honors, and the obsequiousness of those who salute them with an excessive humility, but remember they are men . . . ; if

they prefer to govern depraved desires rather than any nation whatever; and if they do all these things not through ardent desire of empty glory, but through love of eternal felicity, not neglecting to offer to the true God, who is their God, for their sins, the sacrifices of humility, contrition and prayer. Such Christian emperors, we say, are happy in the present time by hope and are destined to be so in the enjoyment of the reality itself, when that which we wait for shall have arrived.[6]

Augustine's notion of individual happiness takes a very limited view of the whole sphere of earthly political pursuits. It is a view that sees no possibility of a reconciliation between the pursuit of temporal glory in the earthly city and the pursuit of eternal glory in the City of God. There was no question of a synthesis between pagan grandeur and Christian humility. The relationship between man's liberation of himself politically and salvation from God would receive particular emphasis later with Thomas Aquinas. In their recognition of God's true greatness, patristic and early medieval theologians negated man's secular grandeur and were unable to accord to it a reasonable or proper place. Not until Thomas Aquinas in the thirteenth century was an accommodation between human grandeur and humility ventured. What Aquinas has to present is a creative tension between Aristotelian virtue and Christian humility and revelation. As reliant as Aquinas is on Aristotle and Augustine for the terms and the structure of his thought, the virtue of magnanimous statesmanship as he defines it turns out to be something quite different from the virtue as Aristotle and Augustine define it.

AQUINAS AND THE MAGNANIMOUS MAN

Aquinas agrees with Aristotle that magnanimity is a virtue dealing with the right-reasoned attitude toward honor; and he agrees, too, that it is concerned with the great honors owing to a great man who is preeminent in all the virtues. Aquinas, like Aristotle, writes of two virtues dealing with honor—one nameless and dealing with the ordinary honors owing to ordinary men and another dealing with the great honors owing to the men who are truly extraordinary. The latter is the virtue of magnanimity.

> We must conclude that the proper matter of magnanimity is great honor, and that a magnanimous man tends to such things as are deserving of honors.[7]

The wording here is quite significant. It suggests that, for Aquinas, the magnanimous man should be more concerned with the great deeds that deserve honor than with the honor that accrues to them. The good deeds are the end of his endeavor; the honor is only the natural consequences of the end achieved.

Nature, claims Aquinas, is not a mere shadow of the supernatural but contains spiritual energies itself. The divine plan of creation cannot be understood without the human race whose existence gives earthly and heavenly meaning to it. Humanity is a partner of God in the building up of the world.

According to Aquinas, the act of creating is the unfolding of a multiplicity of existences. He notes that *Genesis* states that "God created man in his image, in the image of God he created him" (I:27). Whoever speaks of the "image of God" finds himself facing the inevitability of multiplicity. Since God cannot be sufficiently well represented by one finite creature, the diverse multiplication of human creatures provides a compensation for their individual deficiencies. Diverse human beings reflect the multiple beauty of God.

> God has produced things in the human being in order to communicate his goodness to the created things and to represent his goodness in them. And because his goodness cannot be represented efficiently in one single creature, he created multiple and diverse things in such a way that whatever is lacking in one creature in representing the divine goodness may be made up for by another. Thus the goodness which in God is simple and unique is found in countless and differentiated creatures. Consequently it is the entire universe which shares perfectly the goodness of God and represents it more than any one creature by itself.[8]

This interrelatedness among human beings is a sacred ordering of creation in which humanity has a sacred vocation—the humanization of nature. Through the realization of the "image of God" in the world, human persons with specific talents build up the world. Human beings are not totally wretched. Man is responsible for his good actions as well as his evil deeds. As a humble creature, man knows that his powers are gifts of God. Aquinas does not present a drama of God's grandeur as contrasted with puny man. The drama is shifted to man; it is concerned with the tension between human grandeur and human limitations. Magnanimity, for Aquinas, is a virtue of human social and political hope, to be realized through one's own human strength and good deeds; honor must be viewed as the natural consequence of good deeds and not merely as an end in itself.

Man has his own worth not only thanks to God's worth but also "as an inalienable human worth which is peculiarly his own."[9] In an important text, a commentary on *Job*, man is viewed as the ultimate subject. Here Aquinas defends Job's argument with God.

> Thus it seems as though a discussion between man and God is unthinkable because of the eminence with which God transcends man. But in that case we must

remember that the truth is not different depending on who speaks it; therefore one who speaks the truth can never be put in the wrong, *no matter who he is speaking with*.[10]

From the very outset of his discussion of magnanimity, Aquinas is careful to reconcile it with humility. There is no necessary conflict between humility and magnanimity; they are, rather, necessary concomitants in a great man who looks at himself—his talents—truthfully:

> There is in man something great which he possesses through the gift of God; and something defective which accrues to him through the weakness of nature. Accordingly magnanimity makes a man deem himself worthy of great things in consideration of the gifts he holds from God: Thus if his soul is endowed with great virtue, magnanimity makes him tend to perfect works of virtue; and the same is to be said of the use of any other good, such as science or external fortune. On the other hand, humility makes a man think of his own deficiency and magnanimity makes him despise others in so far as they fall away from God's gifts. Yet humility makes us honor others and esteem them better than ourselves, in so far as we see some of God's gifts in them.[11]

Any great gift, such as effective rulership over insufficient human beings, must engender in their possessor not the desire for great honor but rather the desire to do great things on behalf of the community of insufficient persons and in the glorification of God. Aquinas claims that this is what Jesus was advocating when He said: "So let your light shine before men, that they may see your good works and glorify [not you but] your Father who is in Heaven" (Matt. 5:16). Aquinas defines the meaning of magnanimous man in such a way that Aristotle's and Augustine's positions are appropriated, altered, and transformed.

AQUINAS AND MAGNANIMOUS STATESMANSHIP

The desire of the magnanimous man to do great things for God and his neighbor, to realize to their fullest the gifts God has given him, is consonant with a recognition that in himself and left to himself he has many weaknesses and sinful tendencies. This double condition or tension within himself, of strength and weakness, also affects his attitude toward his fellow man and the nature of politics. The desire for social and political honor can be irrational in three ways:

> First, when a man desires recognition of an excellence which he has not; this is to desire more than his share of honor. Secondly, when a man desires honor for himself without referring it to God. Thirdly, when a man's appetite rests in honor itself, without referring it to the profit of others.[12]

The first aberration is that of the excess of mediocre man—the desire for political honor or responsibility for excellence that he actually does not possess. The last two aberrations the magnanimous man may be guilty of. His honored status may tempt him to forget his created status and his obligation to employ those gifts for other insufficient human beings. The political ruler must be motivated by a concern for the political good and not for personal ambition alone. These two limitations on a great man's attitude toward honor demonstrate the importance of the Christian virtues of humility and charity as clear norms for judging the rationality of a true statesman's attitude toward the great honors that *are* his due.

As an infinitely perfect being, God has no need for honor or glory. God did not create the world in order to receive the recognition, the honor, and the glory of human beings. God created in order to communicate and manifest His perfection to someone outside Himself. Rational creatures, seeing the excellence of God manifested in His creatures, do acknowledge it, do honor and glorify God; but that was not the motive for which God created. Magnanimous statesmen should be like God. Their chief concern should be great deeds and they should acknowledge them in others. But the glory and the honor must not be the sole motive of the talented magnanimous statesmen, who administer or create a polity for the common good, any more than glory was the motive for God in creating.[13] Men in high positions of public trust cannot be indifferent about their reputations; but they should secure their reputations by performing the duties of their positions in such a way as to *merit* honor and glory.

Like Aristotle, Aquinas admits that a great man may, out of ignorance of his own abilities or from fear of failure, become guilty of pusillanimity by not doing the great things of which he is actually capable. The repeated cautions that Aquinas gives to men about their attitude toward honor suggests to him that the far more dangerous aberration from magnanimity is by excess rather than by defect. This position reflects his view of both the need for prudent rulership or statesmanship and the need for limits placed on that honorable political task.

Aquinas' approach to the qualities of excellence in rulership and the limited nature of the political task is best discerned in his partial rejection of both the pagan and patristic notions of magnanimity. His standard of magnanimous statesmanship clearly rejects the arrogance of political power. Although it is anachronistic to declare Aquinas to be a precursor of "Whiggery," it shall be shown that he, like Cicero, considered rulership to be a public trust that must not devolve into tyranny. As Aquinas put it:

First it is necessary that the man who is raised up to be king by those whom it concerns should be of such condition that it is impossible that he should become a tyrant. . . . Then, once the king is established, the government of the kingdom must be so arranged that the opportunity to tyrannize is removed. At the same time his power should be so tempered that he cannot easily fall into tyranny.[14]

For Aquinas, civil society was regarded as an integral part of the divine order and, like the whole, as being diversified in degrees. Relations between human beings, as well as between the faculties of the individual human being, reflected the cosmic law by which the higher entity ruled the lower. Thus,

the [power of] reason rules the irascible and concupiscible powers by a political rule, such as that by which free men are ruled, who in some respect have a free will of their own.[15]

A man's bodily power was subject to the "sensitive powers" and both were ruled by the intellect or reason. (In a similar way, in civil society the proper "order among men" was for those who possessed talents in understanding and administration to rule those who were less intelligent but strong in body.) For Aquinas, the power of the magnanimous statesman is never concerned with purely "despotic" methods, but it is better understood in terms of "political" rule. The above analogy claims that the rule of reason within the individual is likewise a "political" rule: each of these lower powers contains within itself a certain freedom of its own, a certain inner power of resistance, and it is the role of prudence and charity to "overcome" this resistance, although never in such a way as to repress the power itself. Likewise the magnanimous statesman is able to distinguish real from apparent greatness.

Prudence as "practical wisdom" found in the magnanimous statesmen rarely "overpowers" the activities of others in civil society in the manner of political manipulation, but rather channels these activities into a prudent mode of response for the common good. A magnanimous ruler, therefore, is not a dictator, even a benevolent one. Rather, he appeals to the citizens in terms of their own nature by trying to do what is just. Civil society is in disorder when a person is in authority "not because of the eminence of his understanding," but because he has usurped the government by "bodily strength" or has been appointed to rule "on the basis of sensual affection." Such a situation is like that in which an individual intellect merely followed the lead of the sensual faculty.

MORAL PRUDENCE AND THE MAGNANIMOUS STATESMAN

The meaning and centrality of prudence in Aquinas' political philosophy is found in the analogy of the Divine Providence in which God is the prudential

Person *par excellence*. Man is at his best as man when, both as rational creature and as created being made in the image of God, he acts according to the measure of practical wisdom that comes to the person, whether by a kind of human or divine inspiration, or by human industry, or by a combination of these elements. Man can learn from prudence not only self-governance, but the management of the affairs of the state as well. For Aquinas, prudence is the master virtue that controls all the rest. Taken as a moral virtue that properly directs man to his final end, prudence presupposes not only a knowledge of the end as well as the means that lead to it, but the "rectitude of the appetite" (or will) insofar as it conformed to the end. Aquinas clearly distinguishes "prudence" in the sense of "cleverness" (*astutia*) from "moral prudence" (*prudentia*) which is a virtue of practical reasoning. Thomas Gilby characterizes Aquinas' view of moral prudence as:

a good habit or settled quality, of the practical reason giving an active bent toward right doing as an individual act; it ranges from our pondering over what should be done through our judgment of what we should choose to do, and is completed in that being made an effective command.[16]

A magnanimous and prudent person is one who makes his decisions in the full light of the moral law as best he can know it through the light of his reason and in consultation with others who are wise. For Aquinas, being prudent means not only knowing the moral law, but knowing also how to apply it in particular material circumstances and in a way that fully respects the right order of means to ends. In effect, for Aquinas, political prudence requires that (a) the ends of one's actions be morally right, and that (b) the means be morally suited to those same ends. An obvious case in point would include "national security" as a legitimate moral end, but not all means can justify its pursuit. For Aquinas, the common good must be aligned with the virtue of *prudentia* whereby public disorder, scandal, and crime are regulated. It is of great importance that *prudentia* be present in the highest degree in the rulers of a state. A magnanimous and prudent statesman is one who (1) assiduously investigates alternative courses of conduct together with the means for accomplishing a moral end; (2) who, beyond the initial process of policy inquiry and investigation, knows how to make practical judgments as to what needs to be done; and most crucially, having made this judgment (3) commands through his will that a given course of political action be omitted or performed. Such a ruler also needs a good memory whereby he can draw from the storehouse of his past experience; circumspection, which involves close attention to the attendant circumstances of a moral decision; and foresight, whereby he can reasonably project into the future certain consequences of a given line of action.[17]

Most importantly, the magnanimous and prudent statesman must be a morally disciplined individual who must be able to distance himself from his own desires so that he can be free of their power and make some judgment about it. Such statesmanship is temperate and questioning; it approves of harmoniousness, proportion, and economy. For Aquinas, this kind of statesmanship also needs both the *esprit de geometrie* and the *esprit de finesse*—the "hard virtues of exact workmanship along with the "disciplines" of courtesy and charity.

MAGNANIMOUS STATESMANSHIP AND THE MIXED REGIME

Prudent rulers can only operate when good government exists, namely, rule that is exercised for the "common good," whereby man's physical needs and the conditions for a good life produce universal (though imperfect) happiness. Those actions are prudent and magnanimous that produce happiness for the "multitude." In the *Summa* when Aquinas asks himself what is the best form of government, he states the following:

> The best form of government is in a State or Kingdom wherein one is given the power to preside over all, while under him are others having governing powers. Yet a government of this kind is shared by all, because all are eligible to govern, and because the rulers are chosen by all. This is the best form of polity, being partly kingdom, since there is one at the head of all; partly aristocracy, insofar as a number of persons are set in authority; partly democracy, that is, government by the people, insofar as the rulers can be chosen from people and the people have the rights to choose their rulers.[18]

There exists a common interest between insufficient persons that goes beyond their legitimate private interests. No one person can determine that interest. As Aquinas states:

> Where there are many men together and each one looks after his own interest, the group would be broken up and scattered unless there were someone to take care of what appertains to the common good. . . . There must, therefore, be something which impels toward the common good of the many, over and above that which impels toward the private good of each individual. Wherefore in all things that are ordained toward a single end, there is something to be found which rules the rest.[19]

This something that rules the rest exists for the community. Statesmanship exists in order for the members of the community to realize their talents and to achieve their perfection. For Aquinas, it is proper for rulers to recognize themselves as their subjects' servants. However, as Jacques Maritain, a great neo-Thomist, warns: "one of the most instructive chapters of a Christian philosophy would deal with what I might call the intermingling of masks and offices. Not only is the part of iniquity often played under the mask of justice for the common good, but masks of iniquity can fill and mar the roles of justice."[20] Serious moral scrutiny must be applied to those who call themselves "servants" of justice and the common good.

There is no doubt as to Aquinas' personal preference for magnanimous monarchical rule, provided that the rule be just and prudent. Aquinas' teaching claims that there is no one form of government that is best in any absolute sense. That form of government is best that under given conditions of time, place, and culture most effectively serves the needs of the people in terms of the common good. Aquinas agrees with Augustine, who expresses the view that in a civil society that is basically pervaded by a sense of responsibility and moderation the people should choose their own magistrates. Otherwise, in a situation where a society is basically corrupt and degenerate, the choice could be reserved to a few men who are both good and wise.[21] Aquinas is also appreciative of the political principle of self-rule that lies at the heart of contemporary liberal democracies. Yet he is cognizant of the dangers of excessive egalitarianism which may fail to consider the need for the "aristocratic" contribution of magnanimous statesmen in politics.

This leads us to the final theme concerning magnanimous statesmen and citizens in government—the question of human equality. Aquinas' political theory views "natural equality" as fundamental to his view of human nature. "In what pertains to the interior motion of the will," says Aquinas, "man is not bound to obey man but only God."[22] Man is bound to obey man in the external bodily actions; but even in such of these as refer to the nature of the body—for example, "whatever concerns the nourishment of the body, and the generation of offspring—man is not bound to obey man but God alone, for *all men are by nature equal.*"[23]

Aquinas teaches that every person is entitled to spiritual freedom and to the exterior conditions of human existence, whether proprietary, personal, or marital. Within this sacred, private sphere no human artifice or organization should intrude. Aquinas strictly limits even serfdom in a way quite "modern" for his time. "A serf," he says, "is his master's property in matters superadded to the natural, but in matters of nature all are equal."[24]

It follows from this that there is no such thing as natural superiority in the spiritual sense. The Aristotelian conception of the natural slave may be ultimately incompatible with Christian philosophical anthropology. Yet some of Aristotle's phraseology is retained but transformed in discussing the particular need for intellectual and moral excellence in magnanimous statesmanship.

Thus the Aristotelian principle of natural inferiority and servitude was reduced by Aquinas to the following axiom of competence: "Those who are preeminent in intellect naturally dominate, while those who are intellectually deficient but corporally strong seem by nature to be adapted for serving, as Aristotle says in his *Politics*."[25] This idea was also applied to politics. "In human government," says Aquinas, "inordination arises from the fact that someone rules not on account of intellectual preeminence, but usurps power for himself by brute force, or someone is appointed to government owing to sensual affection."[26]

Thus while all men are entitled to spiritual freedom and to the exterior conditions of human existence, some hierarchical gradation is essential for human coexistence. This gradation must be based on the existing distribution of disparities and aptitudes if the magnanimous statesman is to have an opportunity to serve. Those persons who excel in active faculties ought to be directed (primarily persuaded) by those who excel in mental faculties. For Aquinas, it is impossible that the common good of the State could progress, unless there is virtue in the citizens, and those magnanimous statesmen to whom the government is entrusted. Although persons are spiritually equal, they are unequal politically. If the principle of the common good is to be made manifest and not result in a chaos of mediocrity and incompetence, the aristocratic principle in the strict and literal sense must be present.

THE MAGNANIMOUS STATESMAN AND THE VICISSITUDES OF POLITICS

For Aquinas the first intention of a ruler must be to establish and maintain the unity of peace among his people. Justice of itself is not sufficient to produce harmony and order that go to make up peace. This effect can only be produced by the virtue of charity. Aquinas says, "Peace is the work of justice indirectly, insofar as justice removes obstacles to peace: but it is the work of charity directly, since charity, according to its very nature, causes peace, for charity is a unitive force."[27] No true rulership is possible without charity.

Charity is thus "the mother" and the foundation of all the virtues, and the moral life is really the life of charity. In charity, we love our neighbors, even where we give different honors in accordance with the worth or excellence of each and where we are unable to love all with the same affection. All virtue, and action, apart from charity is necessarily incomplete. It is in charity that justice, for example, becomes full or complete justice. Aquinas claims that even just decisions involving the promotion of the welfare of the community or state can lack the sanction of the full knowledge of what is good. That is because just acts, such as the distribution and restitution of divisible goods, can be true and fair but also blind and inequitable. Even theft must be seen in the light of charity in order to determine which acts of appropriation are *morally* wrong. Inasmuch as material things are to be held in such a way as to be shared with others, the taking of the goods of another when one is in need is not really theft. Thus justice, which regulates human actions with respect to the claims of others, must truly understand these claims as the claims of neighbors and not simply of social equals or unequals.

In his insistence on charity by the ruler, Aquinas quotes the command of Moses, "Seek out from among the people wise men who fear God, in whom there is charity . . . and appoint from them leaders."[28] As we have emphasized, Aquinas' view of rulership is one of service, and sacrificial service is a manifestation of charity. There can never be charity without service; it is the fruit of charity. Indeed, it is the ultimate test of the statesman's magnanimity.

Charity on the part of the ruler begets love from the people. It inspires them to great acts of unselfishness and devotion. Aquinas relates the example of the great love that Julius Caesar manifested for his soldiers and how this was reciprocated. It is this charity that enables the magnanimous statesman to elevate and maintain without hostility the public authority. Such a ruler is always courteous and pleasant with his people. The prudent statesman is always aware that there is in the bosom of every man a secret rebellion and opposition to all authority. Experience confirms this and original sin explains it. The true statesman realizes this full well. The tyrant may utilize his coercive powers to beat a man to his knees but he will never acquire any internal submission. The magnanimous, prudent, and charitable statesman, instead of creating large numbers of enemies to his rule, diminishes such enmity by making many of them friends by his great love and sacrificial service. No better example of the pursuit of such magnanimity and charity can be found in American politics than in the presidency of Abraham Lincoln:

> With malice toward none; with charity for all; with firmness in the right, as God gives us to see the right, let us strive on to finish the work we are in; to bind up the nation's wounds; to care for him who shall have borne the battle and his widow, and his orphan—to do all which may achieve and cherish a just and lasting peace among ourselves, and with all nations.[29]

It is clear for Aquinas that few persons possess the qualities of magnanimous, prudent, and charitable statesmanship that are necessary in one who takes upon himself the prerogative of making the practical judgments necessary in the governance of the political community. We have seen that for Aquinas prudence and charity are virtues that are basic to making efficacious moral judgments which are measured by the objective demands of the commonweal. It is also clear for Aquinas that political prudence should be cultivated and found in all the citizens of a civil community, since the common good is the concern of them all. But it is required in a special way in those who exercise civil authority.

For Aquinas, political prudence involves not only considering the practical political actions conducive to the common good, but it also involves an understanding of when no political rule is best. Very often some measure which of itself is most desirable must be refrained from because given the concrete sociocultural circumstances, it would be detrimental to the common good or to public peace. Likewise, certain hardships must be tolerated because, given the concrete circumstances, measures against them would undermine the common good. This is not considered an abandonment of principle. Rather, it is an appreciation of the view that if the common good is destroyed for the sake of a particular, legitimate, or even laudable end, the magnanimous statesman is defeating his primary task, the preservation of the public good.[30]

Aquinas' profound concern about the centrality of prudence for the charitable and magnanimous statesman is exemplified quite well in Lincoln's particular approach to the proper tactics of alcohol reform with reference to "temperance" crusades. For Lincoln, persuasion, not denunciation, is the means to be used. Without friendship even truth will fail. "If you would win a man to your cause, first convince him that you are his sincere friend. Therein is a drop of honey that catches his heart, which say what he will, is the great high road to his reason."[31] Lincoln's counsel of persuasion and friendship is not mere expediency; rather it is best to be a friend to both the opponents and supporters of "temperance."[32] Aquinas and Lincoln are one in their concern about how governments can devour themselves in the pursuit of absolute principles without concern for human weakness, present circumstances, or charity. An excessively moralistic approach on the part of the authorities can only lead to greater disorder, to bitterness and resentment in civil society, and is contrary to political prudence. As a modern Thomist, John Courtney Murray, put it:

> society must look to other institutions for the elevation and maintenance of its moral standards, that is, to the church, the home, the school, and the network of voluntary associations that concern themselves with public morality in one or other aspect.
>
> Law and morality are indeed related, even though differentiated. That is the premises of law are ultimately found in the moral law. And human legislation does look to the moralization of society. But, mindful of its own nature and mode of action, it must not moralize excessively; otherwise it tends to defeat even its own modest aims, by bringing itself into contempt.[33]

It is quite difficult to raise up a new generation of magnanimous statesmen with the "hard" virtues necessary to transcend the dogmas of their age. Deference to intellectual and moral excellence, for Thomas Aquinas, can only exist when charity and the intuition of metaphysical reason are understood to be the real sources of human dignity and magnanimous statesmanship. Leo Strauss has stated that human problems arise when political life is deprived of the sacred: "It is hardly necessary to add that the dogmatic exclusion of religious awareness proper renders questionable all long-range predictions concerning the future of societies."[34] For Thomas Aquinas, God's undiminished greatness provides for the preservation and integrity of human community. His approach to magnanimous statesmanship is grounded in the profound commitment to a fruitful relationship between revelation and reason as the basis for a healthy political life.

NOTES

1. A slightly longer version of this chapter originally appeared in *Tempered Strength: Studies in the Nature and Scope of Prudential Leadership*, ed. Ethan Fishman (Lanham, Md.: Lexington Books, 2002). Professor Deutsch had intended to use that earlier piece as the basis for a largely new chapter to be included in this volume, but, unfortunately, health issues prevented his completing the new version. The original is reprinted here with permission. We have, however, omitted the original version's discussion of Ciceronian magnanimity, in view of James Fetter and Walter Nicgorski's extensive treatment of that subject in Chapter 3 of the present volume.

2. Leo Strauss, *Spinoza's Critique of Religion* (New York: Schocken Books, 1965), 50.

3. Larry Arnhart, "Statesmanship as Magnanimity: Classical, Christian and Modern," *Polity* (Winter 1983): 263–65.

4. Aristotle, *Nicomachean Ethics*, 1124.20–1125a. and 1123a. 34 1124.6.

5. W. Nestle, "Die Haupteinwande des antiken Denkens gegen das Christentum," *Archiv fur Religionswissenschaft 37* (1941): 51–100.

6. St. Augustine, *De civitate Dei*, Bk. XXII, Ch. 22, trans. Marcus Dods (New York: Modern Library, 1950), 178.

7. St. Thomas Aquinas, *Summa Theologiae*, trans. by the Fathers of the English Dominican Province (London: Burns, Oats and Washbourne, 1935), IIa, IIae, CXXIX, art. 2.

8. Aquinas, *Summa*, I, q. 47 and 1.

9. Aquinas, *Summa*, I, q. 6. a. 4.

10. St. Thomas Aquinas, *Exposito in Job*, Ch. 13, lect. 2.

11. Aquinas, *Summa*, IIa, IIae, CXXIX, art. 3, ad 4.

12. *Ibid.*

13. Aquinas, *Summa*, IIa, IIae, CXXXII, art. 1, ad Iam.

14. St. Thomas Aquinas, *On Kingship: to the King of Cyprus*, trans. and intro. I. Th. Eschmann, O.P. (Toronto: Pontifical Institute of the University of Toronto Press, 1949), 24.

15. Aquinas, *Summa*, I-II q. 56a, ad 3.

16. Thomas Gilby, *Summa Theologiae* (London: Blackfriar's, 1949), vol. 36, appendix 4, p. 183.

17. Aquinas, *Summa*, I-II, q. 57, art. 6.

18. Aquinas, *Summa*, I-II, 105, 1 in c.

19. Quoted in Wilfred Parsons, "St. Thomas Aquinas and Popular Sovereignty," *Thought* XIV (1941): 473.

20. Jacques Maritain, *True Humanism* (New York: Scribners and Sons, 1928), 223.

21. Aquinas, *Summa*, I-II, q. 97, a.lc.

22. Aquinas, *Summa*, II-II, q. 104, art. 5.

23. *Ibid.*

24. *Ibid.*

25. St. Thomas Aquinas, *Summa Contra Gentiles*, trans. Vernon J. Bourke (Notre Dame: University of Notre Dame Press, 1975), 2–3.

26. St. Thomas Aquinas, *Commentary on the Politics*, trans. A. P. D'Entreves (Oxford: Basil Blackwell, 1947), iii, 17, 1288 a. 15.

27. Aquinas, *Summa*, II-II, q. 29 a. 3, ad. 3.

28. St. Thomas Aquinas, "De Regime Judaeorium," in *Aquinas: Selected Political Writings*, trans. A. P. D'Entreves (Oxford: Basil Blackwell, 1948), 91.

29. Cited in Glen E. Thurow, *Abraham Lincoln and American Political Religion* (Albany: State University of New York Press, 1976), 89.

30. Aquinas, *Summa*, I-II, 96.2 ad 2.

31. *Ibid.*

32. *Ibid.*

33. John Courtney Murray, *We Hold These Truths* (New York: Image Books, 1964) 166.

34. Leo Strauss, *Liberalism, Ancient and Modern* (New York: Basic Books, 1968), 8.

II

MAGNANIMITY AND MODERNITY

5

Hobbes on Magnanimity and Statesmanship: Replacing Virtue with Science

Geoffrey M. Vaughan

At first glance we might think that Hobbes had no use for either magnanimity or statesmanship. How could either fit into his commonwealth, that great Leviathan, king over the children of pride? The word "statesman" or "statesmanship" appears, as far as I can tell, in only two passages of *Behemoth*, neither very significant.[1] Magnanimity, for its part, is defined in *Leviathan* as merely "contempt of little helps and hindrances."[2] A fellow Oxfordian would later describe Aristotle's magnanimous man in terms Hobbes might have approved as "a prig with the conceit and bad manners of a prig."[3] It would be easy to conclude that he considered neither magnanimity nor statesmanship to be worthy subjects of study. We might even go so far as to suggest that they are not worthy of emulation, leading as they might to vainglory and the presumptions that lead to civil war.

It is certainly true that Hobbes had scientific pretensions for his political theory, and this topic has been ably covered by scholars.[4] But it is also the case that he introduced his masterwork, *Leviathan*, with a letter extolling the virtues of his deceased friend, Sidney Godolphin. Hobbes was not insensitive to virtue and virtuous men. But neither was he unrealistic about such men. Sidney died early in the civil war, thus rendering his virtues inaccessible to the royalist cause, and Francis, his brother and the man to whom *Leviathan* is dedicated, turned the Scilly Islands over to the Commonwealth in 1646. Whatever virtues these brothers possessed and however highly Hobbes might have thought of them, their virtues did little good because they were so unusual and short-lived. The reason such virtues are unavailing is to be found in his account of the only two things that can induce men to keep their covenants: "And those are either a Feare of the consequence of breaking their word; or a Glory, or Pride in appearing not to need to break it. This later is a

Generosity too rarely found to be presumed on, especially in the pursuers of Wealth, Command, or sensuall Pleasure; which are the greatest part of Mankind."[5] The Godolphin brothers—or at least Sidney—might have kept their word from a generosity of spirit, but such a rare quality is not solid enough ground for erecting civil society.

The advantage of paying attention to magnanimity and statesmanship in the thought of Thomas Hobbes is that it allows us to see the extent to which his arguments in *Leviathan* and elsewhere develop what is, for him, a suboptimal answer to the questions he sought to address in his work. I shall argue that Hobbes could treat these topics lightly only after regretfully acknowledging that his preferred solution, which would involve both, is unworkable. And it is the impracticality of relying on magnanimity and statesmanship that led Hobbes to develop the arguments that he did, the arguments that do not rely on either.

MAGNANIMITY AND STATESMANSHIP

Before we explore the various ways that magnanimity and statesmanship play out in Hobbes's political theory, we ought first to consider how he understood each of these terms. Again, the biggest obstacle to this is his infrequent use of these terms and short attention to these concepts. Nevertheless there is certainly enough for us to go on at this point.

Taking magnanimity first, we can be grateful for the fact that Hobbes did indeed define the term for us. The first mention of magnanimity in *Leviathan*, however, is not its definition. Rather, Hobbes offered it as an example of the ways in which names can not be the true grounds of any ratiocination. According to Hobbes, one man will call prodigality what another will call magnanimity, as one will call gravity what another would call stupidity.[6] When we come to the definition of magnanimity we find, as noted above, that it is contempt of little helps and hindrances. This arises as part of a description of the various passions which, in the work of other authors, would be called virtues. In Hobbes's account, not only are they passions, but magnanimity merely falls in his list between pusillanimity and kindness.[7] He further refined the definition by offering us two different sorts of magnanimity. The first, which is to be found in the face of physical danger, he defined as valor or fortitude. The second type of magnanimity arises in the use of riches and is called liberality.

These first occurrences of magnanimity in *Leviathan* do not seem very promising. The warnings regarding the use of names may be useful, but there is nothing to suggest that his choice of terms had special significance. Quentin

Skinner, however, has taken the trouble to compare Hobbes's warnings about the use of names to his earlier list in *The Elements of Law*. Almost all the terms changed in *Leviathan*. The only pair that even resembles the earlier list is prodigality:magnanimity, which earlier appeared as liberality:prodigality.[8] What is especially curious is that "prodigality" nowhere else appears in *Leviathan* and is not listed among the passions in chapter 6. Indeed, there seems to be no description of excessive spending, even though Hobbes offers three different words for its opposite. And yet this word is the one that he uses in both lists. It is curious that Hobbes consistently warned that magnanimity or one of its variants could be perniciously misused in a rhetorical struggle, even as he used it repeatedly.

The definition of magnanimity and its two variants is also disappointing, for "greatness of soul" is reduced to a contempt for something bad rather than an attraction to or pursuit of something good. In keeping with its status as a passion it is little more than an aversion.[9] Moreover, the definitions of valor and liberality ring a little hollow. How does a contempt for "little helps, and hindrances" translate into valorous actions in the face of death? Compare this to Aristotle's account: "Still, nobility shines through even in such circumstances, when a man bears many great misfortunes with good grace not because he is insensitive to pain but because he is noble and high-minded [*megalopsuchos*]."[10] There is an incommensurability between, on the one hand, a passion that disdains pettiness and, on the other, those actions that we might associate with valor. Liberality is not much better explained by this contempt for little helps and hindrances.[11] Far more than define these terms what Hobbes seems to do here was define them away. What would otherwise be understood as the virtues of magnanimity, valor or fortitude, and liberality are presented in *Leviathan* not only as passions, rather than virtues, but as minor passions. Reducing courage to the hope of avoiding hurt by resistance as he also did is certainly commensurate with this general diminution of the virtues.[12]

A further and significant refinement arises two chapters later, in chapter 8, where magnanimity is now defined as "contempt of unjust or dishonest helps."[13] The curious shift here is from little to unjust or dishonest. What would account for the sudden moral content of magnanimity? This refined definition of magnanimity arises in the context of Hobbes's definition and account of the intellectual virtues, specifically prudence. He explained that the prudence that uses unjust and dishonest means is "that Crooked Wisdom, which is called CRAFT; which is a sign of Pusillanimity." Thus, however prudent it may be to turn to injustice and dishonesty, the magnanimous man will not do so. But why not? If dishonesty were to be a great rather than a little help, why would the magnanimous man continue to contemn it? Only a few chapters later Hobbes will tell us that "Force, and Fraud, are in warre the two Cardinal vertues."[14] The refinement raises more problems than it answers.

Thereafter, in the four other mentions of magnanimity to be found in *Leviathan*, it is understood in relation to the display or acquisition of power. For instance, on one and the same page magnanimity is said to be both consciousness of power and a sign of power.[15] In other words, while on the one hand it arises from self-knowledge and self-reflection, it is also a signal to others. Following upon the second, we find in chapter 14 that actions can be undertaken for the purpose of gaining a reputation for magnanimity. One would apparently so want such a reputation that Hobbes even said rights would be transferred without reciprocation.[16] And we find, in the final mention of magnanimity, that if not magnanimity itself at least its effects are honorable by nature.

So where does Hobbes stand on the topic of magnanimity? Is it good or bad? On the one hand it would seem to be good, for the magnanimous man disdains injustice and that would be good for the commonwealth. On the other hand, of course, both the awareness of power that leads to magnanimous actions and the desire for power that does the same involves a subject in the very type of contest that destabilizes the commonwealth and can lead to civil war. As much as having power leads to magnanimity, a reputation for magnanimity through repeated magnanimous actions can produce power where none or little existed before. For, as Hobbes tells us, a reputation for power is power.[17] And, as any student of Hobbes can explain, for anyone other than the sovereign to have that reputation or to seek it is dangerous.[18] Therefore, there seem to be two types of magnanimity. There is what we could call the true magnanimity, the type that leads the man to distain both little helps and injustice. But there is also another type, perhaps a false magnanimity that might even inspire injustice. The distinction between the true and the false is not fair because Hobbes never made such a distinction himself. He treated both as magnanimity, perhaps for good reason.[19] How could one judge between an action produced by a magnanimous contempt of little helps and an action merely intended to look as if it were produced by the same? In many cases they would be the same act. Hobbes did not want the state to look into men's hearts, nor did he intend to produce a political science which relied on accomplishing that impossible task.[20]

At best we could say that Hobbes was ambivalent about magnanimity. But this is not strong enough. According to Leo Strauss, Hobbes uniquely makes the claim in *Leviathan* that magnanimity is the origin of all virtue. Strauss attributes this position that Hobbes took only temporarily to the influence of Descartes. Rather, "[f]or Hobbes, except when confused by his own real intentions by Descartes, sees the origin of virtue not in magnanimity, but in fear, in fear of violent death. He considers not magnanimity but fear of violent death as the only adequate self-consciousness."[21] While he might have preferred a world or a commonwealth which could rely upon magnanimous men, relying upon such virtues where they can so easily be feigned was the underlying fault of previous attempts to provide political peace. Hobbes would not allow himself to indulge these fantasies. "Precisely because magnanimity is a form of pride, even though it be the most 'honorable' form, it cannot be accepted by Hobbes as the origin of justice."[22] He dedicated *Leviathan* to Francis Godolphin, but he could not expect an entire commonwealth to be populated by men such as he.

According to Hobbes, the laws of nature are contrary to our natural passions and the terror of some power is needed to compel us to abide by them.[23] In the context of our concerns here, certainly the one law of nature that is contrary to the passions associated with magnanimity is the ninth, against pride. It is here where Hobbes takes a shot at Aristotle for assuming that a natural inequality permitted some to rule over others. Hobbes would have none of this. Accordingly he argued, "If Nature therefore have made men equall; that equalitie is to be acknowledged: or if Nature have made men unequall; yet because men that think themselves equall, will not enter into conditions of Peace, but upon Equall termes, such equalitie must be admitted."[24] Whether or not men are equal by nature, by the laws of nature they must pretend that all are equal, for without such pretense no one will enter the contracts that produce peace. This is not quite the irony that Aristotle so approved of in the magnanimous man, but neither is it quite statesmanship.[25]

The power of the sovereign is designed to compel us to obey the laws we authorized him to make. Therefore, one might think that Hobbes's philosophy had an important place for statesmanship. The overwhelming role of the sovereign within the commonwealth would normally suggest this. However, as I have already pointed out, the term does not appear anywhere it might be expected. In general terms, how would statesmanship as we normally understand it fit into Hobbes's political philosophy?

Because Hobbes did not define statesmanship nor even discuss it in *Leviathan* or his other treatises, there are two possible places for us to look for it. We can look to his analysis of prudence or to his descriptions of civil science. Prudence seems to be a logical place to find something like Hobbesian statesmanship, but it is disappointing. According to Hobbes, "To govern well a family, and a kingdome, are not different degrees of Prudence; but different sorts of business."[26] Prudence is not specific to affairs of state; rather, it is a general ability to predict future events based on the experience of similar events in the past.[27] It is not absolute, and it is certainly not scientific, but it can serve individuals well enough. In fact, it seems to serve individuals better than groups. "A plain husband-man is more Prudent in affaires of his own house," wrote Hobbes, "then a Privy Counseller in the affairs of another man."[28] Prudence may be of some use in politics, but Hobbes sought something more certain.

Hobbes's civil science, a science he characteristically thought first appeared with his publication of *De Cive* in 1642, was to be the place where such certainty could be found. Prudence, again, relies on comparing past events to current ones and extrapolating from that the likelihood of the same results occurring again. Hobbes's civil science relies on much surer methods. The Introduction to *Leviathan* ends thus:

> He that is to govern a whole Nation, must read in himself, not this, or that particular man; but Man-kind: which though it be hard to do, harder than to learn any Language, or Science; yet, when I shall have set down my own reading orderly, and perspicuously, the pains left another, will be onely to consider, if he also find not the same in himself. For this kind of Doctrine, admitteth no other Demonstration.[29]

We shall see below just how difficult it will be for Hobbes to restrict this civil science to the sovereign, and in what ways the subject must also understand some part of it. But for the moment it is important to see that what we might call statesmanship is neither a passion, like magnanimity, nor an intellectual virtue, like prudence. It is something different, it is something new; it is a science.[30]

Nevertheless, Hobbes cannot do without the statesman to the same degree that he thinks he can do without the magnanimous man. The virtues of the magnanimous man are rare and, he tells us, can not be relied upon for our safety precisely because of their rarity. The argument in *Leviathan* and other places, by contrast, seems to suggest that the qualities needed for a statesman can be taught, produced, or somehow developed through civil science. In a curious passage at the end of the second part of *Leviathan*, Hobbes writes "I am at the point of believing this my labour, as uselesse, as the Commonwealth of *Plato*."[31] He regains his hope however when he considers how little is required of the sovereign and his principal ministers, for he does not even ask them to master the mathematical sciences as Plato did. Instead, Hobbes ends this section by imagining a sovereign who would "by the exercise of entire Soveraignty, in protecting the Publique teaching of it, convert this Truth of Speculation, into the Utility of Practice." Here it seems they need only teach it, or allow it to be taught; perhaps they do not even need to understand it fully. Whatever may be the case, Hobbes tried to move away from relying upon the virtues, whether moral or intellectual, and place more stress on science.

One thing that is starting to become apparent is that Hobbes treated magnanimity as a passion and downgraded its status as a moral virtue whereas he treated statesmanship, insofar as he did treat it at all, as the product of his civil science and resembling a civil science. We shall see the significance of this distinction as magnanimity and statesmanship play out among the different roles of sovereign and subject. One fact remains constant, however. Hobbes did not want to rely upon magnanimity in any level of society for the peace and tranquility of the state. This pushed him in the awkward direction of relying upon his new science in such a way that it would have to be somewhat widespread throughout the people in the commonwealth. These general considerations on magnanimity and statesmanship lead us to our more specific considerations of what role they play in the duties of both sovereign and subject.

THE SOVEREIGN

When it comes to the question of magnanimity and statesmanship the sovereign is certainly the most important figure. Both of these virtues would seem to apply to the sovereign far more than any subjects. But here it is important to remember what exactly the sovereign is and what role sovereignty plays in Hobbes's political philosophy. Power defines the position of the sovereign, for the sovereign is authorized to use the collective power of all the members of the Commonwealth.[32] The sovereign is not a philosopher king, as Hobbes made clear in *Leviathan*.[33] The sovereign's right to rule does not rest on his inherent qualities, but rather on the position he holds among the institutions of power. That is to say, the office is more important to Hobbes than is the officeholder. And we can see in several places that when Hobbes argued for the superior merits of monarchy he did not suggest that monarchs are morally superior people. It is suspected that this argument, among others, accounts for the cool reception of *Leviathan* in the court of Charles II.[34]

If magnanimity is the consciousness of power, all sovereigns ought to be magnanimous as a matter of course. But what type of magnanimity? We can hope that they would distain injustice—if the sovereign can commit an injustice—but we know that magnanimity does not always work in that direction. It can easily slip into vainglory. And even when it does not this may still prove to be dangerous to the commonwealth. When we think of magnanimity as a contempt of little hurts, might we not conclude that overlooking many small offenses against sovereignty can lead to much larger ones?[35]

We know that diminishing the power of the sovereign is not good for the state.[36] Rather, the virtue of the sovereign is to be found in retaining the concentration of power, not in adhering to some other concept of justice. For

Hobbes's whole point is that there can be no justice outside of the state, and there is no state without the centralization of power. So, however much the more positive aspects of magnanimity may appeal to us, Hobbes cannot be more than ambivalent about it. It is not consistently positive, it does not always lead to actions that promote peace. Hobbes cannot, therefore, endorse it as a virtue—or a passion—for sovereigns.

Hobbes is well known for arguing that there is no real distinction between a tyrant and a sovereign, and that the very term tyrant merely means a "monarchy misliked."[37] A statesman, therefore, may very well be no more than a sovereign who is liked. Thus tyranny and statesmanship can be dismissed by Hobbes as mere commentary rather than description. But as Kinch Hoekstra has explained, tyranny plays a complex role in Hobbes's work.[38] For instance, in *De Cive* Hobbes tells us that a king rules well and a tyrant does not.[39] This is a very strong comment coming from Hobbes and it is not repeated elsewhere in his work. Nevertheless, we can find something akin to this same statement in *Leviathan*. Consider the argument in chapter 30. Although entitled "Of the Office of the Sovereign Representative" it could as easily have been entitled "Of Statesmanship," for it is a fascinating instruction to sovereigns. Much of this chapter explains how and why the sovereign must justify his rights to his people and why he must execute those rights as he does. Hobbes explains, "and consequently, it is his Duty, to cause them so to be instructed; and not onely his Duty, but his Benefit also, and Security, against the danger that may arise to himselfe in his naturall Person, from Rebellion."[40] In this sense, then, a tyrant does rule poorly for he has not sufficiently explained himself to his people. Thus, a poorly instructed people will consider the legitimate actions of a sovereign to be acts of hostility, "which when they think they have strength enough, they will endeavour by acts of Hostility, to avoyd."[41]

Hobbes opens the chapter by explaining that the safety of the people to which the sovereign is bound by the very purpose of his institution means that he must do much more than simply keep them alive. "But by Safety here," he explains, "is not meant a bare Preservation, but also all other Contentments of life, which every man by lawful Industry, without danger, or hurt to the Common-wealth, shall acquire to himselfe."[42] This rather expansive understanding of safety leads Hobbes to list among the duties of a sovereign not only the equal application of justice or equality of all subjects before the law, but even such policies as a flat tax or sales tax, and the replacement of private charity with state welfare. This is also the chapter in which he famously recommended a reform of the universities for, "the Instruction of the people, dependeth wholly, on the right teaching of Youth in the Universities."[43] The idea running throughout this chapter is that a sovereign who does not rule well or rather, who is not believed to rule well, will be accused of tyranny. But it seems that, however much Hobbes objected to the political and partisan uses to which the term tyrant could be put, he could find some justification for applying it to those sovereigns who provoked their people into rebellion or who never explained the legitimacy of their actions. He wrote: "I conclude therefore, that in the instruction of the people in the Essentiall Rights (which are the Naturall, and Fundamental Lawes) of Soveraignty, there is no difficulty, (whilest a Soveraign has his Power entire,) but what proceeds from his own fault, or the fault of those whom he trusteth in the administration of the Common-wealth."[44] So long as the sovereign does his duty and retains his full rights, he can easily teach the people to respect those rights and, thus, he can continue to retain them.

There is one other argument that runs through chapter 30 of *Leviathan*, and it is that the interest of the sovereign is the same as that of his people. Hobbes writes, "For the good of the Soveraign and People, cannot be separated. It is a weak Soveraign, that has weak Subjects; and a weak People, whose soveraign wanteth Power to rule them at his will."[45] Hobbes uses this same argument elsewhere to argue for the superiority of monarchy over both aristocracy and democracy, so it cannot be dismissed as an idle point.[46] But in the context of this chapter it should also be understood as an instruction to sovereigns who might otherwise overlook it. This second argument in the chapter, therefore, might be understood as complementary to the first. Whereas the first argument instructs the sovereign in the importance of how he is perceived by the people, this second argument instructs him in how he should perceive them. In other words, neither party should see the other as an enemy but as a partner in the common enterprise of procuring safety for all involved, safety in its most broad understanding. Conveniently, of course, it is the duty and in the interest of everyone that this be accomplished.

The sovereign was not expected to act upon the virtue of prudence, but upon the wisdom of Hobbes's science. Prudence extrapolates from past events to predict future ones, so that "The best Prophet naturally is the best guesser; and the best guesser, he that is most versed and studied in the matters he guesses at: for he hath most *Signes* to guess by."[47] But Hobbes was not in the business of guessing; that was not good enough for him. And certainly the sovereign had to do better than simply guess at policy, so the virtue of prudence had to be replaced with the science of politics. Magnanimity, being treated as the opposite, that is as a passion, plays much less of a role in the duty of a sovereign. But all of this accords very well with the suboptimal account that Hobbes presents in *Leviathan* and his other books. He was writing about the duties attendant to sovereignty, not its perfection. Surely Hobbes would have been very pleased with a sovereign who was magnanimous in only the best sense and a true statesman. But could he expect such a figure to rise but rarely? He was not going to entrust public safety to fortune, any more than to guesswork.

THE SUBJECT

Hobbes wrote in *De Homine* that "whatsoever the laws are, not to violate them is always and everywhere held to be a virtue in citizens, and to neglect them is held to be a vice."[48] That says about all that needs to be said on the topic of magnanimity and statesmanship on the part of a subject. At least it would say everything, if it were not for the unfortunate fact that subjects often do not obey the laws and that a good deal of Hobbes's work was an attempt to explain why they should. So we must take a bit more time with this topic.

One of the most intriguing and often difficult parts of Hobbes's argument in the *Leviathan* is that the subjects form the commonwealth through an agreement with one another that includes the sovereign only tangentially.[49] This at least is the argument regarding a commonwealth by institution. And even though the commonwealth by acquisition is, of course, different, Hobbes tried to take the commonwealth by institution as the paradigmatic case. He may not be entirely successful in this attempt, and it may be true that acquisition better fits both the historical record and his own explanation.[50] Nevertheless, it is important to focus upon the commonwealth by institution when considering the duties of the subject because it is the formation of this commonwealth that best explains those duties as more than submission. As Hobbes well knew, if there is something approaching a moral reason for forming a commonwealth, and concomitant moral duties, they are to be found in this account of civil society.

The first duty of the subject when forming a commonwealth is to confer his power onto another.[51] In fact, Hobbes can say that the act of creation and the thing itself are one and the same. For authorizing another to take actions on one's behalf both creates the commonwealth and defines it and, at least in *Leviathan*, the soon-to-be-sovereign plays no role in this process. Through this act of creation the individual becomes a subject by alienating his own power (with certain exceptions)[52] to the sovereign, as do all the others. Relinquishing power defines the subject, so any act that recovers some of it will be an act of usurpation. Here we see that magnanimity, in all but its most benign sense, is incompatible with the duties of the subject. As either a display of power or a means of acquiring it, magnanimity threatens the monopoly of power that, Hobbes argued, is the key to securing peace.

Thus the passion of magnanimity is not good for the commonwealth. For even in those cases where it arises from salutary motives or a true moral virtue, it tends to be admired as a sign of power: "Reputation of power, is Power; because it draweth with it the adhaerence of those that need protection."[53] And whereas having subjects who disdain to commit injustice might be a good thing for the commonwealth, magnanimity is too ambiguous a virtue to trust. Subjects who wield power on their own threaten the peace because the laws cease to bind them effectively. He wrote that "laws are as cobwebs to potent men."[54] Anything that loosens the bonds of the law moves in the direction of returning men to the state of nature. Nevertheless, Hobbes did claim that a sovereign who is popular and beloved of his people has nothing to fear from the popularity of any of his subjects. For such a sovereign relies not only on the good opinion in which he is held but also on the very office of sovereignty which a usurper does not have.[55] There is no contradiction here. Hobbes was thinking of the best possible case where a sovereign understands his role, explains it to his people, and all submit to his rule. In the suboptimal condition which he takes to be the normal one, however, powerful subjects are a cause for concern.

At first glance it would seem that statesmanship is by definition an encroachment on the rights of sovereignty. Wisdom or insight into the affairs of state are not the proper concern of subjects. There are many passages in Hobbes's work that bear this out. He tells us that subjects should not compare their laws with the laws of other states and that they should not seek reform. In *Leviathan*, he unfavorably compared human society to that of bees on many points. One stands out in this context:

> Thirdly, that these creatures, having not (as man) the use of reason, do not see, nor think they see any fault, in the administration of their common businesse: whereas amongst men, there are very many, that thinke themselves wiser, and abler to govern the Publique, better than the rest; and these strive to reforme and innovate, one this way, another that way; and thereby bring it into Distraction and Civill warre.[56]

In *De Cive* he made the point with force: "every king, whether good or bad, is exposed to being condemned by the judgment, and having his throat cut by the hand, of a lone assassin."[57] As Harvey Mansfield has put it, "For Hobbes, then, consent is not a kind of participation in politics; it is, to the contrary, as far as possible an abstention from politics."[58] Excluding the subjects from politics is not that simple, however. Subjects will not spontaneously obey the laws, and they will certainly not know why they ought to obey the laws unless someone tells them. Some amount of understanding, some access to his civil science, is required of subjects for the state to be successful.

This leads to a tension in Hobbes's political philosophy. He wanted his book to be taught in the schools and then those lessons to be transferred to the people through other means. In a most colorful passage, he wrote:

> For seeing the Universities are the Fountains of Civill, and Morall Doctrine, from whence the Preachers, and the Gentry, drawing such water as they find, use to sprinkle the same (both from the Pulpit, and in their Conversation) upon the People, there ought certainly to be great care taken, to have it pure, both from the Venime of Heathen Politicians, and from the Incantation of Deceiving Spirits.[59]

Thus, on the one hand, his argument required that all the subjects of the commonwealth learn their duties and the justifications for the rights of the sovereign. He even placed subjects in the awkward position of rejecting powers that they might be granted when they understand that, instead, they ought to be retained by the sovereign.[60] This places a burden on the subject to understand the science of politics. Yet, on the other hand, these same subjects must not look too deeply into political questions or compare their own laws with the laws of others. For example, Hobbes is frank in admitting that "there is scarce a Common-wealth in the world, whose beginnings can in conscience be justified."[61] Opening-up political questions would both encroach on the rights of the sovereign and stir up discontent. How do you teach people to learn only so much?[62]

Hobbes divided the population of each commonwealth into two groups: the first has little time or interest in discussing or discovering the principles of natural justice; the second forms the opinions of the first group based upon the little bit they studied in the universities. The first group he described as they "whom necessity, or covetousenesse keepeth attent on their trades, and labour; and they, on the other side, whom superfluity, or sloth carrieth afther their sensuall pleasures, (which two sorts of men take up the greatest part of Mankind)."[63] This first group was not distinguished as an economic class, for it included both rich and poor (as did the second group). Rather, it was a class of people too poor, greedy, or hedonistic to devote any time to studying. And this is the vast majority of humanity. Yet these were the same people Hobbes thought had to have just enough of his civil science to know what to do. Perhaps their general distraction or indifference to such studies makes irrelevant any concern about them going too far. But it does not solve the problem of getting them up to the minimum standard, even if they are more easy to instruct than are the rich and potent subjects.[64]

Magnanimity, a passion, is not demanded of the subject and its vices are certainly discouraged. It is more difficult to understand the place of statesmanship, however. Some civil science is required, but only a certain amount.

Too much or too little understanding of politics on the part of the subject imperils the state. It is a difficult balance to achieve, and Hobbes did not provide a great deal of advice on how to strike it. Presumably that is the job of the sovereign as statesman.

CONCLUSION

Hobbes described the commonwealth as an artificial person, and in the Introduction to the *Leviathan* he set out in detail a comparison of all the parts of the human body and all the parts of the state. Ought we, then, to ask if this artificial man might not have the virtues of magnanimity and statesmanship? There is no place in his description of the *Leviathan* for the passion of magnanimity. Hobbes tells us that voluntary motion and the passions arise from imagination,[65] to which nothing corresponds in his analogy. This should come as no surprise, for institutions have no passions; that, it would seem, is their great advantage. By contrast, if the intellectual virtue of statesmanship as either prudence or civil science might be assigned to the faculty of reason in the individual, it has its corresponding feature in the state under the heading of "equity." Even if equity does not exhaust the classical understanding of statesmanship, it certainly captures a great deal of what Hobbes would have understood by it.[66]

Hobbes could largely do without magnanimity because he thought he need not rely on this passion. Statesmanship, however, was much harder for him to abandon. The problem Hobbes faced is that a sovereign could make mistakes that would endanger the commonwealth. Institutions alone could not solve this problem, which is why Hobbes offered very little by way of institutional solutions.[67] Neither could he rely on the virtues of mere men, like the brothers Godolphin, to achieve any more than they had in the past. His promise of the true civil science had to take him beyond that. And yet, however much Hobbes tried to insulate the state from the vagaries and inconsistencies of the human element, they always returned on him.

As a second best solution to fundamental political problems, Hobbes's plans have much to recommend them. Many subsequent authors have recreated some of his solutions.[68] But as his law of equality makes especially clear, much of his solution is based upon a fiction or a pretense. To the extent that magnanimity can be dismissed as a passion and statesmanship subsumed by his civil science, it might just work. But we know that magnanimity may be based on a reasonable assessment of one's abilities, and Hobbes admitted that intellectual virtues were required to implement his science. He might be able to distract us from magnanimity and statesmanship, but he cannot eliminate them from politics. In this Hobbes was right in describing sovereignty in the artificial person as an artificial soul: without the virtues of magnanimity and statesmanship to accompany it, such sovereignty is no more than a very thin body.[69]

NOTES

1. Thomas Hobbes, *Behemoth or the Long Parliament*, ed. and trans. Ferdinand Tönnies, with an Introduction by Stephen Holmes (Chicago: University of Chicago Press, 1990), 22, 119.

2. Hobbes, *Leviathan*, ed. Richard Tuck (Cambridge and New York: Cambridge University Press, 1996), 41 (ch. 6).

3. Quoted in W. F. R. Hardie, *Aristotle's Ethical Theory*, second edition (Oxford: Clarendon Press, 1980), 119.

4. A variety of positions have been staked-out on this topic. For a good sense of the range of possibilities and their development, consider among many others the following: Davide Panagia, "Delicate Discriminations: Thomas Hobbes's Science of Politics," *Polity* 36, no. 1 (2003): 91–114; Noel Malcolm, "Hobbes's Science of Politics and his Theory of Science," in *Aspects of Hobbes* (Oxford: Clarendon Press, 2002); Tom Sorell, "Hobbes's Persuasive Civil Science," *The Philosophical Quarterly* 40, no. 3 (1990): 342–51; Donald W. Hanson, "Science, Prudence, and Folly in Hobbes's Political Theory," *Political Theory* 21, no. 4 (1993): 643–64; David Gauthier, *The Logic of Leviathan* (Oxford: Clarendon Press, 1969); M. M. Goldsmith, *Hobbes's Science of Politics* (New York: Columbia University Press, 1966).

5. Hobbes, *Leviathan*, 99 (ch. 14). Consider also the following: "That which gives to humane Actions the relish of Justice, is a certain Noblenesse or Gallantnesse of courage, (rarely found,) by which a man scorns to be beholding for the contentment of his life, to fraud, or breach of promise." *Leviathan*, 104 (ch. 15).

6. Hobbes, *Leviathan*, 31 (ch. 4); see also Hobbes, *The Elements of Law*, 5.14.

7. Hobbes, *Leviathan*, 41 (ch. 6).

8. Quentin Skinner, *Reason and Rhetoric in the Philosophy of Thomas Hobbes* (Cambridge and New York: Cambridge University Press, 1996), 339–40.

9. See Hobbes, *Leviathan*, 38 (ch. 6).

10. Aristotle, *Nicomachean Ethics*, trans. Martin Ostwald (Indianapolis: Bobbs-Merrill, 1962), 1100b30–33.

11. See here R. P. Hanley, "Aristotle on the Greatness of Greatness of Soul," *History of Political Thought* 23, no. 1 (2002): 13–14.

12. Hobbes, *Leviathan*, 41 (ch. 6).

13. Hobbes, *Leviathan*, 53 (ch. 8).

14. Hobbes, *Leviathan*, 90 (ch. 13). The force of this question might be mitigated if we were to consider the turn to injustice because Hobbes claims that there is no injustice in the state of nature. The question of turning to injustice, therefore, becomes a question of breaking the law. But dishonesty can exist in civil society and the state of nature, and there is no indication that Hobbes was speaking only of one condition when referring to magnanimity. Thus, however much I do think attention to injustice

may complicate the argument I am presenting, sticking fast to dishonesty reveals that Hobbes has got himself into a predicament.

15. Hobbes, *Leviathan*, 66 (ch. 10).

16. Hobbes, *Leviathan*, 94 (ch. 14).

17. Hobbes, *Leviathan*, 62 (ch. 10).

18. Consider here what he calls the "Lawes of Honour," in *Leviathan*, 126 (ch. 18).

19. Aristotle did distinguish between magnanimity and its excess, vanity, and its defect, pusillanimity. See *Nicomachean Ethics* 1107b22–24, 1123b; and Hanley, "Greatness of Soul," 3 and 12 n. 45.

20. Hobbes, *Leviathan*, 10 ("Introduction") and 251 (ch. 31).

21. Leo Strauss, *The Political Philosophy of Hobbes: Its Basis and Genesis*, trans. Elsa M. Sinclair (Chicago: University of Chicago Press, 1952), 57. See also Peter Berkowitz, *Virtue and the Making of Modern Liberalism* (Princeton: Princeton University Press, 1999).

22. Strauss, *The Political Philosophy of Hobbes*, 55–56.

23. Hobbes, *Leviathan*, 117 (ch. 17).

24. Hobbes, *Leviathan*, 107 (ch. 15).

25. See Aristotle, *Nicomachean Ethics*, 1124b20–30; Hanley, "Greatness of Soul," 15–17; Carson Holloway, "Christianity, Magnanimity, and Statesmanship," *Review of Politics* 61, no. 4 (1999): 589.

26. Hobbes, *Leviathan*, 53 (ch. 8). On the difference between a family and a state, see Hobbes, *Leviathan*, 142 (ch. 20).

27. Hobbes, *Leviathan*, 23 (ch. 3).

28. Hobbes, *Leviathan*, 53 (ch. 8).

29. Hobbes, *Leviathan*, 11 ("Introduction").

30. See Noel Malcolm, "Hobbes's Science of Politics and his Theory of Science," in *Aspects of Hobbes* (Oxford: Clarendon Press, 2002).

31. Hobbes, *Leviathan*, 254 (ch. 31).

32. Hobbes, *Leviathan*, 121 (ch. 18).

33. Hobbes, *Leviathan*, 254 (ch. 31).

34. See Geoffrey M. Vaughan, "The Audience of *Leviathan* and the Audience of Hobbes's Political Philosophy," *History of Political Thought* 22, no. 3 (2001): 458–63.

35. Hobbes, *Behemoth*, 94.

36. Hobbes, *Leviathan*, 209 (ch. 27).

37. Hobbes, *Leviathan*, 470 (ch. 46). See also Thomas Hobbes, *De Cive*, ed. Howard Warrender (Oxford: Clarendon Press, 1983), vii. 2, 3.

38. See Kinch Hoekstra, "Tyrannus Rex vs. Leviathan," *Pacific Philosophical Quarterly* 82 (2001): 420–446.

39. Hobbes, *De Cive*, vii. 3.

40. Hobbes, *Leviathan*, 233 (ch. 30).

41. Hobbes, *Leviathan*, 232 (ch. 30). See Hoekstra, "Tyrannus Rex," 437.

42. Hobbes, *Leviathan*, 231 (ch. 30).

43. Hobbes, *Leviathan*, 237 (ch. 30). See also Geoffrey M. Vaughan, *Behemoth Teaches Leviathan* (Lanham, Md.: Lexington Books, 2002).

44. Hobbes, *Leviathan*, 233 (ch. 30).

45. Hobbes, *Leviathan*, 240 (ch. 30). See also Hobbes, *Leviathan*, 244 (ch. 30) and 491 ("Review and Conclusion").

46. Hobbes, *Leviathan*, 131 (ch. 19). See also Hobbes, *De Cive*, xiii. 2.

47. Hobbes, *Leviathan*, 22 (ch. 3).

48. Thomas Hobbes, *De Homine*, in *Man and Citizen*, ed. Bernard Gert (Indianapolis: Hackett Publishing Co., 1991), 69.

49. See Hobbes, *Leviathan*, 122 (ch. 18), 185 (ch. 26).

50. Hobbes, *Leviathan*, 489 ("Review and Conclusion").

51. Hobbes, *Leviathan*, 120 (ch. 17).

52. See Hobbes, *Leviathan*, 151 (ch. 21) and 208 (ch. 27).

53. Hobbes, *Leviathan*, 62 (ch. 10).

54. Hobbes, *Leviathan*, 204 (ch. 27). See also Hobbes, *Leviathan*, 233 (ch. 30) and Skinner, *Reason and Rhetoric*, 390.

55. Hobbes, *Leviathan*, 243–44 (ch. 30).

56. Hobbes, *Leviathan*, 119 (ch. 17).

57. Hobbes, *De Cive*, xii.1 as quoted in and translated in Kinch Hoekstra, "Tyrannus Rex," 432.

58. Harvey C. Mansfield, Jr., "Hobbes and the Science of Indirect Government," *American Political Science Review* 65, no. 1 (1971): 100–1.

59. Hobbes, *Leviathan*, 491 ("Review and Conclusion"). See also Hobbes, *Leviathan*, 237 (ch. 30).

60. Hobbes, *Leviathan*, 209 (ch. 27). See Kinch Hoekstra, "Tyrannus Rex," 444 n. 39.

61. Hobbes, *Leviathan*, 486 ("Review and Conclusion"). The argument that sovereignty by institution is the paradigmatic case is undermined by this line, at least the claim that institution is the historically more accurate route to the commonwealth is undermined. See also Hobbes, *Leviathan*, 143 (ch. 20).

62. Hobbes faced this very dilemma himself. By what right could he, a subject, write on politics? See *Leviathan*, 489 ("Review and Conclusion") and Vaughan, *Behemoth Teaches Leviathan*, 22ff.

63. Hobbes, *Leviathan*, 236 (ch. 30).

64. See Hobbes, *Leviathan*, 233 (ch. 30).

65. Hobbes, *Leviathan*, 38 (ch. 6).

66. As McDowell says: "Hobbes's *Dialogue* is a significant contribution to the tradition of equity jurisprudence in that equity is now joined to a new concept of natural law." Gary L. McDowell, *Equity and the Constitution* (Chicago: Chicago University Press, 1982), 27. See also *Thomas Hobbes: A Dialogue between a Philosopher and a Student of the Common Laws of England*, ed. Joseph Cropsey (Chicago: University of Chicago Press, 1971).

67. See Vaughan, *Behemoth Teaches Leviathan*, 21ff.

68. An idiosyncratic list of works would include the following: Alan Zaitchik, "Hobbes and Hypothetical Consent," *Political Studies* 23, no. 4 (1975): 475–85; Perez Zagorin, "Hobbes on our Mind," *The Philosophical Forum* 33, no. 3 (2002): 393–412; Patrick Neal, *Liberalism and Its Discontents* (Washington Square, N.Y.: New York University Press, 1997).

69. Hobbes, *Leviathan*, 274 (ch. 34).

6

Tocqueville on Greatness and Justice

Peter Augustine Lawler

Two of the most fundamental tensions in human life seem to be between magnanimity and democracy and magnanimity and justice. Our vague but real awareness of these tensions is the reason that we democrats distrust claims for the greatness of particular individuals. We are repulsed by the inegalitarian or unjust tendency of the great-souled or magnanimous person to privilege him- or herself over others. And we notice that historical circumstances that seem to make great men happy—such as wars and revolution—make most people miserable. In a just society, maybe we would neither need nor want displays of individual greatness, and the great modern effort in pursuit of justice seemed to depend upon giving men especially concerned with displaying their political excellence less and less to do. That means, of course, that the more spirited or manly a human being is—the more concerned he or she is with asserting his or her outstanding personal significance or greatness—the more the modern regime of egalitarian justice is going to frustrate him or her. And in fact, great human aspirations and great human deeds have not disappeared, although both may have become both more rare and more misunderstood. As the novelist Tom Wolfe has often portrayed, it is the nature of human beings to be concerned—with widely varying levels of intensity—with their status as individuals and to act in all sorts of ways to establish their personal significance even or especially in our officially egalitarian time.[1]

Nobody has considered with more relentless self-examination and political astuteness the place of greatness of soul in the modern, progressively more egalitarian world than Alexis de Tocqueville. Tocqueville discovered in himself many of the qualities and longings that Aristotle described in his classic description of the magnanimous man, and most of the personal shortcomings

Tocqueville discovered in himself brought to the surface limitations or tensions in any understanding of human greatness, even Aristotle's. Despite what amounts to a claim for divine self-sufficiency, magnanimity is the quality of a human being, not God or even a god. Greatness is based on specifically human accomplishment judged by specifically human standards and even dependent on specifically human limitations. Tocqueville's self-criticism—which led to his choice for God's standard of justice over his own merely human standard of greatness—is already largely present in tensions and contradictions that Aristotle allows us to discover in the character he portrays. My purpose is to highlight certain of Tocqueville's democratic, Christian, and Socratic corrections of Aristotle's presentation of the magnanimous man's self-understanding. I can't do that without saying something about Aristotle first.

ARISTOTLE'S MAGNANIMOUS MAN[2]

Human greatness, according to Aristotle, is the rational perfection of the spirited part of the human soul—the part of the soul concerned with one's own significance or excellence. Greatness or outstanding virtue is necessarily a point of personal distinction or pride; it's more than ordinary or commonplace or average or everyday. Greatness, first of all, distinguishes our species from all the others; even the chimps and the dolphins don't have our capacity to live rationally and excellently, and not even the chimps and the dolphins are that concerned with displaying and discovering their personal significance. Particular members of our species can be ranked according to their greatness, according to the magnificence of their personal accomplishments.

Aristotle describes the great-souled or magnanimous man as rising above the petty concerns of most human beings. He appears to be confidently conscious of his superiority, of his proud detachment from the inordinate pursuit of money, power, and security that characterizes most human lives. He takes pleasures in thinking about what he knows about his own greatness. It pleases him to think that *who* he *is* depends on himself alone. He does accept the honor or praise of others as the least he deserves, but he prides himself in not being overly concerned with it. He doesn't regard any external good—even honor or glory—as *the* point of *his* particularly noble life. This self-confidence is the foundation of what anyone can see is his noble demeanor. He scorns flattery and gossip; he is kind or not haughty to those beneath him, and he only defers to the opinions of others out of friendship.

Because he is in the decisive respect the most secure of men, the great-souled man gives remarkably little attention to his material security. Although he must be aware of the place of luck in human affairs, it pleases him to free his thoughts about his own excellence from any sense of contingency. His stable self-certainty is the cause of what might be his most admirable characteristic—his extraordinary ability to be unaffected by the inevitable vicissitudes of life. Because he doesn't think of himself as defined by his material existence, he readily risks his life. That's not to say his life is defined by risk-taking. There's no point to such courage except to display one's greatness, and such a display wouldn't be virtuous unless it were really needed. So the great-souled man wouldn't go into battle for light and transient causes, and he wouldn't wander in search of adventure like some soldier of fortune. He only engages in activities that will provide evidence of his *lasting* greatness. Because *he* in some sense endures, only such deeds are worthy of *him.* Because such deeds also need to be performed on a scale that corresponds to his greatness, it would seem that he would only act to somehow save the whole community or even the whole world from ruin. His great deeds might even have to be indispensable for the community's salvation—the greatness of Lincoln or Churchill.

The great-souled man regards himself—always with evidence—as the greatest of benefactors. The greatness of the good that he does can in some measure be comprehended and so honored by others, if not so much the experience of greatness of soul that is at the foundation of his activity. But the great-souled man refuses to acknowledge that his greatness actually depends upon this or that deed. It certainly doesn't depend on his success, even if some failure deprives him of the honor which is his due. He's not tyrannically enslaved to some desire for recognition. So his self-conception and his judgment aren't distorted—or at least he doesn't become blindly angry—when insulted or slighted or otherwise misjudged. His true knowledge of his own greatness keeps him from either the anger or the overconfidence that would produce rash action. Because his virtue is real, reason remains in command.

For Aristotle, greatness of soul is a real human pleasure that corresponds in some way to real human accomplishment. Reason is able to confirm that the spirited assertion of one's own transcendent significance is more than mere vanity. Only a very few *names* correspond to beings worthy of being known and remembered for the splendor of who they *are* and what they've done. The experience of greatness of soul is real when it is enjoyed by a really great man—and such men really exist.

Because this experience reaches its height through the perfect cooperation of the rational and spirited parts of the human soul, it depends on neglecting or abstracting from anything that would disturb that cooperation. The experience of greatness of soul suppresses or ignores the erotic part of the soul, the part that reveals to us our dependence on and gratitude to others, our need for love and friendship, our incompleteness as solitary or self-sufficient beings, the perverse futility of all our striving for self-sufficiency, and our wondrous openness to the truth about all things, including other strange and wonderful human beings and ourselves. An erotic being *is* one who is born and will die, and the great-souled man does what he can not to understand himself that way. He is, his critic might say, in willful rebellion against what he really knows about the necessarily ephemeral, contingent, and socially embedded and indebted character of his merely human existence. He may not exaggerate his greatness, but he likes to forget much of its source. By exaggerating the self-sufficiency of *his being*, he downplays the reality and the goodness of his natural sociality or lack of self-sufficiency or personal perfection.

Because he exaggerates his superiority to and self-sufficiency from other human beings, the magnanimous man finds it impossible to take pleasure in or even to acknowledge the goods in life that don't have their source or their cause in him, and he hates to think of himself as having received anything good from anyone else. It pains him to acknowledge who and what has contributed to his greatness, and he would, in fact, prefer to perform great deeds alone, or not with others, perhaps not even with friends. By neglecting what he owes and is owed by others, he is blind or indifferent to the demands of justice. He knows far too well he is owed far more than anyone can give him, but he doesn't even really think he owes his community the great deeds he performs on its behalf. He acts out of magnificent generosity—his greatness can't be required or commanded by others—and not out of justice. It's likely that he acts unjustly by ignoring or slighting the mundane duties that all citizens—including those who have benefited him greatly—share. Aristotle does say that the magnanimous man does to some extent live for his friends, but it's still hard to see why he would have friends and especially why he would enjoy them for who they are.

Despite all these unjust pretensions in the direction of self-sufficiency, the truth is that the great-souled man's standard of greatness is rather social. He assumes the truth of the political opinion that the most divine human activity—the one most worthy of prayer and praise—is benefiting others. He tends to think of himself as a civil theological god, while averting his eyes from the obvious conventionality and falsity of all civil theology. According to Aristotle, an utterly self-sufficient god would be completely indifferent to the affairs of men. He would be unerotic and uncaring, and without any reason to act. Divine perfection, from Aristotle's view, is pure thought; it is the characteristic of a disembodied being that exists apart from the social and moral world of action.

So the great-souled man imagines himself free from the constraints of his social and political world, while remaining stuck with being concerned about

[handwritten margin note: social dependence and transcendence]

honor that he can't help but think he shouldn't need and is unworthy of him. Insofar as he must act, he's stuck with judging himself in some measure by the moral standards of others. He's stuck with some care for *who* other men are and *what* they think, although it doesn't seem that he really cares for, admires, or loves them. He both rises above and depends upon the judgment of ordinary men.

If he had any erotic openness at all, the magnanimous man would have some sense of the neediness that comes with this care. Aristotle reports three times that for the great-souled man "nothing is great." And, Aristotle adds, he's not given to wonder. Wonder, according to Aristotle, is the foundation of philosophy. It points the human being in the direction of something greater than himself, toward a perfection which he lacks and toward which he can both look up and is drawn. He doesn't share in the closest thing to humility in Aristotle's thought—the perception that human beings are not the greatest or most wonderful beings in the world. He's blind to both the wondrous greatness of heavenly order and how strange and wonderful most people are. He doesn't even wonder about himself; he takes his greatness as a given.

The great-souled man neglects the erotic dimension of his nature, in part, to avoid confrontation with the contradiction between his claim that nothing is great and the extreme—even if justified—claims he makes for his own greatness. Nothing is great, it pleases him to think, in comparison to his own greatness. So he lacks the crucial Socratic perception of the gap between his love of the truth and the actual wisdom that eludes him. Loving the truth— not to mention loving other people—ought to be a pleasure, but apparently it's overwhelmed, in the magnanimous man, by what it reveals to him about his own pretensions. Socrates, by contrast, is both erotic enough and courageous enough to think beyond the "who" or concerns about personal significance that animate the great-souled man to the "what" or the impersonal causes of all that exists. The drama of Socrates, in large part, is the anonymous truth being known by a particular person.[3] For the magnanimous man, it's far more important that the truth not be anonymous than it be completely known. *[handwritten margin note: truth / transparency]*

So most of all the magnanimous man may not be given to wonder because he's not completely open to the truth about himself. He's unafraid to speak truthfully to others, but he dislikes completely truthful speech about himself. He's unlikely to be glad to get the gift of well-meaning criticism, even from those who love him. According to Thomas Aquinas, gratitude is the virtue that comes through acknowledging a debt of love, and no man should desire to be free from that debt—that is, unloved.[4] The great-souled man believes he would rather be free from what seems to make human life most worth living for most men and women. By confusing a part of virtue with the whole of virtue—because he is confusing a part of himself with the whole of himself, he is more aristocratic or conscious of his superiority and less democratic or conscious of his duties to and similarities to others than is reasonable. And although he clearly takes pleasure in thinking and hearing about his own greatness, it is very unclear that he's actually happy—or at least anywhere near as happy as a human being might be. By connecting his happiness with virtuous and honorable action, he implicitly acknowledges his mere humanity or some connection with others. By connecting his happiness with a kind of trans-social and trans-erotic self-sufficiency, he must to some extent experience the misery that comes with confusing oneself with a god.

In Aristotle's hands, all the criticisms that should flow from recognizing these human contradictions are ambiguous. They can't be resolved completely on the level of moral or spirited human action, and human beings are stuck with being spirited and with the need for great deeds. Human happiness necessarily includes some consciousness of one's own greatness or personal significance. Although it may not please him, Aristotle makes it reasonable to assume that the magnanimous man's self-consciousness inevitably includes some nagging recognition of his dependence on others. It is impossible, of course, to perform great deeds by or for oneself. Opportunities are needed for such action, and the magnanimous man can't really create them for himself and remain virtuous.

His dependence on political circumstances beyond his control is surely the source of his greatest frustration. What can he do if he's stuck living in a time when there's nothing worthy of him to do, a time in which human beings have no need of great, community-saving action? Nothing might pain him more—although he could never say it—than living in a time blessed with too much real justice—a time when it's best that he remain unemployed. Is it really possible for him proudly to sustain *himself* if nobody notices his excellence because he never has a chance to display it? Even the greatest of men is surely unable to free himself from all knowledge of the contingency of his excellence, and so from all anxious self-doubt. He may be able to bear bad luck better than most men, but Aristotle admits that it's unreasonable to believe that the virtuous man will be happy no matter what his circumstances might be. Aristotle acknowledges—even if he whispers for the sake of virtue—the fact that chance and contingency are characteristic of every human life.

The magnanimous man can, at best, be very imperfectly free from the need to act to establish his self-sufficient personal significance. The inability to escape completely from something of that restless self-awareness is one reason why Aristotle attempted to show that his longing to be free from dependence points beyond itself to the way of life of the philosopher. Aristotle finally acknowledges that lives defined by moral virtue—even magnanimity—are merely human, whereas the way of life devoted to contemplation is the one that actually imitates the divine. God is characterized by a thoughtful self-sufficiency that produces a serene indifference to the affairs of men, of mixed beings composed of both bodies and souls. Insofar we can genuinely imitate such a god through our transcendence of noble action in the direction of contemplative leisure, we achieve an unmixed form of happiness not available to merely moral and political men.

So Aristotle finally acknowledges that magnanimity is a characteristic of mixed beings aiming at a greatness that will remain somewhat beyond them, while adding the pure pleasure of detached thought can also be experienced quite imperfectly by mere men. He causes us to see, of course, if the imperfect pleasure that comes with contemplation of one's own real greatness depends on our mixed existence. Genuine self-sufficiency would free us, no doubt, from the need to act but also from the real pleasure or pride that comes with the real performance of great deeds for beings who really need help. It would also free us from love. Aristotle certainly leaves us with the thought that thinking about the strange and wonderful magnanimous man—and spirited displays of moral virtue generally—are more a proper and pleasurable subject for human contemplation than the stars. In his view, it even seems that the best men are better and worse—and certainly more wonderful—than the impersonal god.

TOCQUEVILLE'S SELF-EXAMINED GREATNESS

The human tensions and contradictions in the self-understanding of the great man are one of Tocqueville's explicit themes. He is less concerned about portraying some great-souled character than with *being* one, with understanding his own great but still merely human longings and accomplishments. Tocqueville's reflections on his own magnanimity are much more conscious and even ironic about the disproportion between his aspirations and his human reality than those of the character Aristotle described. He says he wrote to overcome, through a relentless self-examination, the inevitable partisanship that comes with his concern for his own greatness. He achieved enough self-knowledge to be able to choose justice over greatness, by being able to distinguish between his human perspective and that of the Creator.

Tocqueville's literary experiment for the primary purpose of candid self-examination was his *Souvenirs*, or his recollections of his political participation during the revolution of 1848. He employed a leisurely "solitude" he did not choose—he'd rather be in public life—to turn "my thoughts to myself." He discovered he enjoyed the "solitary pleasure of remembering great events," and so he was able to reflect and write only to please himself. That pleasure, more precisely, didn't depend on the opinions of others, but it did depend on who he was and what he did in the social context of political life. He discovered that his desire for pleasure caused his memory to be selective. It naturally gravitated to people and events that "have something of greatness about them" (3–4).[5] He had an "invincible curiosity," but not about everything, only about greatness (122–23, 257). It's not true for him, as it is for Aristotle's character, that he's not given to wonder and that to him nothing is great. He wonders about what is truly great, about manifestations of great human individuality.

Ordinary human beings and routine or "bourgeois" times, Tocqueville admitted, were too unstriking or boring for him to remember. He admits that he can't remember most names and faces; in his eyes, most people don't really have names or personal significance (82–83). His theoretical curiosity for what people do, he admits, has a profoundly aristocratic bias. But that bias has its theoretical justification. It's only in great or revolutionary times that the full range of human virtue and vice displays itself (4). Greatness is rare but real, and it's impossible to really know human beings without seeing it for what it is. But Tocqueville is candid enough to add that the pleasure he takes in greatness requires his suspension of doubt. To distrust completely his selective perspective would make thought about human greatness—and so perhaps distinctively human happiness—impossible (62, 82).

Unlike the American democrats he describes in *Democracy in America* (2, 1, 1),[6] Tocqueville was no Cartesian—at least most of the time—when it comes to the pleasure of privileging manifestations of greatness of soul. He could even acknowledge that the only contemplation that gave him pleasure was of greatness; metaphysical and theological inquiry filled him with the misery of anxious, disorienting uncertainty about the nature and destiny of man. He could see, with Pascal, that political thought might, in part, be a passionate diversion from his misery in the absence of faith in God. But he would never acknowledge that it was only a diversion; he thought great men, virtuous liberty, and great political accomplishment were real. Great men exaggerate the effects and the goodness of their deeds, but exaggerations aren't to be confused with lies or complete self-deceptions.

We can say, at least on the level of self-presentation, that Tocqueville was much more Socratic than the Aristotelian character in the many ways he acknowledged that his obsession with greatness corresponded, in large measure, to his many human weaknesses, and in the way he really both wondered and was anxious about his own greatness. The reason that he wrote the *Souvenirs* for himself alone was that he knew that it was impossible for him to tell the truth about himself or others in speech or writing meant for others. Great men find it impossible to display their shortcomings to others, and they aren't about to share their doubts even with their friends (80, 81). Tocqueville is only able to tell himself that by nature he's both excessively proud and full of self-distrust. His passion for greatness corresponds to his "innate" weakness of extreme anxiety about his status or significance as a particular man (230), and he acknowledged that even his solitary judgments were suspect, given his self-partisanship (80, 81). His primary fear, he admits, is that he might, in truth, be lacking in distinctiveness or greatness, that his life is merely petty or insignificant (231). Nothing disturbed his "peace of mind" more than threats to his pride. His "pride," he acknowledged, "is as nervous and restless as the mind itself" (84). He claims to be less afraid of danger than of doubt—doubts about *who* he is and *what* he should do. A shortage of self-confidence more than a "weak heart" is what immobilizes him in political life most of the time (84–85).

A revolution that reduced society to a "wretched state" and made most people miserable made Tocqueville happy. It gave him what he most desired—self-confidence. There was, in his mind, "no room for moral hesitation," and his great virtue was suddenly clearly indispensable (84–85). A great man of thoroughgoing excellence and integrity was needed to help save the political community and maybe civilization itself! The opportunity to "rescue society," Tocqueville remembers, "touched both my integrity and my pride" (193). He remembers himself being called to near the center of the political stage for "the great personal consideration he enjoyed outside of politics," a greatness that transcended the doubtful partisanship of political controversy (187). And "consciousness of the importance of what I was doing" elevated his pride still more, making him more "calm and tranquil" in the midst of revolutionary chaos than he was during a middle class time of calm and tranquility (231). He was more calm because he was both more self-confident and no longer morally and politically isolated (46, 47, 222).

But even about his opportunities for great deeds Tocqueville was capable of irony. He admitted he enjoyed a touch of danger, but not too much—and certainly not actually fighting (106, 157). And he himself was never overwhelmed by the seething "chaotic anger" that produces revolutionary brutality (145). We can say that mere courage was far from the whole of virtue for him; he needed a political stage on which to display all his immaterial or moral and intellectual greatness.

The revolution gave Tocqueville an opportunity to prove his indispensable personal significance both to himself and others. He admitted that his self-esteem depended on the esteem of others, or that at least he benefited greatly from their recognition. So he cared about it more than is reasonable and sulked when it was not forthcoming (83–84). He acknowledged that he didn't get or even deserve such recognition in the middle class or bourgeois, parliamentary regime that was toppled by the revolution. There he was both very isolated and very ineffective. To succeed he would have had to make nuanced calculations and detailed compromises among a variety of morally dubious interests, as well as take a genuine interest in the men who advanced those interests. He thought both the men and the choices to be made were unworthy of him, and he could focus his attention on neither well enough to be confident that he really knew what he was doing. And in his unappreciated isolation, of course, he even doubted who he was (81–83).

So Tocqueville was not confident enough to withdraw from a political world where his greatness was unemployed. Because his passion for greatness couldn't be detached from his passion for recognition, he always took advantage of any political role—however petty—that came his way. He was always plagued by anxious misery—personal and "metaphysical"—with nothing political to do. When he was completely denied a place on the political stage—and only then, he wrote books about political life in the service of a future with a worthy place for great men like him. His books are always thought in the service of greatness, and that mixture of theory and practice always limited and directed his curiosity.[7] He, with good reason, tended to think of them as singular contributions to the perpetuation of human liberty—displays of a rare form of redemptive excellence characteristic of magnanimity.

Tocqueville admitted that his contempt for ordinary or middle-class political life was unjustly exaggerated; he couldn't view it from the perspective of the happiness it provided for most men. There is lot to be said for a society that was only "corrupt," but not "cruel" and "bloodthirsty" (36). Although he couldn't remember them, the truth is that just about all men have names and a personal significance slighted by his selective vision. He could only acknowledge in passing that there might be something good natured even or especially in some of the most dullwitted of them. The simplicity of natural goodness rarely—if ever—impressed Tocqueville. The name he gives to the one person he describes with such a character—"Eugene"—is all too clearly a generic reference or not a particular person's real name (157).

Tocqueville's partisanship on behalf of greatness was both somewhat unrealistic and somewhat unjust, but it also had the theoretical merit of revealing the indispensability of greatness even for securing justice. The bourgeois rulers, he showed, were wrong in believing that government could be reduced to an amoral, impersonal mechanism, and the socialists were probably even more wrong to believe that political life could, in justice, just wither away. The coming of revolution was evidence that probably every effort to dispense altogether with greatness and great men is bound to fail, although the unprecedented nature of events in his time was enough for Tocqueville to lack confidence or certainty about the human future. There's enough truth in his magnanimous perspective for him to have spoken boldly and truly that "the real cause, the effective one, that makes men lose power is that they have become unworthy of it" (14). Tocqueville remembers that the bourgeois King Louis-Philippe's "profound disbelief in virtue . . . clouded his vision," keeping him from seeing both virtue's beauty and its utility (6).

Still, Tocqueville's most important contribution to our understanding of greatness of soul is his clear recognition that it depends on human weakness. From Pascal, he learned that our greatness is intertwined with our misery. Tocqueville's passionate immersion in political life rescued him, only in part, from the anxious uncertainty that plagued him when his thought was detached from great action. His solitary pleasure that comes with thoughts of greatness is not the complacent, transerotic solitude of a self-sufficient or self-absorbed being. Certainly Tocqueville experienced none of the serenity of those who can connect divinity with pure thought.

Greatness of soul is characteristic of the being who is neither pure mind nor pure body, and our greatness can't be detached from—it is in many ways rooted in—our miserable awareness of our contingency. It is full of the contradictions and paradoxes constantly displayed by the being who, as Tocqueville says (again following Pascal), is the beast with the angel in him (2, 2, 16). For him, greatness is the ambiguously self-confident assertion of the spirited part of the soul allied imperfectly with reason in pursuit of evidence that one's existence is not merely insignificant, dispensable, momentary, and material. The magnanimous man needs to act and be recognized to quell the doubt that comes with the thought that one's own pride might be vanity—a thought shared by neither the beasts nor the angels, not to mention God. God doesn't doubt His own greatness nor is particularly concerned with it. But that doesn't mean, as Aristotle thought, that God couldn't be just or providentially concerned with the affairs of men.

JUSTICE AND GREATNESS IN *DEMOCRACY IN AMERICA*

Although it was written more than a decade later, Tocqueville's candid account of merely human greatness in his *Souvenirs* actually explains his qualified and reluctant judgment in favor of democratic justice over aristocratic greatness at the end of *Democracy in America*. There he impresses us with the difficulty of judging what his book describes—the movement of the world of men toward equality. He reports that his vision blurs—it is neither clear nor selective enough—and his thoughts vacillate—because they're shaped by more than one perspective. He is confronting the choice between judging by his own human standard and that of the just and providential Creator (4, 2, 8).

Tocqueville's own standard is greatness or, more precisely, the delight he experiences in observing very great men. There seems to be little place for men such as himself in the emerging egalitarian world. There "particular persons" only do "small things," and general causes or impersonal forces explain far more of historical change and human behavior. That's partly because there are only a very few men with "vast ambitions," and "[g]enius becomes rarer." More generally, life seems unelevated and unadorned; nothing seems great. The particular greatness of extraordinary individuals gets lost in the "universal uniformity" of the emerging world (4, 2, 8).

The near-disappearance of great men both "saddens and chills" Tocqueville. It's chilling to consider that men like himself might have no future (4, 2, 8). That possibility might even call into question the claim that they ever existed at all, that human greatness ever explained what people are and do (2, 1, 19). The fate of men might always have been best explained by impersonal forces beyond anyone's real control. For Tocqueville, the unadorned or unmagnanimous life is worthy of neither his thought nor his action. He's both saddened and chilled by the prospect of a life not worth living by him.

Still, Tocqueville truthfully compels himself to think beyond his own partisanship. He admits, as he did in the *Souvenirs*, that the pleasure he receives from the spectacle of greatness is "born of his weakness," and so too is the anxious chill he experiences in its absence (4, 2, 8). It's impossible for a mere man to see everything, but he can admit that his passion for greatness determines what it pleases him to see. So the aristocratic partisan of greatness unjustly diverts his eyes from the poverty, cruelty, and ignorance that characterize most lives in aristocratic times. The choice of greatness over justice comes from attributing too much significance to his particular needs or longings, to his own particular existence, and to the importance of what men like him think and do.

Tocqueville explained the aristocratic perspective that unjustly privileges great men even limited what "the most profound and vast geniuses of Greece and Rome could see." Their thought was too intensely particular "to arrive at the idea, so general but at the same time so simple, of the similarity of men and the equal right to freedom from birth." So they complacently concluded that it was natural that human greatness would always depend on slavery, that the many, out of necessity, would live for the few. They readily diverted their eyes from the remedial injustice of slavery; even the philosophers who were born slaves were far from abolitionists (2, 1, 3).

"Jesus Christ," Tocqueville claims, "had to come down to earth to make it understood that all members of the human species are naturally alike and equal" (2, 1, 3). Jesus made us understand what was already and remains true by nature. God becoming man—showing his personal concern for every particular human being—was necessary to correct effectively the merely human preference for greatness or justice. All human beings are equally more than slaves to nature or their country or other human beings, and they are all equal under and equally not God. Tocqueville is not necessarily affirming his personal faith in the divinity of Jesus. The confidence that faith would give him would counter more effectively, it would seem, than greatness his anxious doubt about his personal significance. But he does refuse to doubt either that man is great or God is just.

Tocqueville chooses the unlimited, undistorted perspective of the Creator-God of the Bible over that of the Greek and Roman philosophers. He explains that only God can see all in both our similarities and differences (2, 1, 3); only an "all-powerful and eternal Being . . . see(s) distinctly, though at once, the whole race and each man." God so understood—as opposed to the indifferent, self-sufficient, and amoral god of the philosophers—is "the *creator* and *preserver* of men." Being a creature is the deepest source of "each man's" personal significance. Because he is the source of the being of each man, God's concern must not be "the singular prosperity of some, but the greatest well-being of all." From his view, the justice of democracy is its greatness, because all men have some greatness about them that deserves to be preserved. That doesn't mean, of course, that all men are equal in their actual displays of greatness. The partial truth of both aristocracy and democracy is preserved in the unlimited vision of the Creator. And only by "enter[ing] into the point of view of God" can Tocqueville see, in justice, the greatness of each particular man, what distinguishes or elevates him above the rest of creation (2, 4, 8).

We can say that the perspective of the Creator elevated Tocqueville above the partisanship of magnanimity in the direction of the true practical wisdom described by Thomas Aquinas. According to Thomas, there's a sort of virtue that allows the magnanimous man to know when he should employ his magnanimity, and when he should contain his impulse toward greatness in the name of reason and justice—"and so ultimately for true human virtue as well."[8] Tocqueville at his best wrote and acted to preserve the creature who could distinguish between himself and the Creator, as well as between himself and merely material existence. He employed his singular greatness to preserve the greatness all human beings—or more clearly all human beings in democratic ages—share in common.

In God's eyes, Tocqueville concludes, what seems like decadence that wounds his pride is actually progress. But he still reserves judgment about the superiority of democracy to aristocracy. That's because God, in some measure, left our future in our own hands, or at least prevents us from knowing our future with any certainty. We're always drawn in one way or another to the errors of either exaggerating or denying our liberty, of regarding ourselves as angels or brutes. The truth is that "Providence has not created the human race either entirely independent or entirely free," and there's still room for human greatness—for properly chastened magnanimous men—in preserving both greatness and justice. God certainly has given us no reason to think that we have no role in preserving ourselves as beings who know themselves as creatures. It's true enough that we can't turn ourselves into gods, but what distinguishes us as human beings from the other animals may or may not have a future. We actually can't be sure that the Creator, without our help, will preserve our greatness—which includes our need for justice—forever (2, 4, 8). By giving us the capability of being both great and just (and so not the necessity of being so), the Creator, for our own good, introduced all sorts of contingency both into our personal lives and into our collective future.

There's reason to doubt Tocqueville's real belief in the Creator-God of the Bible, and we might want to conclude that his references to him are ironic or instrumental in the pursuit of his real goal of perpetuating liberty understood as human greatness in democratic times. "In politics," he explains, "men unite for great undertakings," and the purpose of political life for him seems less the pursuit of justice or the common good than displays of great individuality. And he certainly distinguishes, quite undemocratically, between the "true friends of freedom and greatness" and most human beings, who would, if pushed, choose equality over liberty, choose, if even futilely, against their own greatness. Only a few men "adore" freedom and regard its defense as a "holy enterprise," and that love of greatness, by its nature, transcends every effort to understand human action as predictable and uniform. Tocqueville makes it clear that magnanimity remains a rare, beautiful, and indispensable human quality, and that even genuine devotion to justice isn't possible without it (2, 4, 7).

But great men have to acknowledge, in truth, that "there is no question of reconstructing an aristocratic society," although their "circle of independence" can be larger there. Their task has become "making freedom issue from the bosom of the democratic society in which God makes us live." God, it seems for the moment, seems less just than willful, and he has imposed unprecedented limitations and challenges on the great. From that view, "those of our contemporaries who want to create or secure the independence and dignity of those like themselves," the great who want to preserve some room for the dignity of greatness, have no choice but to "show themselves to be friends of equality." So Tocqueville's seemingly rather selfless choice for God over himself might be a way of "showing" that friendship, although his guiding thought is not about God's justice but human greatness (2, 4, 7).

Even if that were true, his conclusion is still based on accurate observations about the superior comprehensiveness and truthfulness of divine justice to his merely human selective perception and privileging of greatness. Tocqueville never claims to love the Creator he describes, but reflection on His existence is indispensable for explaining why the great man's existence is not so different from that of most human beings that he can justly or reasonably claim that most human beings live for his benefit. Tocqueville concludes that a return to aristocracy is not even to be "wished," because it's unreasonable or unjust to sacrifice "the prosperity of the greatest number to the greatness of the few" (2, 4, 7). The greatness of the few is only legitimately employed to preserve the greatness—the human distinctiveness of partly free creatures under God—that the many and the few share. Because Tocqueville never makes the error of confusing greatness or any manifestation of political life with some perfection of the human soul, he never sunders the connection that unites all human beings under God.[9]

GREATNESS AND DEMOCRACY

Tocqueville has to teach the magnanimous man in democratic times to be attentive to the greatness he shares with all his fellow human beings—the experiences they all have in common that elevate each of them all above all else that exists. This education that reconciles greatness—in some measure at least—to justice is far from easy; it requires, as Tocqueville admits, a sensitivity for the strange and wonderful details in the lives of the seemingly ordinary that he himself, as a political leader, often lacked. The movement toward democracy, he explains, actually dispels the illusions that obscure the true, egalitarian foundation of human greatness.

Tocqueville describes the human effort to idealize existence or portray greatness in his discussion of poetry. Aristocratic poetry idealizes human beings by exaggerating their freedom from material existence for proud transcendence of nobility and contemplation. In a certain sense, Aristotle's *Ethics* is a form of aristocratic poetry. But egalitarian progress discredits aristocratic illusions—such as the ones that supported the serene self-sufficiency of the magnanimous man—and seems, at first, to empty life of all material for poetic adornment. The unadorned human experience of the truth about himself is as someone "wandering" for a moment between "two abysses"; "man comes from nothing, traverses time, and is going to disappear forever in the bosom of God." Man, in truth, is the most "marvelous" being in the universe, full "of infinite greatness and pettiness" and all sorts of contradictions (2, 1, 17). The most poetic being who *really exists* is the unadorned human being. He's the one first described by Pascal, the purest of seekers whom Tocqueville presents as free from both aristocratic and democratic illusions (2, 1, 10).

Our always obscured but never completely absent awareness of the strange, wonderful, and somewhat incomprehensible truth about ourselves is really the foundation of human greatness, and our curiosity really is best directed toward the lives of those particular souls. Our existence is always between ignorance and knowledge, especially about ourselves. We know enough to be proud and anxious and poetic, but not enough to be condemned to wallow in fatalistic despair or ascend to divine wisdom and self-sufficiency. The truthful experience that constitutes our humanity is neither shared with the other animals nor with God. And it produces all sorts of human thought and action that, in truth, can't be incorporated into some materialistic system. All human longing for greatness—and all great deeds—are rooted in some way in our truthful and singular experience of contingency or particularity. Our greatness comes from the fact that we know that we are neither God nor merely one of the unconscious and species-oriented animals; we can't help but experience ourselves as individuals concerned with our less than self-evident personal significance.

The anxious, restless, and miserable concern self-conscious mortals have for their particular being is, by itself, a sign of human greatness. That concern is the source of our immaterial and even immortal longings and hopes, and it leads us to perform great deeds, deeds which are evidence, in fact, of our enduring significance. The characteristic democratic error is to pity excessively contingent beings between abysses by giving insufficient attention to the greatness of what such beings have done with what they know (3,1,1). Great human accomplishments and great human thought withstand the test of time far more impressively than particular human bodies do, and our proud and anxious desire not to be merely contingent and insignificant beings need not go completely unsatisfied (2, 2, 15).

If we really believe everything human is as ephemeral as particular bodies, then great thought and action may become impossible. The truth is that nothing human endures is a self-fulfilling prophecy. People who believe that their existence is in some sense immortal or transcendent really do produce monuments of their greatness in both thought and action. The dogmatic opinion that nothing human is of particular significance really immerses a man in the present—or obliterates his singular concern with his own past and future that distinguishes him from the other animals—and keeps him from being moved by what he really knows (2, 2, 15–17). Perhaps the only thing of any real significance is the liberty—for great thought and action—given to members of our species alone. The only thing of real significance, arguably, is the drama of the human being moved to great thought and action by what he really knows about himself.

Tocqueville defends democratic greatness against the untrue doctrine of materialism—a perennial human temptation that is especially pernicious in democratic ages. Materialism, its defenders say, is useful because it gives people an appropriately modest conception of themselves. They say it dispels haughty illusions that make us think of ourselves as more than we really are. But the truth is that the materialists see us as less than we really are—as indistinguishable from the other animals. And so materialism denies what we can see with our own eyes about our distinctively human behavior. The doctrine of materialism—preached by the materialistic scientist—can't incorporate the real existence of the materialistic scientist, the being who knows, unlike any other animal, the truth about the way things really are. He proudly concludes that by capturing every other human being in his materialistic system he stands above other members of his species like a god. His pride is more unrealistic and more revolting than that of the aristocrats, who usually maintain some "paternalistic" human connections between themselves and those they rule and who in some ways acknowledged the distinction between themselves and God (2, 2, 15).

The doctrine of materialism suggests that members of our species are as readily controlled as those of the other species. It suggests the theory of what Harvey Mansfield calls "rational control,"[10] that would characterize the soft despotism Tocqueville describes, a society in which human beings have docilely surrendered everything great about themselves—any thought or action with the future in view—in favor of an easygoing security or contentment engineered for them by schoolmarmish despots armed with materialistic expertise (2, 4, 6). Partly because they aim to replace greatness with subhuman despotism, Tocqueville calls the materialists the "natural enemies" of any democratic people (2, 2, 15).

Tocqueville's other fear about the pernicious consequences of materialism, the one confirmed by American experience, is that belief in the doctrine of materialism will cause Americans to pursue material well-being with an "insane ardor" (2, 2, 15). The insanity of such diversion, of course, is not characteristic of any other animal and is actually proof that members of our species are more than material beings. The Americans are often miserable because they can distort but not eradicate the needs of their souls (2, 2, 12). They often make the mistake of believing that those needs can be satisfied through material success, partly because they half-consciously believe much of the time that their real longing is for a greatness beyond material determination that can't be satisfied (2, 2, 13).

To Tocqueville, the Americans display their greatness as beings full of contradictions through their obviously incoherent thought and action. The particularly ambitious among them readily risk their lives to secure better their material self-preservation (2, 2, 18). They proudly display their contempt for the
life they work to preserve. They both do and do not identify their beings with
their bodies. They, with some justice, lack the serene self-confidence of the
magnanimous man who knows that he *is* more than a material being. The
magnanimous man neglects the fact that his longing for transcendence has its
roots in his perception of his contingency, and the American neglects that fact
that his singular perception of contingency can be the source of real transcendence.

Tocqueville certainly shows us the incoherent greatness in the Americans'
moral doctrine of self-interest rightly understood. The Americans brag about
their self-sufficiency—their freedom from natural instinct and each other.
Their pride in their enlightened liberty is displayed in their explanations that
what appears to be self-sacrifice on their part is not really self-sacrifice at all.
They both transcend the natural world of animals and proudly refuse to be
pawns in the hands of others by turning every moment of their lives over to
calculation about their own interests (2, 2, 8). But they calculate about material enjoyment, about a purpose all the animals share! And their incoherent
doctrine—if it really governed their whole lives, as they brag—would turn
those lives into hell. They would always be thinking about how to enjoy, but
never take time to enjoy. It is impossible to have a doctrine that both does justice to the human longing for free or transcendent self-sufficiency and identifies human happiness with material enjoyment. The secure reduction of happiness to such enjoyment (as Rousseau explains) is given only to the animals
unaware of their contingency and so unconcerned with their personal significance (2, 2, 16).

Why does Tocqueville seemingly strongly affirm and only gently criticize
the incoherence of the *moral* doctrine of self-interest rightly understood? It's
because he notices that the Americans *are* better than they *say*. The American
boasting about his freedom hides the offense against freedom or self-sufficiency that is the human happiness he really does enjoy. Americans often give
way to their natural impulses to love and be of service to other human beings
(2, 2, 8). Despite their individualistic talk, they often act and think like par-
ents, spouses, children, neighbors, citizens, and creatures. They explain away
the fact of their social involvement in the institutions of local government, a
wide variety of voluntary associations, the family, and the church with their
doctrine. It's in their self-interest, they say, to build alliances through marriage (2, 3, 11), citizenship (2, 2, 4), and going to church, and it's possible,
they claim, to even play let's make a deal with God (2, 2, 9). But the truth is

that, despite their perverse pride in their self-interested liberty, they come to know and love each other (2, 2, 4) and God (2, 2, 9).

Tocqueville presents the Americans as far more successfully combating than succumbing to the democratic "heart disease" of individualism or indifference to the lives of others. Like the magnanimous man Aristotle describes, the American tends to describes himself as an extremely self-involved and unerotic being, but what he says is far from true either about his real personal experiences or what he actually does. A danger Tocqueville shows us, of course, is that what they *say* may gradually transform who they *are*, and that's why he reminds us that Americans unrealistically disparage their capacities for both greatness and justice — for all "great devotions" — by really believing their doctrine is true (2, 2, 8).

MIDDLE-CLASS MAGNANIMITY?

There's a more elementary way of expressing the Americans' contradiction: All the Americans attach themselves to worldly good as if they'll never die, as if they knew that their existence in this world is secure. But they pursue them in such a rush — and with such a feverish ardor — that they also seem convinced that they'll be around only a moment more. With fortunate circumstances that should be the foundation of unprecedented contentment and enjoyment, they're more restless and even sad than people ever have been. The good news is that they certainly remain too serious — and too lacking in playfulness or spontaneity — to be mere animals. The bad news is that their lives can appear to be evidence that there's no such thing as *human* happiness, and so Tocqueville reports that they sustain their liberty more as a matter of will than of reason (2, 2, 13).

Their pursuit of enjoyment is, most of all, really pursuit of self-sufficiency through the imposition of rational control through willful calculation on their material being. It is a confused display of materialistic magnanimity made possible by the illusion that they can look at their bodies and their needs from some undisclosed location apart from them and figure out how to satisfy them from there. They are less beings with material needs than beings with the freedom to work. Middle-class Americans define themselves as free beings who work (2, 1, 3), as beings with interests (2, 2, 8). They see themselves as standing in a truthful location between aristocratic and materialistic illusions; they are different from all the other beings who exist because they are and know they are middle class. Their pursuit, they think, is more realistic or more effective than that of the aristocrats, while still being a proud manifestation of human liberty. It's hard to deny that the middle class American does achieve more real security or freedom from contingency that Aristotle's character, although his confusion about who he is causes him to experience himself as progressively less secure. Arguably today's middle-class Americans are the most secure, anxious, and death- or contingency-haunted people ever.

Part of the justice of democracy is its elevation of work. Aristocrats said and to some large extent thought that, because of their greatness, work was not for them; they were fundamentally better than beings with interests (2, 2, 8). They inconsiderately believed they had no responsibility to make their lives productive. Their lives were mostly for leisure, and even their few great and glorious deeds weren't to be confused with what was required to meet ordinary human need. They proudly thought that their thoughts soared above any concern for increasing human prosperity or reducing human misery (2, 1, 10), and it didn't please them to admit that even they had to secretly give some attention to their material advantage (2, 2, 8). In general, aristocrats had an excessively proud or magnanimous understanding of their freedom from the ordinary work that must be done, because they had a very high opinion of their personal significance. It didn't strike them as unjust that most people are stuck with working for them.

America's middle-class democracy extends both freedom and the duty to work to everyone. Everyone, in justice, is free to work to sustain himself. No man is enslaved to another man's imaginary view of the nobility of freedom or leisure, and both not working for oneself (or not working for money) and not working at all become ignoble. The result, Tocqueville explains, is that "[i]n democracies nothing is greater or more brilliant than commerce." So it's in such productive activity that great ambition and talent usually display themselves, and Tocqueville remarks that the "greatness and audacity"—even the heroism—of American men of commerce is evidence of the contempt such ambitious men would have shown to chosen activity in aristocratic times (2, 2, 18). Magnanimity is displaced from politics and even philosophy into trade, industry, and invention, and the thought behind that democratic change is that nothing is more vital to particular people and the community as a whole than material prosperity.

The magnanimous man has always been stuck, to some extent, with serving some communal standard of excellence, with living for the perpetuation of the way of life of some people or another. In some sense, the magnanimous man has always been a being who works, and the magnanimous democrat who is honored for satisfying the people's vulgar and so real needs is less deluded than his aristocratic counterpart both about the claim justice makes upon him and the real source of his honor. People are surely happier if he is clever enough to satisfy their needs with "the arts of peace," as opposed to the arts of war, even if they are more disposed to honor warriors than commercial heroes. As Tocqueville himself reflected, his preference for revolutionary over bourgeois life could only be completely coherent if revolution could be affirmed as an end in itself. His fear—from the perspective of greatness—that great revolutions will become rare in democratic ages actually expresses the intention of every modern revolution—to be the revolution that will bring revolution to an end (2, 3, 21).

The insane ardor of the men of the 20th century who affirmed permanent revolution was really a "manliness run amok"; they believed that only cruel, bloody frenzy of ideological war could save them from the modern abolition of personal significance in the names of equality, efficiency, and justice.[11] Fortunately for magnanimous men like Churchill, de Gaulle, Solzhenitsyn, Havel, and even Patton, the battles made necessary by the inhuman or anti-human ambition of those fanatics provided a basically unexpected but quite wonderful opportunity to display something like classical magnanimity, to defend a world where reason in some sense is comparatively in command. But nobody in his right mind would thank Lenin, Hitler, and Stalin for giving magnanimous men something great or even redemptive to do.

Maybe we can say that—in *Democracy in America*—Tocqueville underestimated—but didn't completely neglect (2, 3, 19)—the monstrous forms the longing of particular men for greatness would take against a world in which they believed they had no place. But we do see better than ever that "commercial greatness" deserves to be praised as having done infinitely more than Marxian revolutionary greatness in satisfying the real needs of people, and commerce really does give men "a high idea of their individual worth" in a way that "disposes them to freedom but moves them away from revolution" (2, 3, 21). The contempt of the great for middle-class life in the modern world too easily becomes contempt for the real conditions of human life itself. And we admire more than ever Tocqueville's manly and largely successful combat against that temptation in his own case.

That's not to deny that the aristocrat's contempt for the vulgar, material standard of productivity has plenty of advantages when it comes to greatness—some people have the leisure to engage in political life for its own sake and others to pursue artistic, theological, literary, and philosophical greatness for their own sakes. And a weakness of democracy, Tocqueville explains, is that there's no way it can recapture fully the appreciation for greatness of the aristocratic ruling class (2, 1, 3). But, in justice, he can't really object to the democratic injunction that everyone work and find some honor and greatness in personal productivity. The middle-class error—or deficient self-understanding—is to view people as for work and *nothing more*. Our wealth, power, and economic and political freedom can't really either address or satisfy our deepest longings (2, 2, 12; 1, 2, 9). The middle-class way of looking at the world can neither comprehend nor allow us to live well with the true greatness of the being who is stuck self-consciously and even incoherently between the other animals and God. So democratic leaders should "attach less value to the work and more to the worker," thinking even of them as "great men" (2. 4, 7). American religion, Tocqueville explains, is in some measure an authentically middle-class antidote to the American middle-class mistake of seeing people as merely beings with interests.

RELIGION, PRIDE, AND GREATNESS

Religion, Tocqueville says, is a natural response to the interrelated human experiences of contingency and greatness. That's because "Alone among all the beings, man shows a natural disgust for existence and an immense desire to exist: he scorns life and fears annihilation" (1, 2, 9). Man, alone among the animals, desires to *be*. So he's disgusted with his merely momentary existence. His disgust causes him both to long to be and actually be more than a merely biological being; he can display his singular greatness, his freedom from material determination. But he can't free himself altogether from his body; great individuals, like the rest of us, die. This combination of both self-disgust and self-elevation and beast and angel *is* pride.[12] This proud and anxious concern for one's personal significance, more than anything else, is the enduring foundation of religion. Religion, Tocqueville shows us, is the natural human response to the multiple dimensions of the human fear of *not being*. Americans, in Tocqueville eyes, see it as providing help that human beings can't possibly provide for themselves in both chastening and supporting our magnanimous pretensions—the "manliness" we all possess in some measure or another.

Religion helps in Americans the confidence that they're more than bodies, and it does so as a supplement to—not a replacement—for the middle class view of the world. Six days of the week, Tocqueville, observes, the American is immersed in the commercial and industrial life of his country. But on Sunday, he "is torn away for a moment from the small passions that agitate his life and the passing interests that fill it, he at once enters into an ideal world in which all is great, pure, eternal." On Sunday, he learns of the "lofty destiny" the God of "infinite magnificence" has given him; he has been made for virtue and immortality. And Christian sermons that rail against his pride actually sustain that pride against the secular, skeptical view that God, immortality, and disinterested virtue aren't really for a being with interests like himself (2, 2, 15).

Tocqueville explains that religion so understood is not to be praised for its political or even moral utility, but for what it does for the individual in opening him to the truth about his greatness that democracy on its own would deny or neglect. It would be very unrealistic and unjust for the Americans to turn every day into Sunday—into a day of rest and contemplation. Nothing would ever get done. But without a day of rest they might become so restless, disoriented, and perhaps finally deranged, and perhaps they would willingly end up surrendering their miserable and unreasonable liberty (2, 2, 12–16).

Tocqueville praises Christianity, as we have seen, for its egalitarianism. But that praise, more precisely, is for its teaching concerning the immaterial greatness that all human beings share. It is the firmest foundation of the democratic concern with equality without the enervating democratic skepticism concerning the soul and its needs. It combines, properly understood, justice and greatness. So Tocqueville praises Christianity for preserving the partial but real truth about aristocratic pride in democratic times.

He is virtually silent about the Christian teaching concerning humility, because, in his opinion, a key threat to the future of greatness of soul is that particular democrats already think too little of themselves. The democrat, it's true, is proud enough to believe that his neighbor is no better than him. But the problem is his tendency to add that both he and his neighbor were made for no more than "vulgar pleasures," that they both are incapable of greatness of soul (2, 3, 20). In a sense their attraction to materialistic doctrine chains them, despite themselves, to an aristocratic prejudice about the way most people *are*.

Democracy tends to drag the great down to the level of the vulgar, despite its noble intention of universalizing greatness. Christianity, in truth, humbles men by showing them all that they're all equally not God, that even their greatest deeds are merely human and so finally unable to free them from all doubt concerning who they are. But it also raises them up by showing them that they are all creatures with souls or an immaterial dimension of existence oriented in the direction of the Creator. Christianity teaches that much of what the aristocrats inconsiderately regarded as merely vulgar, when viewed more attentively, actually is great (like Jesus and the virtues he extols). And Christianity serves justice while not obliterating greatness by connecting the greatness of the few to the greatness of many through experiences of limitation and elevation that all human beings do or ought to share in common.

The true Christian teaching is about the equal greatness or personal significance of every particular human being. But even if equal greatness is not quite an oxymoron, it does describe two qualities in tension. Even if Christianity is as egalitarian as a religion that distinguishes between creatures and the Creator can be—as a religion that sees the significance of particular individuals can be—it still is based on an inegalitarian privileging of human beings over the rest of the creation, and it depends on an uncritical suspension of the democrat's habitual doubt about all immaterial privileging as a claim to rule (2, 1, 2). The rule of a personal God over all men, the democrat constantly suspects, is about to morph into the claim to rule by particular men over others on the basis of qualities of soul. A consistent democrat can't help but object to the residual magnanimity or aristocratic premises in the Christian view of greatness.

So the idea of a Creator or just, personal God is endangered by the general trend toward impersonality or the tyranny of no one in particular of democracy. Christianity, the danger is, may well give way to pantheism. Pantheism is the perfectly egalitarian theology; everything and everyone become indistinguishably divine. So the human perception of the contingency of one's particular being turns out to be an illusion. The charm of pantheism, Tocqueville explains, is that it "destroys human individuality," or the experience at the foundation of human greatness. It both "nourishes the haughtiness and flatters the laziness of the democratic mind" (2, 1, 7). That combination of haughtiness and laziness flows from the virtually effortless comprehension of one's own divinity. There is no longer the need to think or do anything great, because everything and everyone is already as great as they could conceivably *be*. The purpose of the pantheistic lullaby is to extinguish the human longings that cause the human individual to resist being incorporated into some whole. The tyranny of the majority or public opinion or impersonal material forces is further generalized into the tyranny of the homogenous divine being.

Tocqueville concludes that "all who remain enamored of the genuine greatness of man should unite and do combat against it" (2, 1, 7). Aristocratic lies encourage greatness; the extremely egalitarian or pantheistic lie aims utterly to negate it. Pantheism, as much or more than materialism, is a denial of the significance of the drama of the particular human life. Insofar as our religion today is moving away from the focus on the personal Creator and his particular creatures, it is no longer a real support for human pride or genuine experiences of magnanimity. According to Chantal Delsol, "I would not hesitate to describe the climate that gives rise to pantheism as a wrong turn in the Enlightenment. . . . Human rights will not guarantee the dignity of each human being unless they are grounded in an understanding that ensures his uniqueness. . . . If . . . one wants and hopes for democracy to be a society of unique persons endowed with free wills and minds, then the more appropriate religious partner would be a monotheism that preaches personal eternity, one in which each irreducible being survives in his irreducibility."[13]

Tocqueville writes of pantheism seducing democratic "minds," but not as successfully orienting the lives of whole human beings in democratic times. The linguistic therapy of an untrue and even ridiculous theology—even one that claims to satisfy the mind's real desire for unity—surely can't overcome in particular human beings the truthful experience of their contingent existence between two abysses. There is, of course, an irreducible human tension between the mind's pure desire to know and the particular being's concern for his or her own fate or significance. Pantheism, it seems, is really a failed form of self-help that can only intensify the reality of democratic disorientation or insane materialistic ardor through its futile denial of what we really experience of our particular souls. Pantheism seems, at first, the perfect antidote to the human fear of *not being*, but only if an individual can swallow the tale that he will continue to *be* after he's dead as part of some tree.

Pantheism is no real solution to the individual's anxious concern about his status or significance in a world where he experiences his contingency so intensely. Not many individuals in America today are losing themselves with any great success in pantheistic or new agey reveries, and people in general continue to be more restless or death-haunted than ever. The mind's love of unity or coherence, our materialistic scientist thinks, seems to be best satisfied through unrealistic denial of what anyone can see about human distinctiveness, but if we were simply minds (or for that matter bodies) we wouldn't truthfully experience our momentary existence. And without such experience—and our ability to love the strange and only partly comprehensible beings who share it, it seems to me we wouldn't be open to the truth about anything at all. The human mind, the magnanimous man rightly asserts with his "manly" view concerning the indispensability of *his* great deeds, isn't really self-sufficient at all.

In the final analysis, magnanimity is a far more realistic characteristic of the being open to the truth about all things—including himself—than either pantheism or materialism are. The Christians are right to inspire skepticism about magnanimity as a quality that makes the few fundamentally more significant than the many; all human beings are equally not God and under God. But the democratic danger is that indiscriminate skepticism about all immaterial or transcendent human qualities will cause us not to be able to appreciate merely but really human greatness for what it is.

NOTES

1. On all the points made in this paragraph, see Harvey C. Mansfield, *Manliness* (Yale University Press, 2006) and Tom Wolfe, *I Am Charlotte Simmons* (Farrar, Straus, and Giroux, 2004). I say more in chapter 7 of my *Homeless and At Home in America* (St. Augustine's Press, 2007).

2. This section is nothing more than a reading of what Aristotle says about the magnanimous man in Book 4 of the *Nicomachean Ethics* in light of what he says in that book as a whole. It is very indebted to secondary sources that go beyond that book to Aristotle's other writings for clarification on this man's character. My debts to these sources are too numerous, subtle, and doubtless unconscious in some ways to

be adequately acknowledged in particular notes. So let me just list them with gratitude: Carson Holloway, "Christianity, Magnanimity and Statesmanship," *Review of
Politics* 61 (Autumn, 1999): 581–604; Larry Arnhart, "Statesmanship as Magnanimity: Classical, Christian and Modern," *Polity* 16 (Winter, 1983): 263–83; Susan D.
Collins, "Moral Virtue and the Limits of Political Community Aristotle's '*Nicomachean Ethics*'," *American Journal of Political Science* 48 (January, 2004): 47–61;
and Jacob Howland, "Aristotle's Great-Souled Man," *Review of Politics* 64 (Winter,
2002): 27–56. My greatest debt turns out to have been to Mary M. Keys, *Aristotle,
Aquinas, and the Promise of the Common Good* (Cambridge University Press, 2006),
chapter 6; it took a good Catholic woman to drive home what should have been the
obvious point that Aristotle's character is just unrealistic, and Thomas employed
Christian psychology to make him more genuinely self-conscious and so more genuinely virtuous. I have agreed and disagreed with all these sources and have employed
them in a selective and probably distorted way to provide a "coherent narrative" that
would be a suitable prelude to Tocqueville.

3. Mansfield, *Manliness*, 221–23.

4. As Keys reminds us; see her *Aristotle, Aquinas, and the Promise of the Common Good*, 156–58.

5. Numbers in parenthesis are page references to Alexis de Tocqueville, *Recollections: The French Revolution of 1848*, ed. J. P. Mayer and A. P. Kerr (Transaction
Books, 1987). For a somewhat different and expanded discussion of the theme of
greatness in these *Recollections* (or *Souvenirs*), see my *The Restless Mind: Alexis de
Tocqueville on the Origin and Perpetuation of Human Liberty* (Rowman and Littlefield, 1993).

6. Three numbers separated by commas in the parenthetical citations refer to volume, part, and chapter of *Democracy in America*. This first reference, for example, is
to volume 2, part 2, chapter 1. I've just about always used the translation of Harvey
C. Mansfield and Delba Winthrop (University of Chicago Press, 2000).

7. On the general context of Tocqueville's thought and its relation to Pascal, see
my *The Restless Mind*.

8. See Keys, *Aristotle, Aquinas, and the Promise of the Common Good*, 197.

9. See Harvey C. Mansfield, Jr., and Delba Winthrop, "Tocqueville's New Politcal
Science," in *The Cambridge Companion to Tocqueville*, ed. Cheryl B. Welch (Cambridge
University Press, 2006), 84.

10. See Mansfield and Winthrop, "Tocqueville's New Political Science," 86.

11. Mansfield, *Manliness*, chapter 4.

12. See Mansfield and Winthrop, "Tocqueville's New Political Science," 86–92.

13. Chantal Delsol, The Unlearned Lessons of the Twentieth Century: An Essay on
Late Modernity, trans. Robin Dick (ISI Books, 2006), 194–95.

7

The Magnanimous Overman: On Nietzsche's Transformation of Aristotle's Greatness of Soul

Jeffrey Church and Catherine H. Zuckert

Many readers of Aristotle and Nietzsche have recognized a striking resemblance between Aristotle's depiction of the magnanimous man and the various incarnations of Nietzsche's higher- or over-men. Like Nietzsche's higher men, Aristotle's magnanimous man maintains a godlike superiority over the many; he is aware of an order of rank among human beings; he benefits many others with noble gifts and deeds, but is contemptuous of their opinion and does not, therefore, seek their gratitude or honor; he tells the truth when appropriate and is ironic when appropriate; he cultivates self-sufficiency yet is always oriented toward others. There are clear parallels between the paragons of virtue in both Aristotle and Nietzsche, but are these similarities superficial, or is there a deeper kinship between the two? And if there is a kinship, how are we to understand Nietzsche's debt to and appropriation of Aristotle's concept of magnanimity?

Some Nietzsche scholars deny that there is a resemblance; others claim that the kinship is illusory; still others argue that the resemblance is real.[1] In this chapter, we defend the third possibility, that Nietzsche's overman is indebted to Aristotle's conception of magnanimity. Indeed, we will argue that Nietzsche thinks that magnanimity is the virtue most needed to counteract the anomie, exhaustion, and pettiness of modern social and political life. However, Nietzsche realizes that he cannot simply return to the ancient virtue and apply it to modern life. The historical changes Christianity and modernity have wrought on human beings make it necessary to transform the virtue to fit his time.

In investigating the relation between Nietzsche's and Aristotle's conceptions of magnanimity, we do not focus on what Nietzsche has to say about Aristotle for two reasons. First, Nietzsche has an ambivalent view of Aristotle. On the one hand, he quietly aligns him with Socrates' false and self-destructive task of seeking knowledge of human existence in order to correct it. Nietzsche's analysis of "the birth of tragedy" can been understood, indeed, to be a response to Aristotle's *Poetics,* although Aristotle and his work are not mentioned in Nietzsche's first book. Nietzsche thinks that Aristotle, like Socrates, mistakenly tried to subordinate human passions to reason.[2] On the other hand, Nietzsche applauds Aristotle for wanting to eliminate pity [*Mitleiden*] from human life, since pity undermines the felt distance (or "pathos of distance") between human beings.[3] Second, Nietzsche does not speak directly about Aristotle's concept of magnanimity.[4]

But what about Nietzsche's statements about Aristotle's ethics in general? Since magnanimity is the crown of the virtues, we may be able to discern Nietzsche's view of Aristotle's magnanimity by examining what Nietzsche has to say about Aristotle's account of the virtues. Bernd Magnus argues that Nietzsche views Aristotle's ethics as slave morality. Since Nietzsche rejects slave morality, Magnus concludes, Nietzsche could not have been influenced by the *Ethics.* However, the issue is more complicated than Magnus suggests, both because Aristotle's *Ethics* does not entirely or even primarily promote slave morality, as the figure of the magnanimous man attests, and because Nietzsche does not wholly condemn slave morality.[5] Slave morality has allowed humans to develop distinctively human traits so that humans are now the "most interesting animal."[6] Moreover, the deepening of the soul effected by Christianity and modernity allows humans to shoot for more distant goals than were possible by more primitive, "noble" men.[7]

The best way to discover what Nietzsche thought about Aristotle's conception of magnanimity is not to take our guidance from what Nietzsche explicitly says about Aristotle, because Nietzsche often refers to Aristotle without naming him, selectively, and in a variety of different contexts. We have to look rather at what Nietzsche does with Aristotle's magnanimous man. Nietzsche often vociferously critiques a philosopher to whom he is indebted in his own positive project—for example, Rousseau, Kant, and Hegel. The same proves to be the case with Aristotle.

Nietzsche does not try simply to uproot and transplant Aristotle's magnanimous man into the nihilism-plagued modern times. On the contrary, Nietzsche argues that concepts must be transformed so as to be relevant for changing contexts.[8] In order to understand Nietzsche's transformation of Aristotle's magnanimous man, it thus becomes necessary to examine Nietzsche's understanding of the modern context and what it requires. Since Nietzsche thinks modernity requires the greatness of the magnanimous man, it then becomes necessary to sketch the characteristics of such a man, according to Aristotle. And to understand Aristotle's conception of magnanimity, we have to take account of two other peaks of human excellence, justice and philosophy. Because Nietzsche thinks that the downfall of Christianity and modernity can be traced to their reinterpretations of justice and philosophy, which reject magnanimity, it becomes necessary, finally, to look at the way in which Nietzsche attempts to supersede the Christian and modern reinterpretations of justice and philosophy by crowning them with a radicalized version of magnanimity.

THE PROBLEM POSED BY THE DECLINE OF MODERN VIRTUE

The philosopher's task, according to Nietzsche, is to unearth the "concept of 'greatness'" [*Begriff 'Grösse'*] or what would exemplify "greatness of soul" [*Grösse der Seele*] for the modern era. Greatness consists in the manifestation of noble and beautiful deeds which reveal what a community's common good is. Greatness makes human community possible by enshrining an understanding of noble and base deeds in the consciousness of the community. A community becomes united and retains its vitality only with such a shared understanding. Virtuous activity on the part of leading citizens, then, becomes necessary not only to found but also to maintain a coherent social and political life.[9]

Without a recurrence of great deeds which refound the community by reaffirming such an understanding—a "table of goods" [*Tafel der Güter*][10]—the community begins to fragment.[11] Without referring to such a shared understanding, individuals not only cease to understand each another; they also fail to understand the import of their own deeds. When there is no longer a shared understanding of the noble and good, people are no longer able to make sense of deeds aimed at the common good.[12] Unable to make sense of their external life, individuals turn inward and attempt simply to satisfy their basic bodily needs.[13] They are no longer motivated by a concept of the good or by a notion of the noble, but simply seek pleasure instead.[14]

In aphorism 212 of *Beyond Good and Evil*, Nietzsche declares that modern virtues are "out of date." Modern understandings of virtue no longer contribute to the common good of modern people. Instead, Nietzsche argues, the fundamental animating characteristics of the modern spirit[15]—egalitarianism, the historical sense, and science unfettered by faith—obstruct the cultivation of superior individuals who perform the noble deeds that give a people its definition. As a result, Nietzsche thinks modern life is becoming ever more nihilistic.

Yet, one of these distinctively modern characteristics makes it possible for Nietzsche not only to locate the source of the modern problem, but also to propose a solution to it. A modern historical sense leads Nietzsche to return to the origins of modernity in order to understand the sources of our nihilism and to retrieve alternative paths immanent within our history which we can follow to alter our nihilistic trajectory. As developed in the works of modern philosophers like Hegel and Marx, the historical sense appears to produce an account of a necessary progress in human events and consciousness. By finding lacunae in the development of concepts, values, and beliefs, Nietzsche shows that the development of the spirit of modernity is not necessarily a rational process culminating in self-knowledge, but merely one contingent path among many other possible ones. Because our current path is only one among many other possibilities, we moderns can retrieve ancient virtues (such as Aristotelian magnanimity) and incorporate them into modern practice. However, the retrieval of these virtues is difficult because they are bound up with a system of cultural institutions and meanings that is foreign to us. Any revival involves a translation, which is to say, a transformation, of the original concepts and practices to make them relevant to modernity.

A revival of the Aristotelian virtue of magnanimity would require modern peoples to organize their lives according to the principles of modernity while at the same time vivifying their culture with a nobility of a bygone era. In the next section we thus turn to Aristotle's presentation of the magnanimous man and examine how this concept might help overcome the obstacles to genuine community that modernity has placed in its own path.

THE ARISTOTELIAN VIRTUE OF MAGNANIMITY

Nietzsche was particularly interested in unearthing Aristotle's concept of magnanimity, because he saw its potential power to counteract the peculiar problems of modern existence. When we turn to Aristotle, however, we see that magnanimity has to be understood in relation to all the other kinds or parts of human virtue, especially justice and philosophy. Not merely does a comparison of magnanimity with these virtues help bring the former into sharper relief; it also prepares us to see the way in which Aristotle's ethics were reinterpreted later in light of Christian beliefs and modern philosophy. That reinterpretation sets the context for Nietzsche's own reappropriation and reinterpretation of Aristotle's virtue magnanimity.

The first peak of human excellence Aristotle describes in his *Nicomachean Ethics* is magnanimity. According to Aristotle, a magnanimous man has three main characteristics. First, this man has a natural and cultivated superiority to other men, because he possesses all the virtues. Second, this man not only is superior; he also knows that he is superior. That is to say, he has self-knowledge. Third, a magnanimous man does not merely possess all the virtues in himself and know that he does; he performs beautiful or noble [*kalos*] public acts.

Like the other virtues, Aristotle shows that the virtue of magnanimity is concerned with an object of desire or aversion (e.g., fear in the case of courage, pleasure for moderation). And he assumes "without argument" that this virtue is concerned with "honor" [*time*], because honor is the highest external good that we have, since we give honor to the gods.[16] What makes this virtue problematic is that the mean that is supposed to define this like all the other virtues cannot be attained, because the object of concern cannot be attained. Honor is an external good and thus a good relative to the person who is honoring. Since the magnanimous man outpaces all other men in excellence, no human honor is satisfying to him.[17] Although the magnanimous man is treated like a god, he is nonetheless a man, so he must always measure himself against men.[18] Treated like a god, he strives to be like a god in his search for self-sufficiency; because he is a man, he cannot achieve such self-sufficiency. He remains dependent on other men to sate his desire for honor, but he does not respect other lesser human beings enough to be satisfied with the honors they bestow.[19] In this way, the magnanimous man resembles Nietzsche's Zarathustra, who has two souls, one which seeks godlike self-sufficiency, and the other which seeks to be among men.[20]

The magnanimous man mediates his two desires, the desire to be a god and the desire for human regard, by performing beautiful and noble actions that often involve risking his life. In performing these deeds, he maintains his intermediary position between god and mere man. As Larry Arnhart and Carson Holloway argue, the magnanimous man seeks immortality.[21] He emulates the gods by striving for self-sufficiency and performing beautiful, beneficent actions. But, as Hanley points out, the magnanimous man perfects his humanity by engaging in noble, civic deeds.[22] The magnanimous man engages in noble or beautiful activities both to be more than human and to be the best kind of human. Although the internal motivation and satisfaction of this man is tension-ridden, the external manifestation of the virtue remains the same: civic beneficence.[23]

Justice is closest to magnanimity in being "the practice of perfect virtue" (*NE* 5.1.15, 1129b15–20). Both virtues benefit others; both contain all the virtues and have as their sphere of activity a political community. The ends of these two virtues are different; however; magnanimity aims at self-perfection whereas justice seeks right action for its own sake (or for the sake of upholding the law).[24] By speaking not of the "just man" but only of "justice" and just actions, Aristotle seems to express some doubt about whether human beings are ever completely concerned about doing what is right for others, without regard for themselves. Precisely for that reason, Aristotle shows that habituation to justice is necessary for the maintenance of a stable community. The emergence of a magnanimous man as leader would not be sufficient to hold the community together.

The theoretical man does not concern himself with political and practical activity. His sphere is not that of the changing human community. But, Aristotle states (*NE* 10.7.1, 1177a11–18), the theoretical man performs his activity "in accordance with the highest virtue," the virtue "of the best part of us," intellect [*nous*]. Our intellect is the "highest thing in us" because it resembles and gives us access to the "highest things that can be known," the eternal things of nature.[25] In his contemplation of eternal nature the theoretical man is godlike, moreover, in a way the magnanimous man is not: he is self-sufficient.[26] Aristotle raises doubts, however, about whether human beings can ever be simply or entirely theoretical, because of their natural, bodily needs.[27]

Aristotle suggests that it is difficult if not impossible for all three of these virtues to be combined in one individual human being or exist simultaneously in a single community. At the conclusion of Book 3 of the *Politics* (1288a) he argues that if a supremely virtuous individual were to arise in a city, it would be not be just to subject that person to the rule of any other. But, Aristotle also observes, the rule of one supremely virtuous individual would deprive all other members of the polity of the opportunity to develop their own potential for deliberation and self-rule. The recognition due the supreme virtue of the individual in this case would not unambiguously result in the common good, although the rule of the wise would nevertheless appear to be good for everyone involved. In this case, Aristotle points to a combination of magnanimity and justice when he suggests that the best possible outcome, in these admittedly rare circumstances, would be for the outstanding individual to lay down laws for his fellow citizens to use after his death. In his *Nicomachean Ethics* (5.10.1, 1137a32–35) Aristotle indicates that the just distribution of honors and goods itself has limits, by observing the need for "equity" as well. At the end of the *Politics* (1323a24–1325b32) Aristotle explicitly addresses the question of whether the life of theory or the life of practice is better, and concludes that the life of theory is. The question arises, because human beings can never devote themselves entirely to theory. As mortals, we have recurring bodily needs. Our lives as individuals are also subject to chance events. Although justice can be described as a proportional geometric relation in which equal people receive equal benefits, whereas unequal individuals should be given unequal rewards, human social and political life cannot be accurately ordered or understood in purely mathematical terms. Because human beings have irreducibly different kinds of needs, bodily, emotional, and intellectual, the goods of human life—including preeminently the virtues—are incommensurable. We need some of all the various kinds.

THE TRANSFORMATION OF THE
OLD CONCEPTION OF HUMAN VIRTUE

At first glance, Aristotle's concept of magnanimity seems to fit well into Nietzsche's program. Nietzsche's overman is concerned both about achieving immortality or godlike status and about contributing to a sound, healthy political order. The overman is the kind of character who would strive to be great, to know that he is great, and to do great actions. He would combat the egalitarianism fostered by modern politics and economics by reintroducing natural or cultivated difference among human beings, and by honoring the differing degrees of human excellence attained. However, the magnanimous man fails to respond to the two other obstacles to greatness immanent in modern spirit: the historical sense and the scientific reduction of human beings to material beings.

As a model of excellence, the magnanimous man must be radicalized in order to overcome these obstacles. He has to become the crown of an enlarged set of virtues, including justice and philosophy, as reinterpreted by Christianity and modernity. So understood, the magnanimous man can no longer be solely concerned with his own perfection, but must be motivated by a love for humankind. Out of that love, the Nietzschean magnanimous man seeks to effect an eschatological and ontological transformation of humankind.[28] His justice leads the great man to provide an eschatology or secular theodicy in order to avoid the enervating effects of the historical sense. His philosophy provides a new ontology, which makes possible the creation of a new "world" in which human beings can lead better lives.

Nietzsche's magnanimous man thus brings together the three peaks of virtue Aristotle found so difficult to combine in a single individual or community in order to confront the problems of modernity. Christianity and modernity had prepared the way for Nietzsche by redefining and then combining justice (as redemption) and philosophy (as world-creating). Nietzsche cannot jettison this deeply entrenched reinterpretation. He tries, therefore, to carry the modern reinterpretation of ancient virtue even further by synthesizing the new interpretations of justice and philosophy with an expanded notion of magnanimity.

To understand Nietzsche's attempted synthesis, it is necessary, first, to detail how and why Nietzsche thinks that Christianity and modernity adapted two of Aristotle's peaks of virtue, justice and philosophy, but rejected the third, magnanimity. Second, we will examine Nietzsche's retrieval and translation of the third peak of Aristotle's virtue ethics, magnanimity. Nietzsche's use of Aristotle's magnanimous man shows that he imagined magnanimity as once again the crown of the virtues and an eminently political virtue. Nietzsche's historical and political project becomes most apparent in his *Thus Spoke Zarathustra*, because Zarathustra aims to retrieve and embody magnanimity within a Christianized and modernized worldview.[29]

CHRISTIANITY AND MODERNITY, JUSTICE AND PHILOSOPHY

According to Aristotle, justice requires the distribution of goods and honors on the basis of desert. But the principle of desert varies according to the constitution of the regime, whether it is aristocratic (desert by virtue), democratic (citizenship awarded to all the free born), or oligarchic (offices awarded on the basis of wealth).[30] According to Nietzsche, Christianity delves beneath such conventional, legal notions of justice, because these conceptions of justice support political orders which oppress Christians. But these political orders provide the conditions for the flourishing of noble, serious [*spoudaios*], or magnanimous men. Christianity embraces what Aristotle himself called "natural justice" [*phusikon dikaiou*] by outlining rules of behavior which are immutable and ought to be everywhere valid. Aristotle admits that there is "such a thing as natural justice," but he argues that even this natural justice is "variable."[31] The early Christians (especially Paul) sought to deploy this concept of immutable justice against the regnant order. In order for this strategy to work, the Christians had to incorporate in their view of natural justice an eschatology, which assured potential Christians that even if they did not defeat the reigning order now, they would in the end of history, when Christ returns to reward the virtuous and punish the powerful.[32]

This eschatological view of justice and history required an ontology to support it. There have to be immortal souls which persist until the end of time;[33] there must be a just God who metes out reward and punishments appropriately. This God has to have power over nature, because he must have power over the nobles who had oppressed Christians. The concept of the Christian God thus transforms the concept of ancient *physis,* by submitting nature to God's control, and by making all human beings naturally equal "in the eyes of God," because all human beings are equally creatures of God. The differences among human beings reflect the degree to which human beings obey their creator. The great, magnanimous men of old are stripped of their three main qualities: natural or cultivated greatness, self-knowledge (because they erroneously think they are better than others), and great deeds (because civic deeds are devalued, whereas "spiritual" deeds are elevated).[34]

As a result of the Christian transformation of justice, the magnanimous man had to be rejected as an ideal. The just man replaced the magnanimous man as the example par excellence of human virtue.[35] However, Nietzsche claims that this Christian justice, which displaced the ancient, Aristotelian view of justice, was not intended to ensure the right because it is right. This Christian justice was, instead, fundamentally a smokescreen for the vengeance the inferior wanted to wreak on the naturally great. Justice no longer concerned the harmony of the human order with nature, but rather the retribution the meek wish to inflict on the proud. As a result of this Christian "transvaluation of values" the order of right, ironically, became might makes right, when the "meek" Christians ruled.

Further, as a result of the Christian transformation of justice, the concept of nature was transformed as well. And this transformation had implications for the philosophical life. The creative will of the Christian God replaced the ancient concept of an immutable natural order, which formed the basis of theoretical or contemplative philosophy. The Christian understanding gave rise to an antagonism, rather than an attempted harmonization, between the human mind and nature.[36] The gap between divine will and human reason was reflected, Nietzsche argues, in the oppositions subsequently drawn between reason and the instincts, intellect and the senses, duty and desire.

These Christian transformations of human understandings of justice and nature sowed the seeds of their own dialectical undermining. According to Nietzsche, modern philosophy carried out this dialectical undermining, when modern philosophers took up the challenge of putting together the pieces of the Christian worldview, the eschatology demanded by justice and the ontology of a contingent universe, while faith in God crumbled. Leibniz and others offered a "theodicy" to account for the seeming imperfections of the world. In the "Copernican Revolution," with which he began his project of formal idealism, Kant claimed that human beings are the spontaneous creators of natural kinds and concepts. We construct what is intelligible to us. Hegel radicalized Kant's project by historicizing it. He showed that human beings are the creators of their own worlds, and that the rationality that guides the creative process leads necessarily to a just end. In Hegel, modern philosophy attempted to complete the Christian project of combining eschatology and contingent ontology, while jettisoning the idea of God and replacing God with rational human creation.[37] In order to make sense of an unintelligible manifold, modern philosophy effected a change in the concept of philosophy from the task of the contemplation of an eternal nature to the spontaneous legislation of conceptual norms.

Modern human and natural sciences did not develop, however, simply in reaction to Christian reinterpretations of justice and creation. Like Socrates and other ancient philosophers, modern scientists sought to discover a rational and just ordering of the world. Like Christian eschatology and ontology, the origins of modern philosophy could thus be traced back to Socrates and the political concerns associated with the apparent injustice and oppression of the lower classes.[38] These modern sciences claimed to have discovered that the origins of human life were natural, but unjust, rather than divine and just. As a result, the development of modern science undermined the eschatological and ontological demands posed by the Christian heritage.

We are now in a position to see why Nietzsche thought the "rationalization" of Christian eschatology and ontology in modern philosophy resulted in nihilism. The reinterpretation of Aristotelian justice and philosophy, first, into a Christian eschatology and, then, into modern idealist philosophy produced the three distinctive characteristics of the modern spirit that made a stable political community impossible. First, the Christian notion of the "equality of all human beings before God" became secularized and spread as a doctrine asserting the "natural equality" of all human beings. And the assertion of the natural equality of all human beings (egalitarianism) made modern men skeptical of any claims of natural or cultivated greatness. They became inclined instead to treat all human beings—no matter how gifted—equally. The doctrine concerning the equality of all human beings thus led modern people to lose sight of what they needed the most, the cultivation of inequality, of great individuals, to maintain their communities and hence the equality of all the people in them.[39]

Second, the Christian story of the birth and death of the Savior in time led its adherents to develop a reflexive account of the rational and just direction of history. And their belief in the just order and direction of history led them to inquire into the origins of justice as well as the development of different peoples' understandings or "tables" of goods. However, the incremental development of historical knowledge gradually made it difficult to maintain a Christian theodicy, in which apparently irrational, if not evil events were explained as results of the humanly incomprehensible, but ultimately beneficent will of God. Historical studies revealed the ignoble origins of human communities, and knowledge of those base origins made it difficult for communities to perpetuate themselves by means of noble deeds.[40] At the same time it became difficult to believe in the sanctity of the origins or the possibility of salvation by means of a return to the foundations of the community, increased historical knowledge led to the importation of foreign values, beliefs, and habits from a multitude of sources into the present. As a result, the "table of goods" and the eschatology which had unified communities in Europe was dissolved.[41] No noble deeds or sacrifices could unify such fragmented communities; the concept of nobility no longer had any meaning for the people. As all sense of community dissolved, individuals increasingly engaged in nothing but egoistic behavior.[42]

Modern philosophy had shown human beings that they impose the universals, concepts, or kinds on the manifold of sensation they experience in order to make sense of the world. Much of modern philosophy bows to the constructions of the world by modern natural science, which finds the source of distinctively human things—namely, justice, the good, and history—in nonhuman nature. From modern science human beings learn that they are not qualitatively but only quantitatively different from other animals; the only difference is in the degree of complexity of their organization. The reduction of nature by science to matter-in-motion makes all stable concepts, including the concepts of justice and of the good, historically contingent and actually false, since these concepts attempt to find stability and unity where there is only flux and disharmony.[43] This reduction thus dooms any attempt to legislate a table of goods, because such a deed attempts the impossible, to arrest ceaseless motion.

NIETZSCHE'S TRANSFORMATION OF MAGNANIMITY

We can now appreciate how and why Nietzsche retrieves and deploys Aristotelian magnanimity in order to extricate modern social and political life from the debilitating effects of egalitarianism, historicism, and science. Modern tendencies toward baseness, egoism, and nihilism disgust Nietzsche, yet he sees tremendous possibilities in modernity for a healthy communal future. He thinks both Christian eschatology and modern ontology can and should be used to achieve a better state for human beings in the future for three reasons. First, only an individual savior or redeemer of the kind in which Europeans used to believe will represent a promise modern people will be able to accept as a real and desirable improvement on the present. Second, Nietzsche believes that it is possible for such a savior to arise and not prove to be a mere illusion, because Kant had shown that human beings can create and impose their own meaning on the world.[44] Third, Christianity and modernity have thoroughly deepened the soul, so that great individual activity is once again possible.[45] The Christian subterranean political machinations of gaining power through the promise of salvation, Christian and modern reflections on the soul and the self, the modern philosophy of subjectively created "worlds," and the modern accumulation of tremendously diverse historical and cultural knowledge, have all contributed to deepening and expanding the powers and scope of the individual. An individual no longer needs to engage in physical or even political activity in order to gain power. As the spread of the Christian gospel showed, private individuals can create new worlds by "legislating" new concepts and tables of goods.[46] The individual's power and influence has become greater, because it has become more "spiritual" (philosophical).[47]

For Nietzsche the Christian moral world is ultimately not a burden, but a tremendous opportunity. He seeks to bring together the potent strands of the Christian modern spirit—the moral component of Christian eschatology, the ontological component of modern idealism, and superior knowledge of the self—by combining Aristotle's magnanimous man with a deepened soul. This new radicalized magnanimous man will be able to synthesize the other strands of the Christian moral spirit and thus provide a foundation for a more potent, unified social and political order.

No divine or world-historical progress occurring despite or over and above the intentional deeds of individual actors can provide the needed redemptive justification for human life. Rather, individuals, armed with historical sense and the greatness of soul to move the culture in its necessary direction, provide both the justice (the final justification) and the philosophy (the ontology) necessary to ground a new community.[48] Aristotle's magnanimous man, a great man within a city, becomes in Nietzsche's hand a titanic man concerned with the fate of the earth and the redeeming all of humankind.[49] The Nietzschean magnanimous man is the grand synthesis of a Caesar, a Christ, and a Socrates, the three peaks of magnanimity, justice, and philosophy as translated into modern life.[50]

These, then, are the broad outlines of the goals of the new magnanimous man. But what about the character of this new magnanimous man himself? Can we call this radicalized concept Aristotelian at all, or is the overman a pure Nietzschean creation? There are similarities, but there are also differences between Aristotle's magnanimous man and Nietzsche's overman. The differences result from Nietzsche's need to transform the concept to suit a new historical setting and Nietzsche's attempt to reconcile the inherent tension within Aristotle's concept of the magnanimous man.

Nietzsche's overman has the three main characteristics of Aristotle's magnanimous man: natural or cultivated greatness, self-knowledge, and great deeds. That Nietzsche's overman surely possesses greatness is shown by Nietzsche's repeated insistence on achieving an order of rank among human beings and a "pathos of distance" between different ranks. Like Aristotle's magnanimous man, Nietzsche's overman maintains his superiority and the "pathos of distance." In doing so he appears "haughty" to his egalitarian contemporaries.[51] The overman's insistence on an order of rank is necessary, according to Nietzsche, to counteract the overwhelming egalitarianism that has been leveling human aspiration and engendering envy toward any rare great specimen.[52]

Like Aristotle's magnanimous man, Nietzsche's overman or higher man also knows that he is great. As Laurence Lampert points out, *Thus Spoke Zarathustra* is a kind of *bildungsroman* of a philosopher. Zarathustra's *bil-*

dung has two parts or stages. The first consists in the acquisition of self-knowledge. As Lampert argues, Zarathustra has to learn that he himself is the overman for which he has been longing. Second, in line with the traditional ambiguity of the German term *bildung,* Nietzsche shows that Zarathustra not only has to gain self-knowledge, but that he also has to construct his own self. This process of self-construction is particularly important and particularly problematic, because the magnanimous man is supposed to possess all the virtues. For Nietzsche, the virtues are not transhistorically given, but represent the fulfillment of the concept "human," which varies in history from time to time and place to place. Insofar as virtue consists in knowledge, one has to know what virtue is. But, according to Nietzsche, what virtue is depends on the requirements of the time.[53] Modern life requires greatness, an order of rank, and a pathos of distance, if human beings are not to degenerate into "last men" who know no goal but a painless death.[54] Only a modern man can save his contemporaries from the results of modern egalitarianism, historicism, and natural science by showing them how intellectual discipline and knowledge can be combined with ancient political and personal virtues to create a new, distinctively modern form of human greatness.

Only a man able to combine the apparently contradictory threads of the genealogy of morals in Europe—the master morality of the ancient Greeks with the slave morality of Scripture—will be able to impose order on the sprawling multiplicity of values and beliefs characteristic of a pluralistic modern age. Not merely will he have the strength of intellect and breadth of soul to unify such a multiplicity of principles and outlooks; he will also be able to apprehend what kind of unity is possible and appropriate for this age. The self-knowledge of Nietzsche's overman is not only deeper and more comprehensive, but also more constructive than Aristotle's magnanimous man's recognition of his own greatness.[55] The magnanimous man represented a distillation of the goals of ancient Greek culture; he did not have to invent an entirely new conception of human excellence.

Finally, like the magnanimous man, Nietzsche's overman performs great deeds. The main kind of deed Nietzsche describes in his *Zarathustra* is gift-giving; and in the section on "The Gift-Giving Virtue," in which Zarathustra counsels his students to give out of superabundance, Nietzsche points back to Aristotle. For Nietzsche, as for Aristotle, gift-giving reveals one's superiority. One does not merely have everything one needs. One is not merely self-sufficient. One has more than one needs and can, therefore, give to others. Likewise, receiving gifts betrays one's inferiority, lack of virtue, and dependency.

The gifts Zarathustra offers, however, are not public, civil gifts, but rather philosophical gifts. Philosophical gifts are nevertheless gifts of infinite value, according to Aristotle, because these gifts show people how best to live. According to Zarathustra, the best life consists in preparing for the overman. According to Zarathustra the gift of wisdom also serves as the founding legislation for the just order, which is organized to prepare for the coming of the overman.[56] The founding moment of the new order does not involve violence or open revolution; but it does require the founder, Zarathustra, to share his wisdom with students. They will become the political agents who will bring Zarathustra's cause to fruition.[57]

At the same time, Zarathustra has to restrain his gift-giving by not telling the whole truth about the overman.[58] Zarathustra learns quickly enough what Aristotle's magnanimous man knows: he will "care more for the truth than for what people will think." He will speak and act openly. Because he despises other men, he is outspoken and frank, except when he speaks with "ironical self-depreciation, as he does to common people."[59] Like Nietzsche, Zarathustra cares for the truth, but he knows that the truths and consequences of modern science are terrible for most people.[60] Because these "deadly truths"—the lack of any categorical difference between man and animal and fluidity of all concepts and goods, hence the nonexistence of any gods or divine sources of justice—are so debilitating for most people, Nietzsche's overman has to exercise a greater degree of irony than Aristotle's magnanimous man would ever employ.

What accounts for this difference between the public, civic deeds of the magnanimous man and the private, philosophical deeds of Zarathustra? Nietzsche's great man does not perform great deeds for the city, because he would be thought haughty by the citizens of modern egalitarian regimes. The spread of egalitarian ideas has thus made political activity by great individuals increasingly difficult in the modern age. Zarathustra realizes that Christian assumptions about the equality of all human beings have so penetrated modern political (I.11), economic (I.12), and social (I.13) institutions that a simple transplantation of the magnanimous man into modern life will have as little effect as Zarathustra himself had in the prologue.

Like Zarathustra, Nietzsche's magnanimous man has to cultivate disciples who can direct the community in ways he cannot. He accomplishes this task by means of private, philosophical activity, rather than by means of public speeches and deeds.[61] Although the lack of public deeds may run counter to Aristotle's conception of magnanimity, Nietzsche's Zarathustra is like Socrates in engaging in private dialectical conversations. And Socrates is an example of the magnanimous man given by Aristotle.[62]

In sum, Nietzsche's overman possesses all three characteristics of Aristotle's magnanimous man. Nietzsche's magnanimous man differs from Aristotle's only in his primary mode of activity, which is philosophical more than political. The deepening of the soul and the sublimation of the violent affects by Christianity and modernity has made it necessary to counteract the negative effects of these developments by means of similar tactics. Nietzsche thus proposes an eschatology based on the promise of the coming of the overman coupled with a philosophy that allows for the construction of a new kind of virtue, a distinctively human "gift-giving" virtue, to combat the problematic results of the historical sense and modern science. Although the sources of this eschatology and ontology are Christian and modern, they take their ultimate bearing from the greatness of the individual, first recognized in the Aristotelian conception of the magnanimous man. This new crowning figure is intended to combat and finally to overcome modern egalitarianism.

There are similarities and differences between the two forms of magnanimity in motivation as well as in character. There is an internal tension in Aristotle's magnanimous man insofar as he wishes to be a god, on the one hand, and yet to be the most excellent specimen of man, on the other. This dual motivation makes a magnanimous man long to be self-sufficient and yet expect recognition from others. The same bifurcation exists for Zarathustra, as he attests in his words and deeds. In deed, Zarathustra oscillates between solitude and human company, unable to be content in either condition for very long. In his speech "On Human Prudence," Zarathustra claims that his glance is bound to the overman, bound to becoming a god. But his hand reaches out to man (as God does to Adam in Michaelangelo's famous painting on the ceiling of the Sistine Chapel), to help man help himself, by providing a model of excellence. Like Aristotle's magnanimous man, Zarathustra sees self-overcoming as a noble deed that benefits the public by example.

Unlike Aristotle's magnanimous man, however, Zarathustra's self-overcoming occurs at an abstract, philosophical level. And it is at this abstract level that Zarathustra overcomes the tension inherent in the two conflicting desires of the magnanimous man. The striving to be godlike and to be the best possible man are identical from the standpoint of modern philosophy with its revelation of human beings as creators of their own worlds. According to Zarathustra, the gift-giving virtue is thus "useless." One simply gives oneself, the pattern of one's ego, to become the pattern of the world around one. The founder's soul becomes the soul of the city. As the source of all order and meaning, the new radicalized magnanimous man cannot receive honors in return for his service, because there is nothing outside of himself to bestow such honors. Any honor that he receives would come, ultimately, from himself. In becoming the creator and sustainer of the self-understanding of a community, Nietzsche's magnanimous man cannot expect honor or recognition, because there are no independent egos to recognize him.

CONCLUSION

Nietzsche's new magnanimous man replaces Hegel's *Geist* as the reconciliatory vehicle of Western thought. But unlike Hegel's cumulative philosophy of history, Nietzsche's higher man has to go back and retrieve a long-lost virtue, which had not previously been incorporated in the developing Western spirit. Facing social, political, and philosophical obstacles, this new magnanimous man must combat these forces at a sufficiently fundamental level so as not to be co-opted by them. Nietzsche's unprecedented synthesis incorporates the justice of Christ, the philosophy of Socrates, and the greatness of Caesar.

A good Aristotelian would respond to Nietzsche's world-historical project by inquiring whether it is necessary or even desirable. Like Leo Strauss,[63] a good Aristotelian might ask about the necessity or even possibility of retaining a Christian-inspired theodicy of human life without belief in the Christian God. On the basis of the more modest ethics of the twentieth century, characterized by pragmatism or a turn to the "life-world" of everyday ethical experience, contemporary political moderates might also raise questions about the need for such a redemptive justification for historical human suffering. They would observe that liberal democratic theorists such as John Rawls and Jürgen Habermas have attempted to ground community on an appeal to justice, separate from philosophical and religious concerns. A contemporary "liberal Aristotelian" political theorist, William Galston, has tried to redefine "liberal virtues" within a more narrowly political framework. Along with Robert Pippin, contemporary students of German idealist philosophy would question the validity of Nietzsche's philosophy of history and his adaptation of Kant and Hegel.[64] Students of deliberative democracy like Mark Warren would also ask whether the modern democratic social and political order is as bad as Nietzsche thinks it is.[65]

Aside from questions about the truth of the foundations and the necessity of Nietzsche's project, there is also a question about its desirability. Liberal democrats may be inclined to accept and incorporate magnanimous men like Abraham Lincoln or Winston Churchill in the political sphere, especially in times of crisis. But liberals are apt to reject the desirability of a thinker, much less of a leader, who would break through any legal boundaries established by a liberal order. Taken at its sublimated, philosophical level, Nietzsche's magnanimous man might be acceptable to liberals in the form of Richard Rorty's private irony or as a strong interlocutor in a Millian dialogue with liberalism, as Ruth Abbey and Frederick Appel suggest (although it is difficult to imagine Nietzsche agreeing to the value of a "Millian" dialogue).[66] Yet his magnanimous man is supposed to legislate values. In *Zarathustra* Nietzsche observes that the greatest events occur in the quietest corners of the world, where the thinkers sit, but Nietzsche does not believe that it is possible for someone to have great new ideas and for those ideas not to have an effect, not merely on the life of the thinker, but on the lives of those who come after him.

The alternative Nietzsche poses of overman or last man might not be a necessary one, nor the overman a desirable goal. A good Aristotelian would question the desirability of superseding the old virtue with Nietzsche's more radical notions of redemptive justice and the human "creation" of new worlds. For Nietzsche there are not and should not be any limitations put on human ambition. He does not recognize the Aristotelian virtue of moderation. The limitless scope and ambition of Nietzsche's overman has a Christian origin in the historicization of human beings and the concomitant destruction of nature as a standard for human life. This problem with Nietzsche's ideal shows us that we need to reconsider Aristotle's notion of nature as circumscribing human beings'—not just the magnanimous man's—desire for honor and godlike self-sufficiency.

NOTES

1. Defending the first possibility, Clancy Martin, "Nietzsche's Homeric Lies," *Journal of Nietzsche Studies* 31(2006): 1–9, argues that Nietzsche's higher man is indebted to the Homeric, not Aristotelian hero. Bernd Magnus, "Aristotle and Nietzsche: *Megalopsychia* and *Uebermensch*," in *The Greeks and the Good Life*, ed. David J. Depew (Fullerton: California State University, 1980), 260–295, stakes out the second possibility. He claims that there is a "family resemblance" between Aristotle's magnanimous man and Nietzsche's overman, but that Aristotle did not actually influence Nietzsche's thinking. On the contrary, Nietzsche considered Aristotle's *Ethics* to be an instance of slave morality. Laurence Lampert, *Nietzsche's Teaching: An Interpretation of* Thus Spoke Zarathustra (New Haven: Yale University Press, 1986), 78, also argues for the second position. In the section "On the Gift-Giving Virtue" in *Zarathustra* Lampert argues that this virtue has its origin in Christian charity, not in Aristotelian magnanimity. We agree with Lampert that Christian love plays a large role in Nietzsche's understanding of the overman, but we argue that Nietzsche's reinterpretation of Christian charity is shaped by Aristotelian concerns about magnanimity. Walter Kaufmann, *Nietzsche: Philosopher, Psychologist, Antichrist* (Princeton: Princeton University Press, 1974), 382–384, and Robert C. Solomon, *Living with Nietzsche: What the Great 'Immoralist' Has to Teach Us* (Oxford: Oxford University Press, 2003), chapter 6, argue that Nietzsche's view of the higher man is indebted to Aristotle. Kaufmann connects Nietzsche's use of the concept to his critique of Christianity and morality, but does not show how Nietzsche translates and deploys the concept in a modern setting. We disagree with Solomon's reduction of magnanimity to "pride" (156). Such a reductive reading fails to capture the inherent greatness of the magnanimous man or to take account for Nietzsche's distinguishing of pride [*Stolz*] from magnanimity [*Grossmüt*].

2. BT 7, 12, 14, 22; see BGE 198 on the purgation of the affects. All citations from Nietzsche are from aphorism or section number and all citations from Aristotle are from the standard numbering. In the notes we make use of the following abbreviations of the titles of Nietzsche's works: AC: *The Antichrist*, AOM: *Assorted Opinions and Maxims*, BGE: *Beyond Good and Evil*, BT: *The Birth of Tragedy*, GM: *On the Genealogy of Morality*, GS: *The Gay Science*, NE: *Nicomachean Ethics*, TI: *Twilight of the Idols*, UM: *Untimely Meditations*, WP: *The Will to Power*, Z: *Thus Spoke Zarathustra*.

3. AC 7.

4. Nietzsche does, however, speak of magnanimity [*Grossmüt* or *Grösse der Seele*] at UM 2.6, BGE 212, AC 50, GS 1.3, GS 1.49, GS 4.283, GS 4.340, WP 808, 981, 984; esp. WP 935, in which Nietzsche seems to refer to an Aristotelian kind of magnanimity, one that "proceed[s] from abundance" and does "not give in order to receive," one whose possessors do not "try to exalt themselves by being gracious;" TI 9.46, in which Nietzsche aligns greatness of soul with worthiness and unworthiness, as Aristotle does.

5. Slave morality is sickness, but like "pregnancy" (GM.2.19). On this point see Catherine Zuckert, "Nietzsche on the Origin and Development of the Distinctively Human," *Polity* 16, no. 1 (Fall 1983): 48–71.

6. GM 1.6.

7. AC 14; BGE Preface.

8. See Nietzsche's discussion of the changing concept of punishment in GM 2.12–15.

9. AC 16.

10. Z 1. "On the Thousand and One Goals."

11. Cf. Niccolo Machiavelli, *Discourses on the History of Titus Livy* 3.1. Nietzsche greatly admired Machiavelli (cf. BGE 28). Nietzsche seems, indeed, to have taken over Machiavelli's understanding of the need for periodic re-foundings of regimes by means of the extraordinary acts of individuals, often involving self-sacrifice. In WP 304, Nietzsche comments; "No philosopher will be in any doubt as to the type of perfection in politics; that is Machiavellianism. But Machiavellianism *pur, sans mélange, cru, vert, dans toute sa force, dans toute son aprete,* is superhuman, divine, transcendental, it will never be achieved by man, at most approximated. . . . One discovers, if one has eyes for hidden things, traces in even the most unprejudiced and conscious moralists (and that is indeed the name for such politicians of morality, for every kind of founder of new moral forces)."

12. UM 2.4.

13. UM 2.5, 9: on egoism.

14. Z 1. Preface 5 on the last man.

15. We use "spirit" in this paper in the Hegelian sense which Nietzsche sometimes employs, that is, an historically evolving self-consciousness shared by and constitutive of a community.

16. NE IV.iii.9–11.

17. After mentioning honor, Aristotle does not state that the magnanimous man "claims" honor, implying that no honor is worthy of being claimed. Furthermore, he states explicitly that honor is not worth very much: "he does not care much even about

honor" (4.3.18, 1124a15–18). Cf. Ryan Patrick Hanley, "Aristotle on the Greatness of Greatness of Soul," *History of Political Thought* 23, no.1 (Spring 2002): 5–7; and Jacob Howland, "Aristotle's Great-Souled Man," *The Review of Politics* 64, no. 1 (Winter 2002): 41–43.

18. We thus disagree with Hanley, "Greatness of Greatness," 7, who claims that the "great-souled man is indifferent to the possession or claiming of honor." On the contrary, the great-souled man is very concerned with honor, but cannot find an adequate source of satisfaction—he does not care about the honor that he actually receives.

19. Cf. Aristotle's discussion of the concept of magnanimity in *Posterior Analytics,* 97b.15–25, in which he proceeds by example. Aristotle brings out two kinds of magnanimity, characterized by not brooking dishonor on the one hand and by being indifferent to fortune on the honor. This concern with honor and with self-sufficiency captures the inherent tension within the concept of magnanimity—Aristotle, moreover, seems to be aware of this tension in that he does not reconcile the two kinds in this discussion. We disagree with René A. Gauthier, *Magnanimité: l'idéal de la grandeur dans la philosophie paienne et dans la théologie chrétienne* (Paris: Vrin, 1951) and Larry Arnhart, "Statesmanship as Magnanimity: Classical, Christian, and Modern," *Polity* 16, no. 2 (Winter 1983): 263–283, who argue that these two kinds point toward the difference between political and philosophical magnanimity and concur in the criticisms of this reading by Hanley, "Greatness of Greatness," 3–4 and Howland, "Great-Souled Man," 20, 44–49.

20. Z 2. "On Human Prudence."

21. Arnhart "Statesmanship," 267; Carson Holloway, "Christianity, Magnanimity, and Statesmanship," *Review of Politics* 61 (1999): 593–4.

22. Hanley, "Greatness," 9.

23. See Carson Holloway, "Shakespeare's *Coriolanus* and Aristotle's Great-Souled Man," *Review of Politics* 69, no. 3 (Summer 2007), 365, who attempts to reconcile the two poles of this virtue on the ground of the magnanimous man's "fundamental earnestness about the good."

24. Cf. Strauss's (Leo Strauss, *Natural Right and History* [Chicago: University of Chicago Press, 1950], 140) similar observation that Aristotle's ethics moves between the two poles of magnanimity and justice.

25. NE 10.7.2, 1177a13–15.

26. NE 10.7.4, 1177a25–1178a5.

27. NE 10.7.8, 1177b25–1178a15.

28. It is not possible to discuss Nietzsche's reinterpretation of Christian love in a brief article, devoted to another topic. Nietzsche's construction of the community around the redeeming figure of the overman obviously reflects something of the earlier Christian conception of the savior. Christian love is not sufficient to account for Nietzsche's view of the overman, however—that is, the overman is not simply a secularized Christ. The overman's concerns about greatness, the rank ordering of human beings, the pathos of distance, all characteristics of the community grounded in the promise of the overman, cannot be traced to Christian so much as to Aristotelian sources.

29. Kaufmann, *Nietzsche,* 384 also argues that *Zarathustra* most clearly expresses Nietzsche's debt to Aristotle's magnanimity, but he does not carry out the comparison.

30. NE 5.3.7–8, 1131a25–30.

31. NE 5.7.1–4, 1134b15–20.

32. GM I.15.

33. AC 41, 43.

34. Nietzsche, then, would disagree with Holloway's ("Christianity, Magnanimity") argument that Aristotle's magnanimous man is compatible with Christianity. See Mary M. Keys, "Aquinas and the Challenge of Aristotelian Magnanimity," *History of Political Thought* 24, no. 1 (2003): 37–65 on the changes Aquinas made in Aristotle's conception of magnanimity to make it compatible with Christianity.

35. Cf. Zarathustra's struggles with the "just" [*Gerechte*] throughout the text.

36. Cf. Nietzsche's remarks on the perennial struggle between science and religion, AC 47–48.

37. Cf. GS 5.357 on Nietzsche's account of the development of German philosophy as the historicization of the Copernican revolution in philosophy. See AC 10–12 on the continuity of Christian morality and German philosophy.

38. See BT 13–15, TI, "The Problem of Socrates." In the latter, Nietzsche criticizes Socrates for being representative of the rabble, but in both texts Nietzsche applauds Socrates for providing a way out of incipient nihilism in Greece, although Socrates went too far in emphasizing rationality over the instincts.

39. AC 57, "*unequal* rights are the condition for any rights at all."

40. In AC 57, Nietzsche suggests that founders have to obscure the contingent nature of the founding in order to establish something lasting.

41. See UM 1 on attenuated culture of modern states; BGE 212 on the diversity of the modern age, and how this diversity leads to exhaustion, not strength, yet this is a diversity that, properly cultivated, can lead to powerful new philosophical creations.

42. See UM 2.5–9 on the effect of historical knowledge on community and the slippery slope to complete egoism.

43. See UM 2.9 on the "deadly truths" revealed by modern science which Nietzsche takes to be true.

44. Cf. BT 18.

45. See GM 2 18.

46. Here, again, Nietzsche appears be indebted to Machiavelli. Cf. Leo Strauss, *Thoughts on Machiavelli* (Glencoe, Il.: The Free Press, 1958), 172–73.

47. BGE 9.

48. On the individual providing a justification, see GS 3.143; on the individual philosopher legislating a new table of goods see BGE 211.

49. See Zarathustra's concern with being "true to the earth," Z Prologue, 3

50. WP 983; on Nietzsche's use of Socrates as a modern exemplar, see Jeffrey Church, "Dreaming of the True Erotic: Nietzsche's Socrates and the Reform of Modern Education," *History of Political Thought* 27, no. 4 (Winter 2006): 685–710.

51. NE IV.iii.18, cf. instances of threatened persecution of Zarathustra, the jester's warning and the gravedigger's jeers, Z Prologue 8; cf. Zarathustra's competition with the people over his disciples Z Prologue 9 and Z 1. "On the Flies of the Marketplace."

52. On the leveling tendencies, see the last man discussion, Z Prologue, 5; On the envy of egalitarianism, see Z 2, "On the Tarantulas." On the possibilities created by a pathos of distance, see BGE 257.

53. BGE 212 on the 16th century's need for altruism and Athens' need for self-irony.

54. Z Prologue 5.

55. Cf AOM 223 on historical knowledge as self-knowledge: "thus self-knowledge will become universal knowledge with regard to all that is past."

56. See Nietzsche's early description of such a communal ideal in UM 3.1–3.

57. In recognizing the need to recruit and educate lesser men to carry out his project, Nietzsche also follows Machiavelli. *Discourses* 1. Preface.

58. Robert Pippin, "Irony and Affirmation in Nietzsche's *Thus Spoke Zarathustra*," in *Nietzsche's New Seas: Explorations in Philosophy, Aesthetics, and Politics,* ed. Michael Allen Gillespie and Tracy B. Strong (Chicago: University of Chicago Press, 1988), 45–74, reads Zarathustra's collapse in the second part as a recognition of the historical contingency of Zarathustra's own proposed solution. Zarathustra withholds this truth from his disciples, as indicated by Zarathustra's shaking of his head to his best disciple's interpretation of his dream, Z 2."The Soothsayer."

59. NE 4.3.28, 1124b25–30.

60. UM 2.9 on the "terrible truths."

61. Z 1. "The Flies in the Marketplace."

62. *Posterior Analytics* 97b.20–25. In arguing that Socrates is, finally, *the* Aristotelian magnanimous man, Howland, "Great-Souled," 53–56, emphasizes Socrates' "human" wisdom, i.e., that he knows that he does not know. Socrates is not, in other words, an example of Aristotelian "theoretical virtue," as Gauthier, *Magnanimite*, 104–07, and R. A. Gauthier and J. Y. Jolif, *L'Ethique a Nicomaque* (Louvain: Publications Universitaires, 1970), vol. 2, pt. 1, 272–98, argue. Socrates qualifies as a magnanimous man, rather, because, as he points out in Plato's *Apology of Socrates* (39a–31a) he performed great deeds for the city by interrogating his fellow citizens, asking them why they continued to seek transitory goods like wealth and reputation out of a fear of death rather than truth, prudence, and the good of their soul. Knowing that he had benefited the city more than anyone else, he then told them (36b–e) that he deserved to be fed at public expense in the Prytaneum.

63. Leo Strauss, "Note on the Plan of Nietzsche's *Beyond Good and Evil*," in *Studies in Platonic Political Philosophy* (Chicago: University of Chicago Press, 1983).

64. Robert B. Pippin, *Idealism as Modernism: Hegelian Variations* (Cambridge: Cambridge University Press, 1997), 22–23.

65. Mark Warren, *Nietzsche and Political Thought* (Cambridge: MIT Press, 1988), introduction.

66. Ruth Abbey and Frederick Appel, "Nietsche and the Will to Politics," *The Review of Politics* 60, no. 1 (Winter 1998): 83–114.

III

MAGNANIMOUS STATESMEN

8

Magnanimity and Martyrdom: The Death and Life of Thomas More

James R. Stoner Jr.

INTRODUCTION: MARTYRDOM AND MAGNANIMITY

Taken in themselves, consulting either common sense or authority, it is not obvious that magnanimity and martyrdom should be at odds. To lay down one's life in witness to the truth of the Gospel surely involves a certain elevation of spirit on the part of the Christian martyr, and of course "greatness of soul" is the literal meaning of magnanimity. Thomas Aquinas sees such congruence between the two that he treats them both as elements of the cardinal virtue of fortitude, which he defines in turn as firmness of mind in the face of the threat of death. In martyrdom, death is suffered, but reason remains steady in its adherence to the faith in the name of charity; to die as a martyr for the faith is a supreme act of fortitude. Magnanimity, according to Aquinas, is a virtue rather than an act, and he defines it more or less as Aristotle does, as the habit of seeking the greatest honors, knowing oneself to be worthy of them, while nevertheless not holding human honor to be of much account in the larger scheme of things. Magnanimity, like fortitude, holds firm even in the face of difficulty, not here the fear of death but the winning of great honor, which never comes without a struggle. Though Aquinas does not repeat the term from Aristotle, both martyrdom and magnanimity seem to him to be a crown of virtue, displaying the nobility of the human spirit, the one at the moment of death, the other in success. Both the martyr and the magnanimous man despise small-mindedness and the petty concerns that animate most people. Both rise above their fellows as they rise above themselves.[1]

Aquinas anticipates the charge raised by the partisans of pagan virtue and critics of Christian virtue that (pagan) magnanimity is at odds with (Christian) humility. His response is to admit that the two represent contrary tendencies, but only because they look at the same thing from opposite perspectives:

> . . . magnanimity makes a man deem himself worthy of great things in consideration of the gifts he holds from God. . . . On the other hand, humility makes a man think little of himself in consideration of his own deficiency.[2]

To Aquinas's mind, the greatness of God explains the nobility of human virtue; the latter is not compromised but enhanced by acknowledging the former. To the objection that the contrary attitudes of pride and humility cannot psychologically coexist, Aquinas would reply that the dispositions of the virtues are so thoroughly imbued with reason and their acts so perfectly guided by prudence that what is evident to the rational understanding about the hierarchy of being can determine how one moves about the world; the magnanimous man may reserve a certain disdain for human honor even as he seeks all he deserves of it, but he never thinks of himself as a god among men nor presumes to act as though he were. At the same time, and in contrast perhaps to some Christian practice in subsequent eras, Aquinas thinks the moral life can be lived without small-minded fastidiousness in following rules and a failure to act with confidence even in the face of complexity. To calculate how to act in relation to the claims of others is the business of the virtue of justice, and justice is so far from contradicting magnanimity that Aquinas writes, "When magnanimity is added to justice it increases the latter's goodness; and yet without justice it would not even be a virtue."[3] High-mindedness without justice is haughty and unworthy of the honor it claims; a just man who is not magnanimous fails to step forward and judge as the community needs.

Now while it makes sense that magnanimity is consistent with humility if it is consistent with martyrdom, the question becomes complicated when at issue is the relation of magnanimity and statesmanship. On the one hand, if magnanimity claims the greatest honors, it surely claims to rule, and if statesmanship consists in the art or act of ruling well, it might seem to accompany magnanimity all the time, at least in good regimes where men of virtue are tapped for office. On the other hand, relating statesmanship and martyrdom seems not a little problematic: Surely the state is in a moment of severe crisis if its statesmen are martyred, and insofar as it is the task of statesmanship to preserve the state from severe crisis, the martyred statesman seems to have failed. Whatever can be said about whether the Christian can welcome martyrdom—Aquinas says a man ought to prepare his mind for it and if necessary endure it, but not court it—it might seem that the statesman, who holds others' lives in his hands, ought least of all to wish for such extremity. Moreover, one might wonder whether martyrdom itself can ever be an act of statesmanship, or whether by definition the martyred statesman has already been deposed. And if he has not been—if the statesman maintains a certain influence on the state even out of office, something easy to observe in practice and easy to understand in theory if the honor of office has been given to one who merits it by his virtue—then what does that imply for activity of Christian statesmanship before the crisis? Is there something unique about the Christian statesman precisely because he has prepared his mind to suffer martyrdom? And what might be the meaning of such Christian statesmanship in the context of the modern, secular state?

THE LIFE AND DEATH OF THOMAS MORE

No one I can think of better illustrates the problematic of statesmanship and martyrdom better than Sir Thomas More, now canonized by the Catholic Church and even pronounced the patron saint of statesmen. Let me briefly sketch his life and death, then outline the issues that his writings, speeches, and examples raise for our theme.[4]

Thomas More was born in London in 1478. A lawyer's son, he followed his father into law, but also trained as a humanist scholar, learning Greek as well as Latin, and gaining an early reputation for extraordinary learning, cemented throughout Europe by the publication in 1516 of his brilliant *Utopia*, a playful, ironic reworking of Plato's *Republic* for a Christian age.

Soon after, More accepted full time duties in the court of King Henry VIII, rising to become, in 1529, his chancellor, the highest civilian office of the realm. More was the first non-cleric to hold this post in several centuries—he had considered taking orders as a youth, but decided instead to marry (twice, the second time soon after he was widowed), and he raised a large family of children, stepchildren, and wards—but an important part of his policy as chancellor was to help Henry suppress the spread of Protestant heresy in England, which he did by occasional prosecution and by publishing enormous tracts refuting Protestant authors such as Frith and Tyndale. More had apparently apprised the King of his opinion about Henry's effort to get the pope to annul his marriage to Catherine of Aragon, his longtime queen who had not borne him a surviving male heir. Henry apparently agreed to let More disagree in silence and have no part of the business, while nevertheless pursuing the matter through the efforts of other officers. When these failed, again through efforts of other instruments, Henry sought to declare himself Supreme Head of the English Church—and then grant himself his own annulment or divorce. It was immediately upon Henry's success in getting a convocation of English clergy to agree to one step toward the assertion of royal supremacy that More resigned the chancellorship in May 1532. The resignation was apparently amicable.

Henry accepted back the Chancellor's Medal—it was not dropped at More's feet as in the new statue of More in St. Patrick's Church in Washington, D.C.—and More gave as his official reasons for resigning ill health and a desire to retire from public life. We do not know all he said privately to the king about either the divorce or the supremacy, but he spoke publicly about neither.

In retirement, More kept up his writing against heretics and carefully avoided commentary on the divorce or the supremacy, but soon that was not enough for the king, who decided all officers of the government and all subjects he chose should take an oath acknowledging the king's supremacy in the church. More refused the oath and was imprisoned. Eventually he was tried for treason upon testimony (thought to be fabricated) that he spoke against the supremacy to another, something he vehemently denied. Even to his daughter, Meg, he refused to give his reason for not swearing—though after his condemnation, with the freedom of the doomed, he spoke against both the supremacy and the divorce.

More held out, at the cost of long imprisonment and eventually a trial for treason, on a very narrow constitutional point: his right to silence in the face of the demand that he take an oath that he asserted—but would not explain—that he could not conscientiously take. More opposed the supremacy, but acknowledged Henry's right to punish treason, and thus acquiesced in the legal prohibition against speaking against the king's right: the common law gave him a right not to speak, and so not to swear, though not a right to say what he will. Of course More's objection to royal supremacy in the Church was also in a way constitutional; it depended on his view of the relative spheres of temporal and spiritual, state and church, king and pope. Even his own sphere of conscience was—*pace* Robert Bolt in "A Man for All Seasons"—not absolute; he would not yield his judgment on the right locus of supremacy in the Church either to parliament or to the judgment of his friends, though he indicated he would to a general council of the whole Church. Though he establishes a sort of republic in *Utopia*, More as an English subject is no republican; still, the monarchy he served was constitutional, and in his understanding to keep it so was worth the wager of his conscience and his life. I might add that More was acutely aware all along that to make a display of conscience and throw away his life would not earn him a crown of glory, but risk him a ring of fire for the sin of pride.

MAGNANIMITY AND STATESMANSHIP IN *UTOPIA*

Let me consider the relationship of magnanimity, statesmanship, and martyrdom in Thomas More by several routes: through his book, *Utopia*, through his activities in relation to heresy in England, and through his writings and speeches in his last days.

Today's More's classic work is simply called *Utopia*, but its full original title is *De optimo reipublicae statu deque nova insula Utopia*, which translates *On the Best State of a Commonwealth and on the New Island of Utopia*.[5] Despite the title, or perhaps because of it, this classic of Renaissance humanism begins with an extensive discussion of the question of how wisdom speaks to power; in fact, that is the topic of the whole of Book I of the work, which is fully half as long as the account of Utopia itself in Book II. The answer apparently arrived at—through a description of the best regime—is playfully if not unproblematically established; More, himself an ironic character in his own work, has the traveler-raconteur Raphael Hythloday insist that Utopia actually exists on the other side of the globe and that, consequently, it ought to be taken more seriously than Plato's republic, which exists only in speech. As is well-known, the Utopia thus sketched is characterized above all by the absence of private property. In contrast to Plato's *Republic*, where only the ruling classes are clearly propertyless, and denied families, too, in Utopia there are private families, but no private property for anyone. Everyone is obliged to work—the few scholars entitled to leisure have to work for that right—and, since all work, no one has to work too much; More calculates that a six-hour day will be enough to keep the common storehouses full. The people eat at common tables, and though they live in homes with their families, they trade their homes among themselves every decade and in the interim never lock their doors. Families rotate to the countryside for two-year stints of hard labor, but otherwise they ply whatever trade they want, supplying each other thanks to the diversity of interests and talents. Many choose to spend their ample leisure time in study, especially by attending early morning lectures. Nor do military obligations interfere too much with this life of leisure: Although prepared for service, the Utopians hire foreign mercenaries and assassins to handle most of their security needs outside the homeland. These they easily afford, since gold is public property and actually despised, used for chains and chamberpots.

Even from this very brief recounting, it is clear that the virtue of magnanimity can have little place in Utopia. In summing up his description, Raphael makes clear that what the Utopians have conquered, and what stands in the way of others' adopting Utopian laws and practices, is pride (*superbia*).[6] To be sure, there are a few honors in Utopia, besides the honor to Utopus its founder implicit in its name. Magistrates are elected, the principal magistrate for life (on good behavior), others for one-year terms; they consult extensively with their constituents when transacting public business and are bound by strict rules that regulate public debate, to prevent orators from investing their pride in their first statements and thus from feeling shame in sacrificing their own opinions for the common good. Except in the process of consultation and when matters are referred to a council of the whole island, discussion of public affairs outside the senate or the popular assembly is a capital offense, to prevent conspiracies that issue in tyranny but apparently forbidding anything like a party caucus as well.[7] In philosophy, not honor but pleasure appears at the center of Utopian ethics, with the false pleasures associated with "vain and unprofitable honors" singled out for scorn.[8] When they offer honor for great virtue, even to the point of erecting statues "to preserve the memory of their good deeds," they seem not to escape utilitarian calculation: this is merely the obverse of punishment to discourage crime.[9] In war, practices that European society would have treated as dishonorable form the heart of Utopian policy: offering bounties for the assassination of enemy rulers, hiring mercenaries, and the like, though excess slaughter on the battlefield is discouraged when Utopians themselves are forced to fight and they are said then to die with honor (*honestas*).[10] Even in death, honor seems confined to the simplest proportions: great funerals are forbidden and cremation is the rule. Indeed, it is only the priests in Utopia who receive great honors. While the only privilege of government officials and their wives is to sit at the head of the common tables, the priests (like governors they are elected, but they are very few) are said to deserve and have the highest honors: immunity from criminal prosecution, respect bordering on reverence from Utopians and even foreigners, fine clothes for services, and the finest women as their wives (unless, as is permitted and sometimes happens, an elderly widow is made priest). While they can excommunicate, even from the rather latitudinarian church, and while they attend Utopian battles (to stop massacres of even enemy defeated), they can use no force, only persuasion. Their chief business, besides leading the people in monthly ecumenical public worship, seems to be education of the young; they also prepare people for death, even, in the case of the incurable or in cases of extreme suffering, for suicide.

If there is little room for magnanimity in Utopia as Raphael describes it, the question of its status is also raised in the dialogue in which the description is embedded. In Book I, More (the character) and his friend Peter Giles try to convince Hythloday that he ought to enter the service of a prince, Giles suggesting the benefits to self, family, and friends, More instead appealing to his "generous and truly philosophical nature."[11] Hythloday will have none of it: He has rid himself of his inheritance and possessions, so has no obligations to his family, and he replies to More by illustrating the futility of such a project, first by recounting a past attempt to influence the chancellor of England in determining policy toward theft, second by imagining a war council with the king of France. More isn't persuaded: Scholastic philosophy "which supposes every topic suitable for every occasion" may get nowhere, but "another, more civil philosophy" "takes its cue, adapts itself to the drama in hand and acts its part neatly and appropriately."[12] Raphael again demurs, complaining that such an accommodating spirit would dilute even the teachings of Christ, and it is precisely in this context that he proposes describing the best city as an alternative path to influence. In his utter lack of concern for worldly honor or profit, the character of Hythloday might be said to be reject magnanimity, showing contempt for ordinary human honors—indeed, maybe too much contempt—but failing to see himself as worthy of honor and so of office and responsibility. Raphael contrasts Plato's republic and his Utopia in that the former exists only in speech, while the latter, he says, really exists, but Utopia is at least as perfect a reflection of his soul as Plato's city-in-speech is of Socrates' since Raphael rejects political honor in principle as much as Utopia neglects it in practice, and this despite the fact that Utopia is never said to be an image of the soul, as of course Plato's city is meant precisely to be. Though more thoughtful commentators have, to my mind, refuted the interpretation given Utopia since at least one of its introductory letters as a city of Christians or of Christian virtues without the Christian religion—Raphael and his companions are the first Christians to arrive there, and as they brought along no priest, they could not bring all the Christian sacraments—we have now found a startling new reason why this is so: not only does Utopia include such unchristian (should I say, *then* unchristian) practices as suicide, divorce, and the toleration of heresy, but it lacks the virtue that leads men to step forward and claim responsibility for their common fate.[13]

The character More not only challenges Hythloday's understanding of his duty, but expresses his doubts as to the perfection of the land Hythloday describes; there can be no doubt that in some respect More the author is ironical in *Utopia*, either about the goodness of the featured city or about himself.[14] At the end of Book I, having heard about the Utopians only in general terms as having abolished private property, the character More expresses classical arguments against communism: lack of care for the commons, in the sense that no one will have an incentive to work, and fighting and turmoil, since the authority of (More even says reverence for) magistrates will be gone if there are no visible distinctions among men. After having heard the full description, More the character again thinks to object, this time more entirely on the basis of the consequence for honor of the abolition of property: "This one thing alone utterly subverts all the nobility, magnificence, splendor and majesty which (in public opinion) are the true ornaments and glory of any commonwealth."[15] Calling into question the right of property, More the author of *Utopia* surely asks his readers to reflect on the relation of wealth and virtue; but in pointing out the relation of property to honor, itself the worldly reward of virtue, More raises the question of the human responsibility to step forward to take command of our own affairs.

If magnanimity seems absent from the republic of Utopia and present ironically in the dialogue that presents it, there is no little touch of magnanimity in the literary project of *Utopia* as a book. To present a model of a best regime is to make a claim to be worthy to rule, and to present one's thoughts ironically in literary form rather than earnestly in political councils is to keep political honor in perspective; or is it rather the case that presenting one's views to literary applause is in fact to seek greater honor than most political offices convey, especially to a commoner in a hereditary monarchy where hereditary aristocrats claim or receive many of the highest offices of the realm? More himself—the man, like the character—already held political office when he published the book, and in fact its success helped propel him into full-time service to the king. The availability of literary honor, indeed of international dimension, in Renaissance Europe was in one sense altogether new, made possible by the recent invention of the printing press and so the timely dissemination of literary production, but it also depended upon the unique public established by universal—that is to say, catholic—doctrine on moral and religious matters, upon a common culture of learning that transcended political boundaries and operated through cultural exchange that involved not only Church hierarchy but also university and court. If More's defense of honor might imply a defense of Catholic hierarchy and magnificence, as well as of national political authority, so his willingness to enter the play of humanist discourse was not unconscious of the value of a common, universal faith.

MAGNANIMITY AND STATESMANSHIP *IN EXTREMIS*

Mention of Catholic doctrine suggests investigation and reflection in More's career as a statesman. He was chancellor for only a few years, and, like Socrates in battle, who distinguished himself in retreat, More's most notable activities apparently involved resisting initiatives pressed by others, not leading reforms himself. Most famously he stayed aloof from King Henry VIII's efforts to annul his marriage; as mentioned above, Henry had apparently appointed More well aware of More's objection to the annulment, the two agreeing that More would not be involved in the efforts or their ramifications. Again, as mentioned before, when this proved impossible, More resigned. But perhaps his more extensive activity as chancellor beyond his routine duties in court involved his efforts to support Church authorities in the suppression of emerging Protestantism in England: writing and publishing extensively against William Tyndale, Christopher St. Germain, and John

Frith, and participating in the prosecution of several Protestants for heresy as well. Though perhaps fully in accord with dominant Catholic thinking at the time, defended by Aquinas, that civil peace permitted the suppression of heresy, lest individuals be led into danger of damnation and the unity of the polity be undermined, the intensity on display in More's anti-heretical writings and testified to by his self-authored epitaph—"to thieves, murderers, and heretics, grievous"—appears anything but magnanimous to modern thinking. While the subsequent century and a half of English politics might seem to vindicate the view that fueling religious controversy would be dangerous to the king's peace, More in action—despite some hints at toleration in *Utopia*—was certainly not a proto-liberal. At the same time, as is confirmed by an earlier speech at Oxford defending the study of Greek and thus the liberal arts, his objections were not to genuine dialectic but to popular dissemination of controversy—at least until, by the publication of his books in English refuting the Protestants page by page, he entered public controversy himself. Whatever else might be said of political support for authoritative doctrine, it does not seem to me to contradict the virtue of magnanimity but instead perhaps to confirm it: Only those who really know ought to have the office of determining what can openly be said.

Even among those who condemn More's activities regarding those he saw as heretics, the dignity of his death is undeniable. For all that Protestantism was to make of individual conscience, here was a man who to the point of martyrdom adhered to conscience on the traditional Catholic understanding: applying the known principles of right in the peculiar circumstances of one's particular situation. Can More, already retired from office, be seen to act as a statesman in his refusal first of all to take the oath of succession he was proffered, and second in his condemnation of the king both for the marriage and the supremacy in his speech after condemnation? In one sense, of course not; precisely because he was out of office he could consider it unprecedented to be asked to swear an oath, something an officer might be asked to do or to resign.[16] And yet Henry had demanded the oath of the retired More, recognizing perhaps his continuing influence and moral authority, as if in some sense he acted as a statesman still. More's defense of the privilege of nonjuring in the constitution of England, and thereby his adherence to the larger constitution of Christendom and its distinction of temporal and spiritual authority, was perhaps, so to speak, an ironic act of statesmanship. But irony is not, under Aristotle or Aquinas, forbidden to—indeed, it may even be expected of—a magnanimous man.

Thomas More, in what he surely knew would be his final months in the Tower, reflected on and wrote about the passion of Christ. Whether by design or under the limitation of a brutal deadline, he concentrates almost entirely on the agony in the garden of Gethsemane, commenting of course on the sleepiness of the disciples, but also on the wakefulness of Jesus and on his genuine human fear in the face of his impending death. This visible sharing of human weakness was meant, More writes, as a comfort to those who do not rush to meet martyrdom as glory, but who, despite their belief, flee persecution while they can and meet their fate in a spirit more of submission than of defiance:

> Thus the wisdom of God, which penetrates all things irresistibly and disposes all things sweetly, foreseeing and contemplating in His ever-present sight how the minds of men in different places would be affected, suits His examples to various times and places, choosing now one destiny, now another, according as He sees which will be most profitable. And so God proportions the temperaments of His martyrs according to His own providence in such a way that one rushes forth eagerly to his death, another creeps out hesitantly and fearfully but for all that bears his death none the less bravely—unless someone perhaps imagines he ought to be thought less brave for having fought down not only his enemies but also his own weariness, sadness and fear—most strong feelings and mighty enemies indeed.
>
> But the whole drift of the present discussion finally comes to this: we should admire both kinds of most holy martyrs; we should venerate both kinds, praise God for both; we should imitate both when the situation demands it, each according to his own capacity and according to the grace God gives each.[17]

From his letters it is clear enough that More considered himself among the hesitant and fearful as he faced the increasingly certain prospect of his martyrdom, among the humble, so to speak, rather than the magnanimous. Still there is a certain magnanimity in recognizing the balance of humility and magnanimity itself in Christian martyrdom. If there is irony in seeing in the martyrdom of a great political man an act of Christian statesmanship, there is perhaps also instruction to Christian statesman in how to balance the political and theological virtues, as well as gentle correction of the irritable connection of ancient magnanimity to human pride.

NOTES

1. See Aquinas, *Summa Theologica*, II-II, q. 123 (on fortitude), q. 124 (on martyrdom), q. 129 (on magnanimity).

2. *Ibid.*, II-II, q. 129, a. 3. See also Carson Holloway, "Christianity, Magnanimity, and Statesmanship," *Review of Politics* 61 (Autumn, 1999), 581–604.

3. *Summa Theologica*, II-II, q. 58, a. 12.

4. My summary of More's life and death draws on the following: R. W. Chambers, *Thomas More* (New York: Harcourt Brace & Co., 1935); Gerard Wegemer, *Thomas*

More: A Portrait in Courage (Princeton, N.J.: Scepter Publications, 1997); Peter Ackroyd, *The Life of Thomas More* (New York: Nan A. Talese, 1998); J. A. Guy, *Thomas More* (London: Arnold, 2000).

5. Thomas More, *Utopia: Latin Text and English Translation*, ed. George M. Logan, Robert M. Adams, and Clarence H. Miller (Cambridge: Cambridge University Press, 1995). All subsequent citations are to this edition.

6. *Utopia*, 246.

7. *Utopia*, 120–125.

8. *Utopia*, 168.

9. *Utopia*, 194.

10. *Utopia*, 212.

11. *Utopia*, 53.

12. *Utopia*, 95–97.

13. See Quentin Skinner, "Thomas More's *Utopia* and the Virtue of True Nobility," in *Visions of Politics, Volume 2: Renaissance Virtues* (Cambridge: Cambridge University Press, 2002), ch. 8, 239.

14. Skinner summarizes the current state of the secondary literature on whether (or rather, how) to read *Utopia* ironically in *Visions of Politics*, 213ff. Cf. Eva Brann, "'An Exquisite Platform': *Utopia*," *Interpretation: A Journal of Political Philosophy* 3, issue 1: 1ff.

15. *Utopia.*, 247.

16. See E. E. Reynolds, *The Trial of St. Thomas More* (New York: P. J. Kenedy and Sons, 1964).

17. Saint Thomas More, *The Sadness of Christ*, ed. Gerard Wegemer, trans. Clarence Miller (Princeton, N.J.: Scepter Publications, 1993), 43–44.

9

George Washington's Greatness and Aristotelian Virtue: Enduring Lessons for Constitutional Democracy

Paul Carrese[1]

THE ACHIEVEMENT, AND FATE, OF WASHINGTON

George Washington was hailed by Americans in his own lifetime, and for at least a century after, as a model of greatness in politics—and this reputation carried beyond American shores. He was called the father of his country, and the American Cincinnatus: a commanding leader in war and peace who relinquished great power after a crisis had passed, and who throughout committed himself to private and public virtue, liberty under law, and securing natural rights for all. Washington earned such praise by sticking to high principles during the crises and pressures of supreme command—first in a long-shot war against the world's superpower, then as citizen-farmer in retirement (from which he was roused to lead a constitutional reform movement), and finally as president. He also resisted the temptations arising from the great honors bestowed upon him, and conversely, he resisted stooping to join his detractors and defenders in the partisan fray that engulfed his last years in office. In his final retirement he owned up to the injustice of slavery by emancipating all of his slaves at his death, a deed unique among the slave-owning presidents. Still, why should political scientists or serious citizens in the twenty first century care about Washington or consider lessons he might offer about leadership and liberal democracy? Both progressives and quantitative social scientists, in academia and beyond, would find study of Washington a largely regressive endeavor. How could a Virginia gentryman and slave owner of a bygone era be relevant for our more enlightened or complicated democracies, in vastly different social and technological conditions, other than by suggesting how far we have come or still need to go? That said, the biographies and studies of Washington keep coming, both popular and academic. This fact, along with broader signs in our politics, suggests that recourse to the founders serves a need felt not only by conservatives or history buffs—perhaps especially so regarding *the* Founding Father.

Why is it that in twenty first century America, after two centuries of increasingly populist and democratic politics and a century of Woodrow Wilson's invention of the policy-driven presidency, our presidential candidates still are evaluated by voters first on the criteria of character and leadership rather than policy expertise or positions? How is it that a prominent history professor and public intellectual could publish a book on "presidential courage," and even land on the cover of a major American news magazine for employing the antiquated terminology of the virtues?[2] These phenomena suggest a tension between the somewhat unarticulated demands of the active citizenry and the democratic theory dominant in academia; it also suggests a contradiction among the citizens themselves. Political science and democratic theory in America for over a century have eschewed issues of character and virtue in favor of new conceptions of democratic leadership, of the relations between leaders and citizens, and of the qualities that both leaders and citizens should hold up as models or goals. Modern democratic theory does not notice or address the tensions between democracy and political virtue, or the demands of the highest kind of principled leadership for a liberal democracy in both domestic and foreign affairs—because, in short, it is not democratic or progressive to focus on such topics. The shift in terminology from statesmanship to leadership is one indication of this narrowing of discourse, as is the shift from republic to democracy as the ideal form of the American polity.[3] As for the voters in presidential primaries and the general election, they overlook the tension between their desire for candidates embodying leadership qualities and their demand for an incessant campaign that features constant recourse to polls and measures of popularity; solicitations for money and attention; and demonstrations that the candidate is attuned to the popular mood.

Modern democratic theory and political science, in short, may wish to have invented a new kind of politics that needs little or no focus on the character of its officials, but modern liberal democracies regularly have faced and still today face a need for leadership that at least echoes older theories of statesmanship—including a commitment in both word and deed to the highest ethical principles and an ability to stand against or educate a public opinion that might prefer easier options or short-term vistas.[4] These are the terms in which Michael Beschloss praises selected American presidents, and even in a popular news magazine he has been so bold as to argue that first rank belongs to the first president: "Nothing in the Constitution says we have to elect a leader capable of presidential courage. That expectation was established by George

Washington. . . . This country received no greater gift. We must always struggle to choose presidents capable of Washington's kind of presidential
courage."[5] Indeed, if greatness is still desired even in our now very democratic political culture, it could be that we retain something of the original
constitutional culture that Washington sought to establish, which recognized
the need for sober and even great characters in commanding positions to sustain free, constitutional government—and also recognized the nobility and
virtue of serving as such a leading citizen. It also could be, however, that our
hunger for greatness is a manifestation of the ancient disease of democracies,
chronicled from Thucydides and Plato to Montesquieu and *The Federalist*, in
which the people as dominant power paradoxically seeks to channel its passion through and find comfort in a single, populist leader. This scenario long
has provoked the warning that a Pericles or Caesar, a Cromwell or Napoleon,
is likely to pivot from demagogue to dictator before he can be stopped. The
fact that Washington and his protégés in the founding era warned against just
these rival extremes, and that Washington himself twice could have used his
popularity to seize arbitrary power and twice passed the test, together suggest
that we still have much to learn from study of his ideas and deeds. One of the
first studies of these themes is Aristotle's delineation of the virtue of magnanimity or greatness of soul, and there seems to be a resemblance between
Washington and the character Aristotle sketches in the *Nicomachean Ethics*
as at once worthy of great honors yet disdaining both populism and abuse
of power. Moreover, the greatest observer of the modern democratic spirit,
Tocqueville, pronounces unqualified praise for Washington as a great statesman and founder even while he worries that modern democracy undermines
moral greatness in both citizenry and office holders.

We might also wonder what can we learn about the constitutional democracy that Washington founded by reflecting upon the ambivalent view in which
he is held by scholars and citizens today. There remains admiration for the
Founding Father among the citizenry, but recent academic and elite opinion
probably resonates more with the subtle demotion-via-contextualization offered by Joseph Ellis than with the praise offered by Gordon Wood. In an essay on "The Greatness of George Washington," Wood, a leading intellectual
historian of the American founding era, laments that the founder "no longer
seems to be first in the hearts of his countrymen," and he firmly chastises our
era: Washington "fully deserves the first place he used to hold. He certainly deserved the accolades his contemporaries gave him. . . . Washington was truly
a great man and the greatest president we ever had."[6] Still, the hearts of most
academics probably respond more to Ellis's effort to place Washington as just
one among the *Founding Brothers*, a work that echoes the historiography of
the past century in praising Jefferson and his democratic-republican protégés

as far more worthy of study—certainly regarding enduring aspirations for the republic and its continual evolution—than are Washington-the-proto-Federalist and his protégés. Ellis later turned to Washington alone but continued the typical demythologizing of our era, portraying him as a distant, merely historical character. He entitled his study *His Excellency,* and indulged an autobiographical opening in which Ellis as a boy views Washington's authoritative but remote status as akin to "the man in the moon." His effort at "a fresh portrait focused tightly on Washington's character" in fact yields a series of backhanded compliments by one who cannot fathom the traditional, Aristotelian conception of character that Washington himself held. His fabled moderation is really an "obsession with self-control" that masks his "bottomless ambition" and "interior urges;" his fabled prudence was an accidental product of a mind devoid of "sophisticated intellectual preconceptions;" he turned down absolute power because he aspired "to live forever in the memory of future generations;" and, his policies luckily guessed "where history was headed."[7]

His Excellency turns out to be dumber than many a recent politician, and basically just as consumed by needs for sexual and popular adulation—albeit more obsessed with controlling such urges. The democratic historian tells a democratic age just what it wants to hear: that we have nothing much to look up to, no real greatness to ponder in Washington, and no real failings in our more democratic culture.[8] If, however, voters still seem to value greatness in presidential candidates, and at least some leading historians still can trumpet the greatness of Washington, perhaps studies of American liberal democracy can be open-minded enough to the question of greatness in politics as to give Washington not a fresh look but a sober, appreciative one.

MAGNANIMITY, STATESMANSHIP, AND DEMOCRATIC INDIVIDUALISM

It is striking for a democratic mind to consider that Aristotle ranked magnanimity or greatness of soul (*megalopsychia*) one of the peaks among the eleven moral virtues he analyzes and endorses in the *Nicomachean Ethics,* with only magnanimity and general (complete) justice embodying "complete virtue."[9] Many scholars find an ascent in Aristotle's assessment of the moral virtues, one indication of which is the higher praise given to justice (last of the eleven) than magnanimity (the fifth in order). Justice "is regarded as the highest virtue," and is "complete virtue in the fullest sense because it is the practice of complete virtue," while magnanimity receives a more circumspect appraisal: it is "the sort of crown of the virtues: it magnifies them and it cannot exist without [all of] them."[10] Nonetheless, the magnanimous man is praised as the *kalos kagathos*, the good and noble man, and "the best man" (4.3, 1123b27–29 and 1124a3–4). Indeed, the recent effort by the analytical schools of classical and moral philosophy to rediscover Aristotle and "virtue ethics" errs in not taking seriously the peak represented by magnanimity, as evident in its omission from a collection of essays on the *Ethics* by leading scholars.[11]

One reason that those of an analytical or liberal-democratic bent might overlook this virtue is its evident association with a more aristocratic conception of politics, or at least with a role for a genuinely aristocratic or excellent citizen in a mixed regime who serves to temper the democratic spirit. Aristotle curiously proposes that this virtue can be investigated either by examining the characteristic of the soul or the man characterized by it (1123a36–1123b1). The ensuing discussion reinforces the proximity of this particular moral virtue to political life or actual rule, perhaps more political in character than any other virtue except justice. Moreover, modern analytical and liberal philosophies are inclined to separate the public from the private, and politics from ethics, in a manner foreign to Aristotle's philosophy— and thus these schools are puzzled by or tend to demote magnanimity. It is challenging for moderns to notice or make sense of the fact that Aristotle's *Ethics* opens and closes with political concerns and assesses them throughout, and conversely that his *Politics* opens with ethical concerns and closes with two books on ethical education for citizenship and rule.[12]

Further obstacles today to seriously considering magnanimity arise from the later influences that define liberal modernity, ranging from Machiavelli's ruthless realism to the emphasis in the Christian tradition on charity and the other-regarding virtues. One element of the modern disposition is the tendency to absorb Machiavelli's view that virtue is really just posturing or the self-assertion of certain qualities for the agent's advantage. Machiavelli's great efforts to redefine *virtù* in *The Prince* seem to be directed at overthrowing precisely Aristotle's ethics, and thus we moderns might be skeptical of Aristotle's emphasis on a magnanimous man who "thinks he deserves great things and actually deserves them" (1123b1–2) and who truly is good, noble, and virtuous.[13] Conversely, greatness of soul is complete virtue in relation to oneself, having the right judgment and self-knowledge to discern what great external goods or honors one deserves and does not (1123a34–b25), whereas justice is virtue in relation to others. The emphasis in the Christian tradition on love of neighbor led philosophers like Aquinas to emphasize justice and the other cardinal virtues over magnanimity because the former are more other-regarding, or, alternately, to adapt magnanimity toward a concern for the common good.[14] Both Christian and liberal philosophy place less emphasis on honor than does classical philosophy—although Montesquieu is a complicated exception—while Aristotle finds a distinct virtue in magnanimity as the right attitude toward the honor one is owed.[15]

These difficulties we have in approaching magnanimity, or comprehending the role of a magnanimous officeholder in any conception of liberal democratic politics, perhaps find a summary in the perplexity a modern would find with Aristotle's definition of the two opposing vices that this virtue avoids. He defines magnanimity as steering between vanity and smallness of soul (or undue humility): the vain man foolishly believes that he deserves great honors which his soul does not in fact merit, while the unduly humble man deprives himself of the good or honor he deserves (1125a17–35).[16] The Machiavellian part of modernity cannot believe anyone really is unduly humble, at least not anyone in political life. Conversely, the Christian and liberal parts of modernity have difficulty understanding why Aristotle ultimately defines undue humility as the more defective extreme, more truly opposed to magnanimity, because undue humility "occurs more frequently and is worse" (1125a33–35; see generally 2.9, 1109a19–b28).[17] Aristotle argues that most human beings will need to err on the side of vanity in order to arrive at the virtue of self-knowledge about the state of one's soul and the appropriate honor we deserve from others, whether in public or private life. Such self-knowledge keeps one on the path of virtue amidst the storms of life, and calibrates one's reaction to the external goods and temptations of public life so as to maintain the appropriately dignified tenor of one's relation to fellow citizens and officeholders.

Aristotle's deems that fewer of us will be vain in the proudly foolish, public manner that he chastises when discussing the haughtiness that some see in the magnanimous man. The truly magnanimous in fact will "bear the gifts of fortune gracefully," even the applause of those beneath them, and it is only the vain who will fail to "have a moderate attitude toward wealth, power," and any other external good that comes their way (1124a5–11224b7). Indeed, one might consider how many citizens in liberal democracy today put themselves forward as candidates for office or for other serious attention and honors— and, then, what proportion of these citizens are buffoons who think too much of themselves in contrast to those who exhibit a proper public-spiritedness. Among the great things of life Aristotle associates with magnanimity are the highest honors, of the sort we render to divinity (1123b16–20), and also war or other mortal dangers, since the magnanimous man "will face great risks" and "will not spare his life" in doing so (1124b7–9). Surely for the classical polis and much of human political history, and to some extent still in modern liberal democracy, both the highest honors and the act of putting one's life at risk in the name of virtue or honor largely fall in the realm of politics.[18]

Here we approach the direct relevance of Aristotelian magnanimity for conceptions of leadership or statesmanship in liberal democracy. Tocqueville advanced similar arguments two millennia after Aristotle amid his astute observations on both the soul of modern democracy and the fate of souls within modern democracy. After turning from his examination of American institutions, laws, and political mores to examine what kind of character such laws and politics produce, Tocqueville warns that pettiness or small-mindedness among the citizenry poses a threat to liberty and to human decency in our era.[19] This echoes Aristotle's judgment that pettiness of soul is more of a vice than is vanity, since failure to even aim toward great things, great honor, or great risks is a failure to aim at what nature intends as the full development of the human soul.[20] Tocqueville had earlier raised this subject in his striking observations about a new condition arising in modern democracy, an "individualism" or low-minded self-regard that yields a narrowing of one's soul. The unintended, unexpected consequence of mass equality and democracy for many souls is a disposition for each citizen "to isolate himself from the mass of those like him and to withdraw to one side with his family and friends," indeed, "to lead him back toward himself alone . . . [and] finally to confine him wholly in the solitude of his own heart."[21] Subsequent studies have directly confirmed Tocqueville's concerns, whether Durkheim and other sociologists of alienation and anomie assessing the rising rates of suicide and marital divorce in modern liberal democracies, or Robert Putnam and political scientists debating the extent of a "bowling alone" culture in which even the American tradition of civic engagement through private associations withers. Of course, Tocqueville's view still is distinct and refreshing, for he insists upon addressing the soul while later social scientists tend to overlook a central point of his diagnosis by assessing only the self, presuming a natural atomism and isolation.[22] Perhaps the senseless but premeditated murders by students of fellow students and teachers in recent decades, such as at Columbine high school in Colorado or Virginia Tech university, also have a root in the demise of any concern or teaching about moral virtue, public spiritedness, and the ideal of magnanimity. The increasing regularity of these crimes may jar us back to thinking about the possibility that there is a natural inclination to society and politics that any political society must nurture, and our familiarity with the greatest recent philosopher on these themes, Tocqueville, in turn should point us back to Aristotle's considerations on similar phenomena.

It may be that *Nicomachean Ethics* ascends from the peak of magnanimity toward virtues that correct the reality or public persona of haughtiness in the great-souled man, starting with friendliness and wittiness (later chapters in Book 4), and moving to the ultimate peak of moral virtue in justice as oriented toward the common good (Book 5). The *Ethics* may further ascend toward the intellectual virtues, including the statesman's need for prudence or practical wisdom (Book 6), and beyond that to the virtue-like quality of friendship (Books 8 and 9) and the great question of whether the active or contemplative life is the best life for humankind (Book 10). Magnanimity provides for Aristotle and for us the lesson that a proper development of our nature requires an ambition to develop and perfect one's soul, including the self-knowledge to assess one's standing in relation to virtue and to others. This last point certainly points toward politics in the sense that Aristotle holds out to us the model of a soul that in turn holds up itself as a model of virtue and greatness for others. The magnanimous will be properly moderate in their responses to honors and to fellow citizens, neither too remote and severe nor too obsequious and flattering. Plutarch perpetuates this understanding of greatness and moderation by analyzing an array of types to admire or avoid in human affairs, and by arguing for the edification gained for oneself through such analyses and comparisons. Thus, Caesar was a cunning manipulator and flatterer of popular opinion, which revealed his vanity (and urge for absolute rule) rather than true greatness; conversely, Cato the Younger often was a model of magnanimity and virtuous resistance to corruption but was too severe—unwilling to compromise or to seek popular support—at crucial moments as Rome slid toward Caesarism.[23] *Lives of the Noble Grecians and Romans* once was standard reading in the Western liberal democracies for any who aspired to leadership in public or private life, and the intellectual foundation for the Plutarchan endeavor had been laid by Aristotle.

WASHINGTON'S MAGNANIMITY AS
GENERAL AND CONSTITUTIONAL FOUNDER

It is no accident that the best recent study of Washington's character and statesmanship, and of his relevance for understanding or improving our politics, seeks to offer "a moral biography, in the tradition of Plutarch."[24] Richard Brookhiser's *Founding Father* is the best of the recent studies because this approach echoes that of the first serious biography of Washington, by John Marshall. Marshall brought to his task a long personal experience with his fellow Virginian and fellow founder in both war and peace, as well as the perspicacity and intellectual rigor which still mark him as the greatest of chief justices of the U.S. Supreme Court.[25] Among the virtues of Marshall's biography is that he captures Washington's own understanding of character, and also that of the eighteenth and nineteenth century Americans who heaped honors upon the man they deemed their Founding Father and Cincinnatus. Marshall's Plutarchan approach is most evident in the closing section of all the editions of *The Life of George Washington*—a work he returned to and revised over three decades—offering what a recent editor calls "a brief character sketch," an "economical précis" of Washington's "intellectual and moral virtues that in itself calls for much pondering."[26] We might ponder that, as Marshall turns from summarizing Washington's generalship to his career as constitutional founder and president, he singles out magnanimity as one of the virtues of republican statesmanship that the great man embodied:

> Respecting, as the first magistrate in a free government must ever do, the real and deliberate sentiments of the people, their gusts of passion passed over without ruffling the smooth surface of his mind. Trusting to the reflecting good sense of the nation, he had the magnanimity to pursue its real interests in opposition to its temporary prejudices; and, in more instances than one, we find him committing his whole popularity to hazard, and pursuing steadily the course dictated by a sense of duty, in opposition to a torrent which would have overwhelmed a man of ordinary firmness.[27]

This may have been one of the passages which drove Jefferson to commission a rival history of the American founding period and of Washington's administration, for Marshall sought to revive the constitutionalism and republican theory of *The Federalist* and Washington in opposition to the more democratic theory of Jefferson. Indeed, it is no accident that in his final years, in Jacksonian America, Marshall sought to produce a one-volume edition of the biography for use in schools, so as to keep the lessons of Washington's constitutionalism and statesmanship in front of teachers and pupils alike.[28]

To understand what we might learn about Aristotelian magnanimity and its relevance for liberal democracy today it is best to focus on a few episodes and writings from Washington's four decades of public service as colonial officer, commanding general, constitutional founder, and president.[29] As Marshall indicates, and in accord with Aristotle's view of moderation and a balance between haughtiness and populism in relations with fellow citizens, Washington's magnanimity reveals itself in his commitment to balanced constitutional government and in resisting popular pressures to adopt policies he deemed unwise.

Around the world today and throughout human history, liberty mostly either never arises or is short lived because military despots squash any genuine politics or rule of law. America and the world owe to Washington the principle that a professional military is necessary to protect liberty and can be safe for it through subordination to laws and civil authority. This accorded with his political moderation: real liberty is ordered liberty, securing self-government and political decency under law. In the darkest hours of the war, Marshall argues that the American cause was saved by the moral greatness of a commander who kept his out-manned, under-supplied, ill-equipped army in the war until victorious: "To this unconquerable firmness—to this perfect self-possession under the most desperate of circumstances, is America, in a great degree, indebted for her independence."[30] America and the cause of liberty in the world also are fortunate that Washington was not tempted by absolute power when the war's prospects brightened. After the victory at Yorktown, an American colonel suggested that he should be king, an offer that might tempt a general deeply admired by his army and—like a Caesar, Cromwell, Napoleon, or Benedict Arnold—also ambitious himself. Colonel Lewis Nicola sought to exploit Washington's sympathy for his troops, proposing that disorganization in Congress and suffering in the army proved to all "the weakness of republicks, & the exertions the army has been able to make by being under a proper head"; hence, many in the army would support him if he chose to be king.[31] Washington replied immediately in writing, expressing "abhorrence" and "astonishment" upon learning of "such ideas existing in the Army." He used Nicola's regard for him against such a plan, connecting principles to the character needed to animate them: "Let me conjure you then, if you have any regard for your Country, concern for yourself or posterity, or respect for me, to banish these thoughts from your Mind" (*W* 468–69).

Trouble in the army arose again in 1783, with a peace process under way that might disband the army before being paid its due. Officers at Washington's headquarters in Newburgh, New York thought he might finally support a threat of mutiny against Congress: the States would not provide their requisitioned funds, Congress could not compel them, and the army suffered. An anonymous letter summoned all the officers to a meeting and suggested they seek the support of their "Illustrious Leader" for this plot (*W* 1107–9 at note 490.13–14). Washington denounced that meeting but called for an official one at which "mature deliberation" should develop "rational measures" for Congress to consider (*W* 490). He implied he would not attend; the element of surprise, then, was his when, in the officers' meeting house—called the Temple of Virtue—he strode in. His speech contrasted the "unmilitary" character and "blackest designs" of the plot with the "rules of propriety" and "order and discipline" more fitting to "your own honor, and the dignity of the Army" (*W* 495–500). His final appeal was to both reason and emotion: "let me conjure you, in the name of our common Country, as you value your own sacred honor, as you respect the rights of humanity, and as you regard the Military and National character of America," to reject this plot to "overturn the liberties of our Country" through civil war. This would prove them models of "unexampled patriotism and patient virtue" and "afford occasion for Posterity to say . . . 'had this day been wanting, the World had never seen the last stage of perfection to which human nature is capable of attaining'" (*W* 498–500). Washington sealed his efforts with another dramatic gesture, again using the army's devotion to him not for his own advantage but for law and liberty. He began to read a letter from a Congressman and then stopped: "Gentlemen, you will permit me to put on my spectacles, for I have not only grown gray, but almost blind, in the service of my country" (*W* 1109 at note 496.12). Some of the officers, no longer rebellious, were in tears. After he left, they unanimously repudiated the plot and reaffirmed their allegiance to civil authority.

Washington's magnanimity had not only immediate but also lasting consequences. Indeed, the main doctrinal statement of the U.S. Army today opens by recounting "Washington at Newburgh: Establishing the Role of the Military in a Democracy," finding in these deeds and words "the fundamental tenet of our professional ethos."[32] Principled to the end, Washington disbanded the army once the peace treaty was official. After a last "Circular Address" to the states recommending policies for the future (including constitutional reform), he resigned his commission before Congress in December of 1783: "Having now finished the work assigned me, I retire from the great theatre of Action; and bidding an Affectionate farewell to this August body under whose orders I have so long acted, I here offer my Commission, and take my leave of all the employments of public life" (*W* 547–48). Jefferson soon wrote to him: "the moderation & virtue of a single character has probably prevented this revolution from being closed as most others have been, by a subversion of that liberty it was intended to establish."[33]

Washington was not left for long in quiet retirement, for within three years he was drafted to lead the constitutional reform movement. Younger leaders such as Madison and Hamilton turned to him not only because they hoped to use his fame but because he already had articulated, in deeds and words, principles about union, constitutionalism, and statesmanship that the reformers sought to advance. Many who became Federalists, arguing for balance between union and states, looked to him as a defender of liberty and the Revolution who also had published a plea for rescuing liberty from anarchy. His 1783 "Circular to the States" had proposed a more perfect union by rebalancing state sovereignty with the common good and by forging a national character. The crisis in domestic and foreign affairs at the war's close was, he wrote, America's "political probation"; it will be either "respectable and prosperous, or contemptuous and miserable as a Nation." Only if it established a "national Character" and stopped "relaxing the powers of the Union, annihilating the cement of the Confederation," could America be independent. Now is "the favorable moment to give such a tone to our Federal Government, as will enable it to answer the ends of its institution": at stake was not only whether "the Revolution" was "a blessing or a curse" for Americans and "the present age" but more—"for with our fate will the destiny of unborn Millions be involved" (*W* 517–18). The "Circular" closes by invoking the deeper principles that had already informed Washington's character and statesmanship, and which he sought to impart to his country—"the immutable rules of Justice" and the civic duty to leave a "Legacy" that will be "useful to his Country." As with his later addresses, the "Circular" balances liberalism and republicanism, liberty and fraternity, human agency and belief in the transcendent. Washington bids "adieu" to "public life," and the soldier-statesman's last act is to elevate the gaze of his fellow citizens, toward a more magnanimous conduct of affairs. In an echo of Aristotle's observation that the highest honors in human affairs are devoted to the divine, Washington invokes the broad principles of natural theology but also, beyond Aristotle's theology, Biblical beliefs in Providence and virtue:

> I now make it my earnest prayer, that God would have you and the State over which you preside, in his holy protection, that he would incline the hearts of the Citizens to cultivate a spirit of subordination and obedience to Government, to entertain a brotherly affection and love for one another, for their fellow Citizens of the United States at large, and particularly for their brethren who have served in the Field, and finally, that he would most graciously be pleased to dispose us all, to do Justice, to love mercy, and to demean ourselves with that Charity, humility and pacific temper of mind, which were the Characteristicks of the Divine Author of our blessed Religion, and without an humble imitation of whose example in these things, we can never hope to be a happy Nation (*W* 524–26).[34]

It was this role as the nation's statesman that led Madison to simultaneously advocate for a constitutional convention in the Virginia legislature and to nominate Washington as a delegate. Once the convention had been called, and after lobbying by Madison, Governor Edmund Randolph, and others across the nation, Washington reluctantly agreed to be a delegate from Virginia. He placed at risk his unrivaled national prestige, his hard-earned honor and reputation, to support the Convention's success and genuine constitutional reform. Washington then sustained this drive for a newly ordered liberty not only at the Convention but in the crucial years ahead. His public statements or speeches at the Convention do not reveal his full role in the birthing of a new order. His prudent use of overt and subtle support for a constitutional revolution was indispensable, such that Madison might be asked to share the honor of fathering the Constitution. Tocqueville's analysis of the Convention praises the delegates as including "the finest minds and noblest characters that had ever appeared in the New World," and he lists "Washington, Madison, Hamilton, the two Morrises" as attending; still, he emphasizes one above all: "George Washington presided over it."[35] The larger political context reveals the importance of this largely hidden hand guiding the Constitution to life. Even though the Confederation Congress had authorized the Convention, Rhode Island's refusal to participate meant that the amendment provision of the Articles, requiring approval of all the states, would not sanction any product of the Convention. Washington's imprimatur was crucial, and he let it be known that he would attend nonetheless. He arrived weeks before a quorum formed and worked with his delegation to refine the opening salvo for reform, the Virginia Plan. Only one other delegate, Benjamin Franklin, could legitimize the Convention so much; yet it was Franklin who spoke of the propriety and necessity of electing Washington to preside. Both in symbolic and practical ways, Washington then kept the Convention and reform on track by attending every session for four months and voting on all motions; by enforcing the rather undemocratic secrecy rule that permitted — as Madison's notes reveal — extraordinarily candid deliberations; and, finally, by signing the Constitution and the letter transmitting it to Congress.

Washington also must be credited for restraint at the Convention, because his moderation bolstered the viability of its product. He could have used his prestige to enact pet ideas, especially on the single executive for which, it is widely recognized, he was the delegates' model; instead, he was careful not to abuse his authority. When he rose on the last day for a rare intervention, Madison notes that he addressed this point first: "his situation" as presiding officer "had hitherto restrained him from offering his sentiments on questions depending in the House, and it might be thought, ought now to impose silence on him." Nonetheless, in a spirit of compromise, he backed a motion to enlarge the House of Representatives to ensure a more democratic representation: "it was much to be desired that the objections to the plan recommended might be made as few as possible," and this motion was "of so much consequence that it would give him much satisfaction to see it adopted." This idea had been debated and defeated regularly in the final weeks; now it was approved unanimously, without debate.[36] A less principled man might have used such influence quite differently; a less moderate one might have felt the people were beneath his dignity and did not need more representation. Washington stood upon, and for, a principled middle ground. In the end, both sides in the ratification debate thought that his public support tipped the scales toward the Constitution's narrow victory. As Marshall put it, "had the influence of character been removed, the intrinsic merits of the instrument would not have secured its adoption" (*LGW* 325). James Monroe wrote to Jefferson that "his influence carried this government."[37] It was an era in which magnanimity counted.

MAGNANIMITY AS CONSTITUTIONAL
EXECUTIVE AND THE FAREWELL ADDRESS

Although he had pledged his reputation to perfecting the Union through constitutional reform, Washington only reluctantly assumed the office of President. His "First Inaugural Address," to "Fellow Citizens" of the Senate and House, opens by noting his "anxieties." Having been "summoned by my Country," he surrendered what had been an "immutable decision" to retire (*W* 730). Given his even more reluctant acceptance of a second term in 1792, his decisions to serve stem not only from civic duty but also from two principles he had long advocated: the executive statesmanship needed in republics, and deference to popular consent. Washington knew from the war that effective statesmanship and popular opinion did not always harmonize; during his presidency he would hazard his happiness and reputation in balancing them as he judged best for American constitutionalism.

The first inaugural address he delivered in 1789 includes many an overtone of Aristotelian ethics and politics, establishing his view that both private and civic virtue would be indispensable for the success of the nascent national government. He praised the "talents, the rectitude, and the patriotism which adorn the characters" of those elected, since such "honorable qualifications" should ensure that "no local prejudices" or "party animosities, will misdirect the comprehensive and equal eye which ought to watch over this great Assemblage of communities and interests." Thus, "the foundations of our national policy, will be laid in the pure and immutable principles of private morality," and such "preeminence" would win for free government "the respect of the world." Since "the preservation of the sacred fire of liberty, and the destiny of the Republican model of Government, are justly considered as *deeply*, perhaps as *finally* staked, on the experiment entrusted" to America, the government must abide by "the eternal rules of order and right, which Heaven itself has ordained." For "there is no truth more thoroughly established, than that there exists in the economy and course of nature, an indissoluble union between virtue and happiness, between duty and advantage, between the genuine maxims of an honest and *magnanimous* policy, and the solid rewards of public prosperity and felicity" (*W* 731–33, emphasis added). Washington closed by reiterating the humility, civility, and moderation fitting for American politics, and just as with the 1783 Circular, Biblical virtues temper classical ethics. The "benign Parent of the human race" once again favored America's "happiness" by promoting tranquil deliberations about reform of the Union, and now he hoped "this divine blessing may be equally *conspicuous* in the enlarged views—the temperate consultations, and the wise measures on which the success of this Government must depend" (*W* 732–34).

The great themes of Washington's presidency were that executive power was safe for republicanism, and that constitutional government, not populism or parties, should guide the way through domestic and foreign trials. These principles animated his speeches and deeds, including his final act of adherence to republican honor, that a republic's chief executive should not hold office for life. The Constitution he helped to fashion and ratify provided a strong keel and rudder, but the final phase of his career proves how crucial his practical wisdom, character, and adherence to constitutionalism were in guiding the ship of state past storms and siren songs. His commitment to making the Constitution work by fleshing out the powers sketched for the chief executive and the entire government still shapes our politics today, beyond his efforts to protect the republic from European powers and visionary creeds. Ideas of presidential power and of statesmanship or leadership have changed in two centuries, but Washington's principles remain a benchmark for evaluating whether these are improvements.

From the beginning he balanced republican dignity and republican simplicity in the presidency, as exemplified in the simple but formal ceremony of his inaugurations—to include supplementing the oath of office prescribed in the Constitution with "so help me God," sworn upon the Bible. This view of character was the basis for Washington's conduct amid the partisanship that rocked his presidency, offering lessons of prudence and moderation still worth pondering. The two great domestic disputes concerned national finances: first, opposition to the Bank and other parts of the economic plan devised by Treasury Secretary Hamilton; second, the protest in western Pennsylvania against the tax on distilled spirits, known as the Whiskey Rebellion. The two great foreign policy disputes involved the upheaval of the French Revolution and the radically egalitarian, antimonarchical theory France sought to impress upon the world, even upon America. Washington's two measures to protect America from such international turbulence—his 1793 Neutrality Proclamation and 1795 treaty with Britain (the Jay Treaty)—occasioned bitter partisan attacks. His policies on this range of domestic and foreign issues were remarkably consistent, informed by his view that liberty is best secured by a complex constitutionalism balancing popular consent with competent offices, and by moderation regarding the theoretical and practical temptations always haunting politics.

One example from his conduct of foreign policy bears this out. Great partisan and popular resistance arose to Washington's neutrality policy and to the treaty with Britain that prevented war with that great power, for he sought accommodation with Britain at the risk of offending the revolutionary French republic and its zealous supporters in America. He withstood charges of monarchism and of groveling to Britain, defending the policy as the best way to maintain both America's true independence and a just peace. In both his "Seventh Annual Message" (as the State of the Union address was then called) and his letter to the House rejecting their request for the Jay Treaty documents, he defended the Framers' principle that foreign policy should not bow to current popular sentiments or abstract creeds. Rather, it should be debated and formulated by the branches somewhat insulated from popular opinion, the indirectly elected Senate and indirectly elected executive. Indeed, despite his reservations about the treaty, he pressed to ratify it in part to quell partisan and popular disorder from the same sorts of local clubs that had stoked the violence of the French Revolution and the Whiskey Rebellion. The "prudence and moderation" which had obtained and ratified the treaty sought an honorable peace as the foundation for America's future prosperity and strength: having been "[f]aithful to ourselves, we have violated no obligation to others" (*W* 920–22, 930–32). Tocqueville considered this achievement particular worthy of comment in 1835, and his observation provides a striking lesson to consider for any liberal democracy in the twenty-first century:

> The sympathies of the people in favor of France were . . . declared with so much violence that nothing less than the inflexible character of Washington and the immense popularity that he enjoyed were needed to prevent war from being declared on England. And still, the efforts that the austere reason of this great man made to struggle against the generous but unreflective passions of his fellow citizens almost took from him the sole recompense that he had ever reserved for himself, the love of his country. The majority pronounced against his policy; now the entire people approves it. If the Constitution and public favor had not given the direction of the external affairs of the state to Washington, it is certain that the nation would have done then precisely what it condemns today.[38]

Perhaps the best known writing from Washington's career is his "Farewell Address" of 1796, which encapsulates and elevates the principles he had stood for during his presidency and entire career. True to his concern about demagoguery, he published the text in a newspaper, foregoing a ceremonial speech. True to his republicanism, it had no grand title, only "United States, September 19, 1796," to "Friends, and Fellow-Citizens" (another newspaper later termed it his "Farewell Address"). The harmony with his earlier writings is striking: the "Address" opens by invoking republican virtue and civic duty; patriotic devotion to the common good; gratitude to Heaven for the country's blessings and prayers for continued Providence; and the need for prudence and moderation to sustain such goods (*W*, 962, 964). Of course, it is famous in part for announcing his withdrawal from consideration for a third term and his final retirement from public life, but it also is worth study for the parting advice Washington offers to his country while affirming the principles that guided him in office. It is indispensable for studies of American politics and history, and of republicanism and statesmanship more broadly.

For the second time in a long career, Washington relinquished near-absolute power when equally ambitious yet less principled men usually have grasped for more. Such deeds, and his statements of principle about them, led his countrymen to rank him with an ancient, quasi-mythical Roman renowned for twice relinquishing absolute power once the threat to his country passed: he was the American Cincinnatus. Today, however, we tend to dismiss Washington's political testament as campaigning for the history books because, as everyone knows, James Madison and Alexander Hamilton really wrote it. As careful study of the Farewell in fact shows, Washington revised every argument or draft provided to him and made it his own.[39] Another ground for dismissing the Farewell is that more democratic voices today find a Machiavellian cunning in it and in his entire career—that Washington saw the need, in a democracy, to resign power or to pretend not to want it so as to gain greater power or glory. Confident in our rational analyses of power and interest, we miss the central lesson of the Farewell about subordinating these drives to higher principles. However satisfying these skeptical views are to some, in reality each principle in the Farewell affirms earlier deeds and statements on the same point. Such consistent dedication to liberty, constitutionalism, and moderation bespeaks a practical wisdom serving higher principles in particular circumstances. Indeed, study of Washington challenges the Machiavellianism pervading much political analysis now, for his moderation and commitment to principle made him an extraordinarily effective statesman. Such study is also indispensable for educated citizens concerned with the statesmanship that translates constitutional principles into sound policies, both domestic and foreign. This is why Tocqueville praised this "admirable letter addressed to his fellow citizens, which forms the political testament of that great man," as the basic charter of American foreign policy.[40]

The larger argument of the Farewell echoes Aristotle by more explicitly grounding the principles of liberty and constitutional order, to which Washington had devoted his career, in the moral and political virtue of moderation. Regarding political practice, moderation means that the democratic principle must be balanced by institutional complexity and space for prudent judgment in specific offices. Concern for liberty and individual rights must be balanced by commitment to the complex rule of law entrenched in the Constitution in order to distinguish liberty from license in domestic or foreign policy. Provision for special offices and talents in government must balance the commitment to equality and popular representation in order to keep the Republic on an even keel and steady course. This constitutionalism is at least neo-Aristotelian, a modern version of the mixed regime, one that works through the mechanism of separation of powers to achieve the rule of law and not of men, but which also features the character of certain offices and men in its complex balance of powers and functions. If we read *The Federalist* at all today it is for the negative, checking conception of factions (plural interests) and separated powers in numbers 10 and 51. We overlook its call in the later essays on the Senate, the Executive, and the Judiciary to foster a particular character, especially qualities of prudence and courage, that would moderate the more democratic and interest-based mechanism.[41] Indeed, it is no accident that Hamilton as Publius invokes magnanimity in expounding the theory of republican executive power embedded in the Constitution, or that Washington himself used the term, since Washington was for Publius the model of the office holder who would sacrifice popularity or honors if duty required a tough decision.[42] This complex constitutionalism is the foundation for the two most famous ideas of Washington's Farewell, his maxim "to steer clear of permanent Alliances" in our foreign policy, and his call to inculcate religion and morality in a self-governing citizenry (*W* 975).

Regarding foreign policy, many people today mistakenly confuse Washington's complex views with Jefferson's later stricture to avoid all "entangling alliances," and they mischaracterize the Farewell as launching a doctrine of isolationism.[43] In fact, Washington criticized the French Revolution and its effects in America for imposing visions and doctrines when knowledge of human nature and practical realities supported more moderate views. His view of prudence is more akin to Aristotle's than Machiavelli's, whereas we tend to side with the latter in defining it merely as self-interested calculation to rationalize expedient deeds. Washington's main principle was that a secure, independent nation must surrender to neither low interest nor abstract justice, but must balance the two. In this prudential spirit, he cites the specific circumstance of the 1790s that suggests America should be a "slave" neither to hatred of Britain nor adoration of France: "a predominant motive has been to endeavor to gain time to our country to settle and mature its yet recent institutions, and to progress without interruption, to that degree of strength and consistency, which is necessary to give it, humanly speaking, command of its own fortunes" (*W* 973, 977). If his main concern was that a nation be independent enough to act wisely and justly, his fundamental principle was to be able to "choose peace or war, as our interest guided by our justice shall Counsel" (*W* 975). He balanced a realist concern about American interests and security with a more liberal call for his nation to "[o]bserve good faith and justice towards all Nations. Cultivate peace and harmony with all. Religion and morality enjoin this conduct; and can it be that good policy does not equally enjoin it?" He cited the utilitarian maxim that "honesty is always the best policy," but he exhorted America to "give to mankind the *magnanimous* and too novel example of a People always guided by an exalted justice and benevolence" (*W* 972, 975, emphasis added). These balanced principles lie within the just war tradition of classical philosophy, Christianity, and modern natural law and international law, which developed guidelines for informing, not replacing, the prudence of statesmen. America's challenges may be different in the twenty first century given our immense power, but most would agree that our aim is still Washington's, to benefit both mankind and ourselves by respecting "the obligation[s] which justice and humanity impose on every Nation." America today seeks justice, and government by and for the citizenry, while being a global hegemon. The ancient Romans, of course, lost their republic to empire; the modern British gave up their empire to preserve the republicanism of a constitutional monarchy. These broad challenges, on top of the more particular ones of our new world of globalized technology and communication, call out for recurrence to Washington's counsels and principled prudence (*W* 977).

ARISTOTELIAN AND CHRISTIAN MAGNANIMITY, AND THE DEMOCRATIC CAVE

The very fact of Washington's Farewell Address prompted, as Brookhiser astutely notes, a generous comment from his old nemesis George III—who said that Washington's two retirements from power "placed him in a light the most distinguished of any man living," and that he was "the greatest character of the age."[44] Such testimony along with many other elements of Washington's career suggest that he embodies an Aristotelian magnanimity, and the titles of Founding Father and Cincinnatus bestowed upon him bespeak a widespread judgment placing him in the rank of the great characters chronicled by Plutarch. Still, Brookhiser notes that while Washington knew of classical virtue especially in the form of Cato the Younger, as conveyed through Addison's play (which Washington had staged during the brutal winter of 1778 at Valley Forge), there are elements of Washington's character that temper the severity of Cato's conduct toward subordinates and fellow citizens. This leads Brookhiser to reflect on the role in Washington's youthful education and mature statesmanship of the "Rules of Civility and Decent Behavior in Company and in Conversation," a work penned by French Jesuits in the sixteenth century to educate for private and political life. One of the earliest documents we have from Washington is his hand-written copy of the 110 rules, which seem to have instilled both ethical principles and an intellectual trait of clarifying the ultimate principles to guide one in any stage of life (*W* 3–10).[45]

The exhortations in the Farewell to instill religious faith as well as moral and intellectual virtue, which accord with similar references to divine guidance and higher principles throughout his career, embody this admixture of classical and Biblical or Christian virtue. Washington endorses neither a secularist wall of separation between religion and government nor the sectarian view that America is a Christian nation. Similarly, a republic should neither ignore the mutual influence between governmental and private morality nor use nocturnal tribunals to review the morals of citizens. Throughout his career, he balanced respect for Christian churches with liberal, enlightened forbearance from any coercion of belief. His "Thanksgiving Proclamation" of 1789 is an extraordinary exhortation to the citizenry, invoking piety, republicanism, religious liberty, and liberal enlightenment.[46] His letters to two minority religions in America, Jews and Roman Catholics, are meditations on the harmony between Biblical faith and the "natural rights" of peaceful citizens to pursue their own piety. A just government "gives to bigotry no sanction, to persecution no assistance" and thus transcends mere "toleration," but it should exhort citizens to "the cultivation of manners, morals, and piety."[47] As with all his major addresses, his Farewell opens and closes by invoking Providence in a manner inclusive of all believers in a transcendent deity without threatening those of other views. He balances the utility of piety and morals with genuine appreciation for them: "Of all the dispositions and habits which lead to political prosperity, Religion and morality are indispensable supports"; "A volume could not trace all their connections with private and public felicity"; just policies are "recommended by every sentiment which ennobles human Nature" (*W* 971, 972–73). These exhortations on religion, which fall just before the section on foreign affairs, confirm that the guiding spirit of the Farewell is moderation—that a higher prudence should guide domestic and foreign affairs, private and public life. He closes the Farewell by hoping that these "counsels of an old and affectionate friend" would "controul the usual current of the passions" and "moderate the fury of party spirit" (*W* 976; see also 832, 851, 924). An element of Christian Aristotelianism tempers his enlightened liberalism and classical republicanism, and suggests the mark of the "Rules of Civility" he imbibed as a youth—the last of which states: "Labour to keep alive in your Breast that Little Spark of Celestial fire Called Conscience" (*W* 10).[48]

It may be that Washington, and the Jesuit philosophy of Christian magnanimity that in part informed his character, does not repudiate but develops elements of Aristotle's conception of magnanimity.[49] Those today who stress a great disjunction between classical and Christian virtue might point to the great statesman of the last century, Churchill, who argued that leading Europeans failed to confront Hitler's designs on Czechoslovakia because of a turn toward Christian pacifism and away from sterner, more traditional conceptions of political honor.[50] The clean antithesis that Churchill draws does not account, however, for the just war tradition in Christian thought, nor for a long tradition of statesmanship, including Washington's, that sought an amalgam of classical and Christian virtue in politics. Churchill also overlooks the efforts by his contemporary De Gaulle to achieve this fusion in both theory and practice.[51] Indeed, it may be that there are seeds of this amalgam even in Aristotle's account. The magnanimous man seems haughty, but in fact is gracious, for only the vain man lords it over others. The great-souled man will not stoop to be concerned with common opinion, and he will not adjust his life to the views of others, but he will adjust his life for a friend (1124b29–1125a1). Since the books on friendship in the *Ethics* contain the first sketch of Aristotle's taxonomy of regimes, including the mixed regime that finds a role for the magnanimous few as well as for the many, it is possible that Aristotle would recognize Washington's emphasis on political friendship and civility in a modern version of the mixed regime. The paradox of late-modern or postmodern liberal democracy is that we may have more difficulty than Aristotle would in recognizing and at least appreciating—if not affirming—these not-simply-democratic elements of Washington's statesmanship and constitutionalism.[52]

As noted, Marshall's biography concludes by emphasizing the bond between a statesman's moral and intellectual virtue. He advises all "candidates for political fame" to study Washington's "sound judgment," his "incorruptible" integrity, and "the texture" of a mind that balanced "modesty" with "dignity" and "an unvarying sense of moral right" with prudence about the possible (*LGW* 465–69). Democratic republics always will look for leaders to ascend from campaigning to governing, from popularity to statesmanship. It may be more of a question whether a democratic academia and intellectual culture in the late-modern liberal democracies is willing to take seriously that need and study it.

NOTES

1. Views expressed are those of the author, not of the Air Force Academy or U.S. Government. I am grateful to Daniel Mahoney and Carson Holloway for comments on an earlier draft of this essay.

2. See Michael Beschloss, "Exclusive Excerpt: The History of 'Presidential Courage'," *Newsweek*, May 14, 2007, cover; and *Presidential Courage: Brave Leaders and How They Changed America, 1789–1989* (New York: Simon & Schuster, 2007).

3. See Herbert Storing, "American Statesmanship Old and New," in *Toward a More Perfect Union: Writings of Herbert J. Storing*, ed. Joseph Bessette (Washington, D.C.: AEI Press, 1995), 403; see *Federalist* no. 10 for Madison's arguments on the advantages of republic versus democracy for securing rights and good government, in

Alexander Hamilton, John Jay, and James Madison, *The Federalist*, ed. Robert Scigliano (New York: Modern Library, 2000), 58–59.

4. Recent works expressing a range of theoretical perspectives on this theme include Marc Landy and Sidney Milkis, *Presidential Greatness* (Lawrence, Kan.: University Press of Kansas, 2000); *The Permanent Campaign and Its Future*, ed. Norman Ornstein and Thomas Mann (Washington, D.C.: Brookings Institution Press and AEI Press, 2000); and *Leading and Leadership*, ed. Timothy Fuller (Notre Dame, Ind.: University of Notre Dame Press, 2000).

5. Beschloss, "A President's Ultimate Test," *Newsweek*, May 14, 2007, 32; the first four chapters of Beschloss' *Presidential Courage* examine Washington's unpopular decision to ratify the Jay Treaty with Britain in 1795.

6. Gordon Wood, *Revolutionary Characters: What Made the Founders Different* (New York: Penguin, 2006), 31.

7. Joseph Ellis, *His Excellency: George Washington* (New York: Random House, 2004), x, xiii, 38, 78, 271 (270–75 *passim*).

8. The *locus classicus* for diagnosing this tendency of democratic historians to eschew great figures and find only egalitarian or structural forces as significant in human affairs is Tocqueville, in "On Some Tendencies Particular to Historians in Democratic Centuries," in *Democracy in America*, trans. Mansfield and Winthrop (Chicago: University of Chicago Press, 2000), Vol. II, Part 1, ch. 20.

9. *Nicomachean Ethics* Book 4, ch. 3, 1123b26–1124a4 (magnanimity), Book 5, ch. 1, 1129b26–30 (complete justice). All translations are from the Martin Ostwald edition (Indianapolis, Ind.: Bobbs-Merrill/Library of the Liberal Arts, 1962), with some modifications. Subsequent references to the *Ethics* are parenthetical in the text of the chapter, to book, chapter, Bekker number.

10. On the ascent through the virtues, among other sources see Susan Collins, "Justice and the Dilemma of Moral Virtue in Aristotle's *Nicomachean Ethics*," in *Aristotle and Modern Politics: The Persistence of Political Philosophy*, ed. Aristide Tessitore (Notre Dame, Ind.: University of Notre Dame Press, 2002).

11. *Essays on Aristotle's Ethics*, ed. Amelie Oksenberg Rorty (Berkeley, Cal.: University of California Press, 1980).

12. This is the structure of the *Politics* in the traditional ordering of its books, but see also the argument for a different ordering in *The Politics of Aristotle*, ed. Peter Simpson (Chapel Hill, N.C.: University of North Carolina Press, 1997).

13. See Harvey C. Mansfield, "Machiavelli's Virtue" and "Machiavelli's Politics," in Mansfield, *Machiavelli's Virtue* (Chicago: University of Chicago Press, 1996), 6–52.

14. See Mary Keys, "Remodeling the Moral Edifice (I): Aquinas and Aristotelian Magnanimity," in *Aquinas, Aristotle, and the Promise of the Common Good* (Notre Dame, Ind.: University of Notre Dame Press, 2006), 143–72. See also Kenneth Deutsch's account in chapter 4 of the present volume.

15. Sharon Krause analyzes the important place for honor in Montesquieu's philosophy, including a comparison of Aristotle and Montesquieu on honor, and argues for liberalism's need to rediscover these issues in *Liberalism With Honor* (Cambridge, Mass.: Harvard University Press, 2002).

16. "Undue humility" is the translation used by David Ross, revised by J. L. Ackrill and J. O. Urmson, *The Nicomachean Ethics* (New York: Oxford University Press, 1980).

17. On this issue see also Carson Holloway's discussion in chapter 2 of the present volume.

18. On the theme of risk and greatness, and its implications for politics—including the implications of overlooking or denigrating the need to educate those inclined by nature toward taking risks and seeking greatness—see Harvey C. Mansfield, *Manliness* (New Haven, Conn.: Yale University Press, 2006).

19. Tocqueville, *Democracy in America*, Vol. II, Part 3, ch. 18, "On Honor in the United States and in Democratic Societies," and ch. 19, "Why One Finds So Many Ambitious Men in the United States and So Few Great Ambitions."

20. Carson Holloway similarly draws upon Tocqueville in reflecting upon Aristotle, in "Christianity, Magnanimity, and Statesmanship," *Review of Politics* 61 (Fall 1999): 581–604, at 597–604; he writes in response to Larry Arnhart, "Statesmanship as Magnanimity: Classical, Christian, and Modern," *Polity* 16 (Winter 1983): 363–83.

21. Tocqueville, *Democracy in America*, Vol. II, Part 2, ch. 2, pp. 482, 484.

22. Among other works see Robert Bellah, "The Quest for the Self: Individualism, Morality, and Politics," in *Interpreting Tocqueville's Democracy in America*, ed. Ken Masugi (Lanham, Md.: Rowman & Littlefield, 1991), 329–47; Peter Augustine Lawler, *The Restless Mind* (Lanham, Md.: Rowman & Littlefield, 1993) and *Democracy and Its Friendly Critics: Tocqueville and Political Life Today* (Lanham, Md.: Rowman & Littlefield, 2004); Pierre Manent, *Tocqueville and the Nature of Democracy*, trans. John Waggoner (Lanham, Md.: Rowman & Littlefield, 1996).

23. See Plutarch, *Lives of the Noble Grecians and Romans*, trans. John Dryden (New York: Modern Library, 1992), Vol. II, on Caesar, 201–203, 208, 214, 234–36; Cato the Younger, 289, 298, 302–3, 307.

24. Richard Brookhiser, *Founding Father: Rediscovering George Washington* (New York: Free Press, 1996), 11.

25. Marshall revised and compressed his multivolume study into a single volume in the final three years of his life, and this edition recently returned to print as John Marshall, *The Life of George Washington: Special Edition for Schools*, ed. Robert Faulkner and Paul Carrese (Indianapolis, Ind.: Liberty Fund, 2000).

26. Faulkner, "Foreword," *Life of Washington: Special Edition for Schools*, xxi.

27. Marshall, *Life: Special Edition*, 467.

28. Further evidence of Marshall's debt to Plutarch and a classical view of moral and political virtue arises in his analysis of Washington's generalship as a combination of two Roman characters studied by Plutarch—that Washington knew how to delay like Fabius, but also how to attack like Marcellus, both of whom fought the great general Hannibal. Marshall, *Life: Special Edition*, 467 and note 17.

29. The analysis in this section and the next draws upon my essay "Liberty, Constitutionalism, and Moderation: The Political Thought of George Washington," in *History of American Political Thought*, ed. Bryan-Paul Frost and Jeffrey Sikkenga (Lanham, Md.: Lexington Books, 2003), 95–113. Portions of that essay are used here with permission. Throughout I am indebted to the works by Marshall and Brookhiser,

and also to Glenn Phelps, *George Washington and American Constitutionalism* (Lawrence, Kan.: University Press of Kansas, 1993); Matthew Spalding and Patrick Garrity, *A Sacred Union of Citizens: George Washington's Farewell Address and the American Character* (Lanham, Md.: Rowman and Littlefield, 1996); and Robert Faulkner, "Foreword," in Marshall's *Life of Washington*, and "Washington and the Founding of Constitutional Democracy," in *Gladly to Learn and Gladly to Teach: Essays on Religion and Political Philosophy in Honor of Ernest L. Fortin, A. A.*, ed. Michael P. Foley and Douglas Kries (Lanham, Md.: Lexington Books, 2002).

30. Marshall, *Life: Special Edition*, 75. Subsequent references to this edition are cited parenthetically in the text as *LGW* with a page number.

31. In *George Washington: Writings*, ed. John Rhodehamel (New York: Literary Classics of the United States, 1997), 1106 at note 468.3. All further quotations from Washington's writings are cited parenthetically in the text as *W*, with page number; writings are quoted as in the originals, with spelling and emphases retained. Another useful one-volume edition is *George Washington: A Collection*, ed. William B. Allen (Indianapolis, Ind.: Liberty Fund, 1988).

32. Department of the Army, *Army Field Manual 1* (2005), chapter 1, at http://www.army.mil/fm1/chapter1.html.

33. Jefferson to Washington, April 16, 1784, in *Thomas Jefferson: Writings*, ed. Merrill D. Peterson (New York: Literary Classics of the United States, 1984), 791. Compare Marshall's extraordinary tribute in *LGW* 301.

34. Compare the Book of Micah 6:8, and the Gospel of Matthew 23:23.

35. Tocqueville, "History of the Federal Constitution," in *Democracy in America*, Vol. 1, pt. 1, ch. 8, 107.

36. James Madison, *Notes of Debates in the Federal Convention of 1787*, ed. Adrienne Koch (New York: W. W. Norton, 1987), 655.

37. Monroe to Jefferson, July 12, 1788, in *The Papers of Thomas Jefferson*, ed. Julian Boyd et. al. (Princeton, N.J.: Princeton University Press, 1950–), 13:352.

38. *Democracy in America*, Vol. 1, pt. 2, ch. 6, 220. Tocqueville cites Marshall's *Life of Washington* as his authority on this, quoting it at length.

39. See Spalding and Garrity, *A Sacred Union of Citizens*, 46–57.

40. Tocqueville, "The Manner in Which American Democracy Conducts External Affairs of State," in *Democracy in America*, Vol. 1, pt. 1, ch. 5, 217.

41. See Harvey C. Mansfield, "Separation of Powers in the American Constitution," in *America's Constitutional Soul* (Baltimore, Md.: Johns Hopkins Univ. Press, 1991), 104–5, 123–25, and Carrese, *The Cloaking of Power: Montesquieu, Blackstone, and the Rise of Judicial Activism* (Chicago: University of Chicago Press, 2003), 190–210, especially at 207–210.

42. Publius argues: "There are some who would be inclined to regard the servile pliancy of the Executive to a prevailing current, either in the community or in the legislature, as its best recommendation. But . . . [t]he republican principle demands that the deliberate sense of the community should govern the conduct of those to whom they intrust the management of their affairs . . . it does not require an unqualified complaisance to every sudden breeze of passion, or to every transient impulse which the people may receive from the arts of men, who flatter their prejudices to betray their

interests. . . . When occasions present themselves, in which the interests of the people are at variance with their inclinations, it is the duty of the persons whom they have appointed to be the guardians of those interests, to withstand the temporary delusion, in order to give them time and opportunity for more cool and sedate reflection. Instances might be cited in which a conduct of this kind has saved the people from very fatal consequences of their own mistakes, and has procured lasting monuments of their gratitude to the men who had courage and *magnanimity* enough to serve them at the peril of their displeasure." *Federalist* no. 71, in Scigliano edition (Modern Library), 458–59 (emphasis added, spelling as in original).

43. I discuss these issues, and the range of views on Washington's foreign and security policies, in "American Power and the Legacy of Washington: Enduring Principles for Foreign and Security Policy," in *American Defense Policy*, 8th edition, ed. Paul Bolt (Baltimore, Md.: Johns Hopkins University Press, 2005), 6–16.

44. Brookhiser, *Founding Father*, 103.

45. Brookhiser, *Founding Father*, 126–31.

46. "Thanksgiving Proclamation," October 3, 1789, in Allen, ed., *Washington: A Collection*, 534–35.

47. To Hebrew Congregation, August 18, 1790 (*W* 766–67); to Roman Catholics, March 15, 1790, in *Washington: A Collection*, 546–47.

48. See *George Washington's Rules of Civility: Complete with the Original French Text and New French-to-English Translations*, Second Edition, ed. John T. Phillips, II (Leesburg, Va.: Goose Creek Productions, 2000), 7–14.

49. See Holloway's discussion in "Christianity, Magnanimity, and Statesmanship," and also Keys, *Aquinas, Aristotle, and the Promise of the Common Good*.

50. Winston Churchill, "Preface" and "The Tragedy of Munich," from *The Gathering Storm*, vol. 1 of *The Second World War* (Boston, Mass.: Houghton Mifflin, 1949), especially the closing of the Munich chapter.

51. See Daniel J. Mahoney, *De Gaulle: Statesmanship, Grandeur, and Modern Democracy* (Westport, Conn.: Praeger, 1996).

52. Recent works addressing these broader themes, in addition to those cited earlier, include Joshua Mitchell, *The Fragility of Freedom: Tocqueville on Religion, Democracy, and the American Future* (Chicago: University of Chicago Press, 1995); Patrick Deneen, *Democratic Faith* (Princeton, N.J.: Princeton University Press, 2005), and Jon Meacham, *American Gospel: God, the Founding Fathers, and the Making of a Nation* (New York: Random House, 2006).

10

Lincoln and Biblical Magnanimity

Joseph R. Fornieri

But whoever would be great among you must be your servant.

Matthew 20:26 (RSV)

Pagan and modern critics alike have blamed Christianity for emasculating political greatness. Statesmanship, they argue, depends upon the Greco-Roman virtue of magnanimity, a disposition contrary to the Christian virtue of humility.[1] During the twilight of the Roman Empire, St. Augustine was compelled to defend Christianity from the charge that it undermined manly spiritedness. During the Renaissance, Machiavelli revisited the pagan indictment against Christianity. In contrast to pagan rites that aroused the martial imagination through the spilling of blood and burnt sacrifices, Christian practices were pacific, involving genuflection and quiet meditation.[2] They instilled the effeminate quality of idleness (*l'ozio*), stigmatized by Machiavelli as the very antithesis of *virtu*—those manly traits that enabled a prince to attain power and glory. Insofar as the Florentine praised "Christian Princes," he did so with a view to their ability (*virtu*) to exploit religion for its political utility.[3] During the Enlightenment, Rousseau added his voice to the nostalgic chorus bemoaning the eclipse of pagan greatness. Like Machiavelli, he claimed that Christianity had destroyed the social unity of the ancient polis by dividing citizens between spiritual and secular authority, between "the things of God and the things of Caesar." Indeed, Rousseau speaks for both ancient and modern critics alike when he says: "Christianity preaches nothing but servitude and dependence. Its spirit is too favorable to tyranny for tyranny not always to take advantage of it. True Christians are made to be slaves; they know it and are scarcely moved by it; this short life has too little worth in their eyes."[4]

171

To be sure, the Gospels radically challenge conventional "wisdom," both ancient and modern, about manliness and its crowning virtue of virility— magnanimity or greatness of soul. The teaching of Jesus Christ reproves the destructive self-centeredness and inordinate worldliness of both the pagan longing for glory and the modern bourgeois love of material comfort. Eschewing political honors, Jesus claimed that his "kingdom was not of this world." Unlike Socrates who conversed primarily with the budding political youth of the Athenian aristocracy, Jesus embraced the outsiders of his society—those on the political margins—women, the poor, lepers, outcasts, Samaritans. To the disappointment of some and to the incomprehension of others, the long-anticipated messiah revealed himself as a Prince of Peace, not a Warrior Prince. Testifying to this, he rode through Jerusalem on a donkey, not a chariot. Before his humiliating death, he washed the feet of his disciples, a symbolic gesture inconceivable to the likes of a Pericles, an Alexander, or a Caesar. His message was initially spread through the blood of martyrs, not by fire and sword. He taught his followers to "take up his cross"; to "turn the other cheek"; and "to love one's neighbor." Moreover, he expanded the term neighbor to include all human beings created in the image of God, not merely those of the same race or tribe. His Sermon on the Mount, the very core of Christian ethics, taught that the meek, the poor in spirit, the peacemakers, and the persecuted are blessed. Perhaps most remarkably, he taught that we should love and pray for our enemies! Turning the traditional manly virtues of self-assertion, self-sufficiency, and the spirited love of honor upside down, Jesus preached humility, dependence upon God, and the charitable love of all—outsider and enemy alike. Succinctly put, in his heavenly kingdom, "the first would be last and the last first." Can such practices be reconciled with magnanimity?

In his most recent account of manliness, Harvey C. Mansfield decries the gender neutrality of modern bourgeois society.[5] To find the true measure of manliness, he "refer[s] back to Plato and Aristotle" who "have always been the master teachers of virtue."[6] Significantly, Mansfield's otherwise excellent and important study omits the profound influence of Christianity in challenging, modifying, and even transforming our notion of virile virtue. Admittedly, his prescription of a philosophical manliness is drawn from pagan sources, as if Christianity played no role in redefining—for better or worse—ancient teachings.[7] Such a glaring omission cannot be accidental, especially to one of the foremost scholars of Machiavelli of our time, not to mention one of the most notable students of Leo Strauss, a political philosopher who spoke of "the Christian mistrust of purely human virtue, for the sake of humiliating pride in its own virtues."[8] In sum, Mansfield's silence lends credence to the ancient and modern critique that "Christianity necessarily undermines magnanimity" and is therefore "responsible for the lack of great statesmanship in the modern world."⁹

Referring back to St. Thomas Aquinas as my guide, a guide Mansfield overlooks, I seek to reveal the potential harmony between greatness of soul and humility, and to show further how these seemingly incompatible qualities are personified in the statesmanship of Abraham Lincoln. In combining these qualities, Lincoln epitomizes what may be described as a biblical magnanimity in the context of the American regime. His greatness of soul corresponds not only with Aquinas's teaching, but also with Hamilton's understanding of magnanimity in the Federalist Papers.[10]

Aquinas considers the virtue of magnanimity in Question 129 of the *Summa Theologica, II-II.*[11] As part of his wider synthesis between faith and reason, he seeks to reconcile Aristotle's conception of greatness of soul with Christian revelation. Like Aristotle, Aquinas defines magnanimity as a virtue or moral excellence concerning "great honors." Amongst "external goods," he notes, "honors takes precedence over all others." Aquinas likewise considers magnanimity to be "the ornament of all the virtues." It crowns, adorns, and displays resplendently the qualities of excellence embodied by the manly man of action.

Because "the essence of human virtue consists in safeguarding the good of reason in human affairs," the particular virtue of magnanimity "observes the mode of reason in great honors." Accordingly, for Aquinas, the virtue of magnanimity strikes the rational mean between the vicious extremes of (1) vanity, whereby one overestimates the honor due to him; and (2) smallness of soul, whereby one underestimates it. However, as will be seen, Aquinas modifies Aristotle's teaching on greatness of soul by incorporating the Christian norms of humility and charity into his understanding of magnanimity. The great souled person does not seek honor as an end in itself, but seeks to be worthy of honor insofar as he or she serves the public good and others who are in need.

Both Aristotle and Aquinas emphasize that magnanimity concerns *great honors*, in contradistinction to "ordinary honors." Aquinas states: "But with regard to great honors there is magnanimity. Wherefore we must conclude that the proper matter of magnanimity is great honor, and that a magnanimous man tends to such things as are deserving of honor."[12] Indeed, the great souled person is "intent only on great things." These are "few and require great attention." Unlike the restive activity of the small souled person who gains satisfaction in accumulating petty honors, riches, and creature comforts; the great souled person is stirred only when some momentous issue is at hand, one that is worthy of great honor. The epic task of founding or saving a regime draws him out of his self-imposed exile from mundane affairs.

To be sure, "the tending of things worthy of great honor" presumes a great ambition. This trait, for better or worse, is one of the defining features of the epic rulers in history—Alexander, Caesar, and Washington. Lincoln was no exception. William Herndon, his former law partner memorably described his colleague's ambition as "a little engine that knew no rest." In point of fact, Lincoln candidly and frequently acknowledged his own thirst for distinction. In 1832, at the age of twenty three in his first run for political office, he confessed, "Every man is said to have his peculiar ambition. Whether it be true or not, I can say for one that I have no other so great as that of being truly esteemed of my fellow men, by rendering myself worthy of their esteem."[13]

In describing his own ambition, Lincoln was inspired by the magnanimous example of his hero George Washington. In a letter dated October 26, 1788, Washington stated: "It is said that every man has his portion of ambition. I may have mine, I suppose, as well as the rest, but if I know my own heart my ambition would not lead me into public life. My only ambition is to do my duty in this world as I am capable of performing it and to merit the good opinion of all man."[14] Indeed, while there may be rival claims to the same honor, the annals of history provide no greater of magnanimity than George Washington—a fitting role model for Lincoln. Here as elsewhere, Lincoln self-consciously modeled his speech and deeds after the Founding Father.[15]

In his campaign biography of 1860, Lincoln recalled his election as Captain of Volunteers in the Black-Hawk War as a "success which gave me more pleasure than any I have had since."[16] Lincoln's greatness of soul was anticipated during his short-stint in the Black Hawk War when he intervened to save the life of an Indian scout who had stumbled into his camp. He stood up to the blood lust of his fellow volunteers who wanted to kill the Indian, perhaps as a trophy to prove that they had seen action—as yet they had not. A lesser man would have given into the rabble. Lincoln could have found cause to hate Indians since his grandfather was killed by one. A lesser man would have justified the execution to avenge family honor, as is practiced in far too many parts of the world today. Thus, at an early age he displayed the strength of character to break the vicious cycle of hatred and revenge, and the moral fortitude to confront the ugly impulses of the mob.[17]

The theme of ambition also figures prominently in Lincoln's first great speech—the *Lyceum Address* of 1838.[18] In it, Lincoln warns against the designs of a "towering genius" who would make common cause with the people to further his own ambition upon the ruins of the nation's republican institutions. Repeating Washington's admonition in the *Farewell Address,* Lincoln forewarned of a demagogue who would undermine the Union by exploiting sectional animosities for personal gain. Lincoln's description is worth quoting in full:

The field of glory is harvested, and the crop is already appropriated. But new reapers will arise, and *they*, too, will seek a field. It is to deny, what the history of the world tells us is true, to suppose that men of ambition and talents will not continue to spring up against us. And, when they do, they will naturally seek the gratification of their ruling passion, as others have *so* done before them. The question, then, is, can that gratification be found in supporting and maintaining an edifice that has been erected by others? Most certainly it cannot. Many great and good men, sufficiently qualified for any task they should undertake, may ever be found, whose ambition would aspire to nothing beyond a seat in Congress, a gubernatorial or a presidential chair; *but such belong not to the family of the lion, or the tribe of the eagle*,[.] What! think you these places would satisfy an Alexander, a Caesar, or a Napoleon? Never! Towering genius disdains a beaten path. It seeks regions hitherto unexplored. It sees *no distinction* in adding story to story, upon the monuments of fame, erected to the memory of others. It *denies* that it is glory enough to serve under any chief. It *scorns* to tread in the footsteps of *any* predecessor, however illustrious. It thirsts and burns for distinction; and, if possible, it will have it, whether at the expense of emancipating slaves, or enslaving freemen. Is it unreasonable then to expect, that some man possessed of the loftiest genius, coupled with ambition sufficient to push it to its utmost stretch, will at some time, spring among us?[19]

Is great ambition necessarily malignant? Does the thirst for distinction necessarily lead to the wellspring of despotism? Characteristic of those possessed by a longing for greatness, the towering genius will never be satisfied with the "ordinary honors" of "a seat in Congress, a gubernatorial, or a presidential chair." However, the fact that there is no outlet for his great ambition (the field of glory has been harvested) leads him to seek other, less salutary outlets for his notoriety. Without the opportunity to build up, the towering genius must tear down, resorting to the most unscrupulous means to surpass the Founders' glory.

Lincoln's reference to Alexander and Caesar in the *Lyceum Address* was no doubt influenced by his reading of Plutarch's *Lives*. Notably, Plutarch couples these two as parallel Greek and Roman lives. Indeed, it was the *unbounded ambition* of Rome's leaders that led to the bitter rivalries amongst the triumvirates, civil war, and, ultimately, the loss of the republic. The inordinate desire for honor so vividly portrayed by Plutarch is diagnosed more profoundly by St. Augustine as the *libido dominandi*—the lust for power. In contrast to the magnanimous example of Washington, Lincoln depicts Alexander and Caesar as members of the "family of the lion" and "tribe of the eagle"— "noble" yet ruthless predators with an instinct to kill and lord over others. This is the dark side of pagan manliness. And in the *Lyceum Address* Lincoln applies its lesson to the circumstances of the American republic.

Scholars have provocatively argued that Lincoln's description of the towering genius is self-referential; that he projected himself into the very role he was warning against; and that his subsequent actions during the Civil War prove that he was willing to gratify this master passion "at the expense of emancipating the slaves, or enslaving freemen."[20] Regardless of whether or not Lincoln had himself in mind when he composed the *Lyceum Address* (perhaps he was conducting a thought experiment in exploring his darker impulses), the speech nonetheless reveals a preoccupation with "the tending of things to great honor" so characteristic of magnanimity and its less noble perversion by unbounded ambition. Indeed, one detects in the youthful yearnings of Lincoln an aspiration for greatness that rivals that of the Founders and the corresponding disappointment that "the field of glory is harvested." Lincoln could not then have known that he would be confronted with the monumental task of preserving the Union, an honor that rivaled the glory of the Founding. This great and honorable deed, however, would come at an awful cost to himself and to the nation.

The theme of ambition is likewise found in Lincoln's reading of Shakespeare. In a private letter to James Hackett, a Shakespearean actor, Lincoln listed his favorite plays as follows, "Lear, Richard Third, Henry Eight, Hamlet, and especially Macbeth. It is wonderful."[21] Not surprisingly, the common denominator amongst these plays is their vivid depiction of unbounded ambition. Did Lincoln see these tragedies as mirrors that reflected his own tyrannical longings or as cautionary tales of what to avoid?

Lincoln's self-described ambition was revealed throughout his adult life as well. After he had lost a senatorial bid in 1855, he pondered:

> Twenty-two years ago Judge Douglas and I first became acquainted. We were both young then; he a trifle younger than I. Even then, we were both ambitious: I, perhaps quite as much so as he. With *me*, the race of ambition has been a failure—a flat failure; with *him* it has been one of splendid success. His name fills the nation; and is not unknown, even, in foreign lands. I affect no contempt for the high eminence he has reached. So reached, that the oppressed of my species, might have shared with me in the elevation, I would rather stand on that eminence, than wear the richest crown that ever pressed a monarch's brow.[22]

Notably, Lincoln did not publish this candid statement. Perhaps it was too revealing; for it betrays more than a hint of envy towards his political rival and nemesis—Stephen A. Douglas.

At first glance, Lincoln's self-described ambition may seem incompatible with Christian humility. To be sure, Aquinas counts both ambition and vainglory as vices that are contrary to the virtue of magnanimity. However, by ambition Aquinas does not mean the desire for honor *per se*; but rather "the inordinate love of honor."[23] Quoting the Roman historian Sallust, he explains that "the good as well as the wicked covet honors for themselves, but the one, i.e., the good, go about it in the right way, whereas the other, the wicked, through lack of the good arts, make use of deceit and falsehood."[24] Likewise, quoting *Matthew 5:16* "Let your light shine before men," Aquinas notes that "the desire for glory does not, of itself, denote a sin: but the desire for empty or vain glory denotes a sin." Glory is vain when the one who seeks glory "does not refer the desire of his own glory to a due end, such as God's honor, or the spiritual welfare of his neighbor."

Aquinas thus distinguishes the virtue of magnanimity from the vices of ambition and vainglory. In the case of the former virtue, the magnanimous man refers his gifts to God and uses them to "profit others." Aquinas explains that "a man ought so far to be pleased that others bear witness to his excellence, as this enables him to profit others." In the case of the latter vices, however, the love of honor is inordinate—that is, honor is sought as an end in itself without regard for what is truly honorable.

To appreciate more fully what is meant by the "inordinate love of honor" we can turn to no better guide than St. Augustine, who, in the *City of God,* diagnoses the Roman love of glory as a spiritual pathology rooted in sin of pride and *amor sui*—the disordered love of self that is contrary to the charitable love of God and neighbor. Indeed, Aquinas refers to Augustine throughout his discussion of vainglory. Relying on the testimony of Rome's own historians, especially Sallust, Augustine's *City of God* provides a cautionary tale of how original sin slowly yet steadily transforms an admirable yet imperfect virtue—the manly love honor—into a shameful vice—the lust for power.

Augustine rebutted the pagan charge that Christianity was responsible for the fall of Rome by revealing that the seeds of its destruction were contained in its very founding. He points to Rome's fratricidal origins. Romulus, the city's namesake, murdered his brother Remus in competition for sole dominion. "Since the goal was glory in domination," he explains, "there would of course be less domination if power was limited by having to be shared. Accordingly, in order that all power might accrue to one single person, his fellow was removed; and what innocence would have kept smaller and better grew through crime into something larger and inferior."[25] Instead of repudiating this wicked deed, the Romans shamelessly revered Romulus as a god, thereby inculcating the love of domination through their own religious cult!

The "manly" Romans coveted praise, hoping to attain some share of immortality through fame that would outlast their death. Augustine explains:

> This glory they most ardently loved. For its sake they chose to live and for its sake they did not hesitate to die. They suppressed all other desires in their boundless

desire for this one thing. In short, since they held it shameful for their native land to be in servitude, and glorious for it to rule and command, their first passion to which they devoted all their energy was to maintain their independence; the second was to win dominion.[26]

Insofar as the Romans suppressed baser lusts for the sake of glory, their actions were still somewhat admirable and deserving of praise. Without the purification of Christian humility and charity, however, Augustine warns that their inordinate love of honor was prone to degenerate into the lust for power—a greedy zeal for dominating and controlling others for its own sake. Blinded by their own pride, the pagans were scandalized by a God who revealed himself in the form of a servant and emptied himself upon a cross. This revelation of sacrificial love did not comport with *their* understanding of manly self-assertion.

Indeed, Lincoln's warning of the towering genius in the *Lyceum Address* is highly reminiscent of the African saint's critique of the Roman *libido dominandi* in the *City of God*. This is not to say that Lincoln had read the *City of God*. It is simply to note, however, the presence of an Augustinian strain of human fallibility implicit to the Calvinism that influenced both the political thought of the Founding and Lincoln.[27]

The overall tenor of Augustine's thought emphasizes the dangers implicit to a pagan manliness that is not chastened and purified by Christian humility and charity. Augustine was compelled to critique the pagan claim to worldly glory because it obscured the true heavenly glory of God.[28] While acknowledging the possibility of a great souled Christian Prince,[29] Augustine underscores the tension between the love of honor and Christianity, not to mention the utter irreconcilability between the inordinate love of glory and service to Christ. In sum, he warns of ambition's slippery slope toward pride and *amor sui*.

If Augustine focuses upon the dangers of an excessive love of honor, Aquinas (who by no means ignores these dangers) points to the hopeful possibilities of Christian greatness. Indeed, Kenneth L. Deutsch correctly explains that "Aquinas defines the meaning of the magnanimous man in such a way that Aristotle's and Augustine's positions are appropriated, altered, and transformed."[30] It is the particulars of this reconciliation and its embodiment in Lincoln that we will now explore in greater detail.

In Article Three of Question 129 on Magnanimity, Aquinas considers the objection that magnanimity cannot be a virtue since it is contrary to the virtue of humility. "[I]t belongs properly to humility," he explains, "that a man restrain himself from being borne towards that which is above him. For this purpose he must know his disproportion to that which surpasses his capacity. Hence knowledge of one's own deficiency belongs to humility, as a rule guiding the appetite."[31] The objection is based on the supposition that a virtue (humility) cannot be opposed to another virtue (magnanimity).

In response to the stated objection, Aquinas distinguishes between humility and magnanimity as different yet compatible virtues:

> There is in man something which he possesses through the gift of God; and something defective which accrues to him through the weakness of nature. Accordingly magnanimity makes a man deem himself worthy of great things in consideration of the gifts he holds from God: thus if his soul is endowed with great virtue, magnanimity makes him tend to perfect works of virtue; and the same is to be said of the use of any other good, such as science or external fortune. On the other hand, humility makes a man think little of himself in consideration of his own deficiency, and magnanimity makes him despise others in so far as they fall away from God's gifts: since he does not think so much of others as to do anything wrong for their sake. Yet humility makes us honor others and esteem them better than ourselves, in so far as we see some of God's gifts in them. Hence it is written of the just man (Ps. xiv. 4): *In his sight a vile person is contemned*, which indicates the contempt of magnanimity, *but he honoreth them that fear the Lord*, which points to the reverential bearing of humility. It is therefore evident that magnanimity and humility are not contrary to one another, although they seem to tend in contrary directions, because they proceed according to different considerations.[32]

Aquinas attributes the apparent contradiction between magnanimity and humility to their "contrary directions." That is to say, they appear to be at odds because they proceed from different considerations or standpoints. Magnanimity considers the person's worthiness of honor *in comparison to the deficiency of others*. Humility considers the agent's own deficiency *in comparison to the perfection of God*. In sum, "[h]umility restrains the appetite from aiming at great things against right reason; while magnanimity urges the mind to great things in accord with right reason. Hence it is clear that magnanimity is not opposed to humility."[33]

Thus, it bears repeating that it is not the desire for honor *per se* that is a vice; but rather the *inordinate desire* of honor that is vicious.

According to Aquinas, the desire for honor can be inordinate in three ways: "First, when a man desires recognition of an excellence which he has not; this is to desire more than his share of honor. Secondly, when a man desires honor for himself without referring it to God. Thirdly, when a man's appetite rests in honor itself, without referring it to the profit of others."[34] In the first case, the mediocre person overestimates his talent; in the second, he attributes his gifts to his own self-sufficiency without reference to God; and in the third, he ignores his charitable obligation to use his gifts to serve the insufficiency of others.

Thus understood, Aquinas makes clear that if the love of honor is not to derail into the vainglorious pride, then the magnanimous man must remember his creaturely status and must rule for the sake of the political good, not for personal ambition alone. "These two limitations on a great man's attitude toward honor," notes Deutsch, "demonstrate the importance of the Christian virtues of humility and charity as clear norms for judging the rationality of a true statesman's attitude toward the great honors that *are* his due."[35]

Moreover, to despise honors is just as wrong as to love them inordinately. Just as Aquinas counts vainglory as a vice, so he counts pusillanimity or smallness of soul as one too.[36] Both irrational excesses are counterpoised to the rational mean of magnanimity that regards honor in due proportion. The pusillanimous man "shrinks from great things out of littleness of soul."[37] This smallness of soul prevents him from serving others. By contrast, magnanimity tends "to perfect works of virtue."

Deutsch further expounds Aquinas's teaching on magnanimity as a virtue of "social and political hope":

> Through the realization of the "image of God" in the world, human persons with specific talents build up the world. Human beings are not totally wretched. Man is responsible for his good actions as well as his evil deeds. As a humble creature, man knows that his powers are gifts of God. Aquinas does not present a drama of God's grandeur as contrasted with puny man. The drama is shifted to man; it is concerned with the tension between human grandeur and limitations. Magnanimity, for Aquinas is a virtue of human social and political hope, to be realized through one's own human strength and good deeds honor must be viewed as the natural consequence of good deeds and not merely as an end in itself.[38]

A magnanimous man is worthy of honor insofar as he serves and ministers to honorable political goods that transcend his own personal ambition and reputation. This places a moral boundary upon ambition. Aquinas explains:

> Those are worthy of praise who despise riches in such a way as to do nothing unbecoming in order to obtain them, nor have too great a desire for them. If, however, one were to despise honors so as not to care to do what is *worthy of honor*, this would be deserving blame. Accordingly magnanimity is about honors in the sense that a man strives to do what is *deserving of honor* yet not so as to think much of the honor accorded by man.[39] (Emphasis mine)

Lincoln's self-described "ambition" was therefore not a vice to the extent that he acknowledged principles that were higher than his own reputation; and to the extent that he sought to be worthy of honor in the service of these principles.

Indeed, a more careful look at Lincoln's first campaign speech above, shows that consonant with Aquinas's understanding of magnanimity and

Washington's example, he sought to be "worthy" of the people's "esteem." In point of fact, his candid acknowledgments of personal ambition were consistently qualified by his commensurate fidelity to a nobler calling and a higher purpose.[40] "While pretending no indifference to earthly honors," he confessed, "I do claim to be actuated in this contest by something higher than anxiety for office." During the Lincoln-Douglas debates he reiterated the twin motives of ambition and principle:

> Ambition has been ascribed to me. God knows how sincerely I prayed from the first that this field of ambition might not be opened. I claim no insensibility to political honors; but today could the Missouri restriction be restored, and the whole slavery question replaced on the old ground of "toleration["] by *necessity* where it exists, with unyielding hostility to the spread of it, on principle, I would in consideration, gladly agree, that Judge Douglas should never be *out*, and I never *in*, an office, so long as we both or either, live.[41]

The true measure of Lincoln's magnanimity was the noble political ends for which he lived and died—namely, the preservation of the Union and the principles for which it stood. The worthy moral ends that defined the American regime were promulgated by the Declaration of Independence. Indeed, Lincoln regarded the principles of the Declaration as sacred and worthy of honor given their status as rational participations in the Divine Law that governed the universe. Accordingly, he described them in comparable terms as the nation's, "political faith," "ancient faith," "Old Faith," "the early faith of the Republic," "political religion."[42]

Lincoln was stirred to reenter public life by the momentous threat of slavery to a Union dedicated to these principles. "I was losing interest in politics," he explained "when the repeal of the Missouri Compromise aroused me again."[43] In his first notable confrontation with the Little Giant at Peoria in 1854, Lincoln proclaimed the core principles that animated his statesmanship and called for a political renewal of these founding principles: "Let us re-adopt the Declaration of Independence and with it, the practices, and policy, which harmonize with it. . . . If we do this, we shall not only have saved the Union, but we shall have so saved it, as to make, and keep it, forever worthy of the saving."[44] Notably, Lincoln demands not the preservation of any Union, but one that is "forever worthy of the saving." That is to say, a Union bound to the promise of freedom in the Declaration.

Lincoln refused to surrender this core principle even if it meant war. As a result, as president elect, he repudiated any compromise that would capitulate to the extension of slavery—most notably, the Crittenden Compromise that would have extended the Missouri Compromise line to the West. In a private letter written shortly after his election and with secession looming, Lincoln ordered his political operatives to remain firm: "Prevent, as far as possible, any of our friends from demoralizing themselves, and our cause, by entertaining propositions for compromise of any sort, on '*slavery extention*.' [sic] There is no possible compromise upon it, but which puts us under again, and leaves all our work to do over again. Whether it be a Mo. line, or Eli Thayer's Pop. Sov. it is all the same. Let either be done, & immediately filibustering and extending slavery recommences. On that point hold firm, as with a chain of steel."[45]

Before Lincoln's inauguration, seven states had seceded from the Union. In Independence Hall, Philadelphia, *en route* to the White House and under the cloud of assassination, Lincoln courageously reaffirmed his commitment to a Union pledged to the principles of the Declaration and the equality of all human beings.

> I have never had a feeling politically that did not spring from the sentiments embodied in the Declaration of Independence. I have often pondered over the dangers which were incurred by the men who assembled here and adopted that Declaration of Independence—I have pondered over the toils that were endured by the officers and soldiers of the army, who achieved that Independence. I have often inquired of myself, what great principle or idea it was that kept this Confederacy so long together. It was not the mere matter of the separation of the colonies from the mother land; but something in that Declaration giving liberty, not alone to the people of this country, but I hope to the world for all future time. It was that which gave promise that in due time the weights should be lifted from the shoulders of all men, and that all should have an equal chance. This is the sentiment embodied in that Declaration of Independence.
>
> Now, my friends, can this country be saved upon that basis? If it can, I will consider myself one of the happiest men in the world if I can help to save it. If it can't be saved upon that principle, it will be truly awful. But, if this country cannot be saved without giving up that principle—I was about to say I would rather be assassinated on this spot than to surrender it.[46]

Lincoln's desire to be worthy of honor was tempered by humility. To understand that humility, however, we must consider the biblical faith that informed his political ethics and how the corresponding Christian norms of humility and charity held his desire for honor within moral boundaries. That Lincoln was an avid reader of the Bible is beyond dispute. The sincerity and depth of his mature biblical faith has been noted elsewhere by scholars.[47] Though Lincoln eschewed formal church membership and though he inclined to skepticism as a youth—at times vacillating between belief and unbelief—he nonetheless turned to the Bible for moral guidance and spiritual solace throughout his entire life—even during the period of his youthful questioning.

Moreover, Lincoln's faith extended beyond the use of religion for mere political utility. In a letter to his friend Joshua Speed, Lincoln bears witness to the role that Providence played in their lives:

> You make a kind acknowledgement of your obligations to me for your present happiness. I am much pleased with that acknowledgement; but a thousand times more am I pleased to know, that you enjoy a degree of happiness, worthy of an acknowledgement. The truth is, I am not sure there was any merit, with me, in the part I took in your difficulty; I was drawn to it as by fate; if I would, I could not have done less than I did. I always was superstitious; and as part of my superstition, I believe God made me one of the instruments of bringing your Fanny and you together, which union, I have no doubt He had foreordained. Whatever he designs, he will do for *me* yet. "Stand *still* and see the salvation of the Lord" is my text just now.[48]

While the youthful Lincoln refers to his strong predestinarian beliefs in terms of both "superstition" and "fate," what he actually describes is likewise consistent with the Bible's description of trust in God's Providence. Lincoln describes the dynamic tension of faith as being existentially poised between the humble acceptance of God's will and an agnosticism concerning God's ultimate purpose. He thus quotes *Exodus* 14:13 to affirm his own trust in a living God who is overseeing events toward some ultimate good. Indeed, the biblical faith displayed in this early letter to Speed is consistent with Lincoln's mature articulation of his faith as President.

Notably, in the letter to Speed, Lincoln displays his self-understanding as "an instrument of God," a term he consistently used to describe his divine calling. Years later, as President, in response to the prayers of Mrs. Gurney, a Quaker woman who came to the White House in 1862 to provide him with spiritual consolation, he was moved to make the following confession of faith, one that further revealed his self-understanding as an instrument of God:

> In the very responsible position in which I happen to be placed, being a humble instrument in the hands of our Heavenly Father, as I am, and as we all are, to work out his great purposes, I have desired that all my works and acts may be according to his will, and that it might be so, I have sought his aid—but if after endeavoring to do my best in the light which he affords me, I find my efforts fail, I must believe that for some purpose unknown to me, He wills it otherwise.[49]

Lincoln's spontaneous confession of faith is also a poignant testimony of his humility before God. First, he acknowledges that all are called, albeit in different ways, to serve as "instruments of God." Second, in striving to work out God's "great purposes," he seeks God's aid. Thirdly, he avoids self-righteousness by acknowledging the gulf between the human and Divine Will. Finally, he submits to the Divine Will by accepting whatever purpose God has in store for him.

While it is beyond the scope of this essay to recount here in great detail the dynamics of Lincoln's biblical faith, it will be instructive to provide one more example of it in a subsequent private letter to Mrs. Gurney, dated September 4, 1864. Recalling their initial meeting two years past (cited above) and its spiritual import, Lincoln stated:

> I have not forgotten—probably never shall forget—the very impressive occasion when yourself and friends visited me on a Sabbath forenoon two years ago. Nor has your kind letter, written nearly a year later, ever been forgotten. In all, it has been your purpose to strengthen my reliance on God. I am much indebted to the good Christian people of the country for their constant prayers and consolations; and to none of them more than to yourself. The purposes of the Almighty are perfect, and must prevail, though we erring mortals may fail to accurately perceive them in advance. We hoped for a happy termination of this terrible war long before this; but God knows best, and has ruled otherwise. *We shall yet acknowledge His wisdom and our own error therein.* Meanwhile we must work earnestly in the best light He gives us, trusting that so working conduces to the great ends He ordains. Surely He intends some great good to follow this mighty convulsion, which no mortal could make, and no mortal could stay.[50] (emphasis mine)

The biblical faith expressed privately in Lincoln's Letter to Mrs. Gurney is further consistent with the piety expressed in other private reflections such as his *Meditation on the Divine Will*, dated Sept. 4, 1864:

> The will of God prevails. In great contests each party claims to act in accordance with the will of God. Both *may* be, and one *must* be wrong. God can not be *for*, and *against* the same thing at the same time. In the present civil war it is quite possible that God's purpose is something different from the purpose of either party—and yet the human instrumentalities, working just as they do, are of the best adaptation to effect His purpose. I am almost ready to say this is probably true—that God wills this contest, and wills that it shall not end yet. By his mere quiet power, on the minds of the now contestants, He could have either *saved* or *destroyed* the Union without a human contest. Yet the contest began. And having begun He could give the final victory to either side any day. Yet the contest proceeds.[51]

The Meditation is particularly noteworthy since Lincoln's secretaries Hay and Nicolay published it as testimony of the depth and authenticity of the President's faith. They explained that, "It was not written to be seen of men.

It was penned in the awful sincerity of a perfectly honest soul trying to bring itself in closer communion with its maker."[52]

In sum, the private writings quoted above manifest the following core elements of Lincoln's biblical faith: humble submission to the Divine Will; reliance upon a higher power; the efficacy of prayer in bringing one into closer communion with God; an affirmation of God's benevolence in the face of suffering; and an ironic contrast between human pretense and Divine omniscience.[53] Bearing witness to God's justice, Lincoln faithfully trusts in the Divine Will even though its ultimate workings are inscrutable.

As will be seen, the private expressions of humility and biblical faith in the above speeches correspond remarkably with Lincoln's public articulation of this faith in his Second Inaugural Address. Commenting upon the profundity and sincerity of Lincoln's faith, the theologian Reinhold Niebuhr observed that, "An analysis of Abraham Lincoln's religion in the context of the prevailing religion of his time and place and in light of the polemical use of the slavery issue, which corrupted religious life in the days before and during the Civil War, must lead to the conclusion that Lincoln's religious convictions were superior in depth and purity to those held by the religious as well as by the political leaders of his day."[54]

As Aquinas noted, magnanimity does not shrink from great deeds. Lincoln's manly determination to preserve the Union stands in stark contrast to James Buchanan's cowardice in allowing the Union to be dismembered. In his *Farewell Speech to Springfield* on February 11, 1861, Lincoln humbly acknowledged the great task before him while also publicly acknowledging his reliance upon Divine Providence to sustain and guide him through the impending national ordeal:

> I now leave, not knowing when, or whether ever, I may return, with a task before me greater than that which rested upon Washington. Without the assistance of that Divine Being, who ever attended him, I cannot succeed. With that assistance I cannot fail. Trusting in Him, who can go with me, and remain with you and be every where for good, let us confidently hope that all will yet be well. To His care commending you, as I hope in your prayers you will commend me, I bid you an affectionate farewell.[55]

Notably, Lincoln compares his task to that of Washington—his model of magnanimity.

With the first shots fired, secession completed, the Confederacy formed, and federal property seized, Lincoln girded the nation for war in his *Special Message to Congress* on July 4, 1861: "And having thus chosen our course, without guile, and with pure purpose, let us renew our trust in God, and go forward without fear, and with manly hearts."[56] Historian Douglas L. Wilson reveals that in the original draft of this message Lincoln wrote, "let us renew our trust in the justice of God." This was deleted in the final draft, however, which was changed to, "let us renew our trust in God." Wilson correctly infers that Lincoln did this to avoid self-righteousness. He states that Lincoln's "apparent reluctance here to claim the justice of God for his cause, which he emphatically believes is just, is a telling discrimination."[57] Put another way, this telling discrimination perfectly illustrates Aquinas's view of the reconciliation between humility and magnanimity.

Lincoln's manly determination to preserve the Union in his July 4th Address corresponds with the magnanimity displayed by Winston Churchill during the Battle of Britain to save his regime from the Nazi menace. The Union's preservation, however, required a concerted effort between its leaders, its army, and the public. Success was threatened not only by rebels on the battlefield, but also by northern antiwar Peace Democrats sympathetic to the South. These subversives were known as the Copperheads, named after a poisonous snake. At times they resorted to treasonous measures to thwart the Lincoln administration, like fomenting a breakaway Northwest Confederacy that would join the South. Lincoln referred to this threat as "the fire in the rear."[58]

The city of Baltimore, Maryland, was a hotbed of Copperhead insurgency. Before the outbreak of war, agents uncovered a plot to assassinate Lincoln in Baltimore while he was *en route* to his inauguration in Washington. After first blood was spilled at Fort Sumter, Baltimore insurgents obstructed the government's efforts to suppress the rebellion, destroying bridges and railroads that would carry reinforcements to Washington. In a statement that captures the justifiable contempt that a magnanimous man has for the pusillanimous, Lincoln chided the leaders of Baltimore for their failure to perform their duty in saving the Union:

> You, gentlemen, come here to me and ask for peace on any terms, and yet have no word of condemnation for those who are making war on us. You express great horror of bloodshed, and yet would not lay a straw in the way of those who are organizing in Virginia and elsewhere to capture this city. The rebels attack Fort Sumter, and your citizens attack troops sent to the defense of the Government, and the lives and property in Washington, and yet you would have me break my oath and surrender the Government without a blow. There is no Washington in that—no Jackson in that—no manhood or honor in that.[59]

Consciousness of one's superiority over others is yet another attribute of magnanimity displayed by Lincoln. Historian David Donald observes that, "Lincoln was not a modest man and, as John Hay astutely observed, he quite inadvertently exhibited towards [his Radical] critics an 'intellectual arrogance and unconscious assumption of superiority' that mortally offended them."[60] To be sure, Lincoln's decision as president to appoint a cabinet of talented and ambitious competitors—a "team of rivals"—further testifies to his magnanimous self-assurance.[61] A small souled insecure leader would have been threatened by such talent and would have selected "yes men" to serve him. Indeed, tyrants are notorious for surrounding themselves with sycophants and incompetents who flatter their every whim. Instead, Lincoln placed the good of the country before his ego by surrounding himself with the most talented and ambitious members of the Republican Party.

While Lincoln was conscious of his intellectual superiority over others who failed in their duty, he also was capable of great humility in putting his ego aside when it came to serving the common good of the nation. This is particularly the case with his forbearance of the continual slights and insults that he received from General George B. McClellan who contemptuously referred to the President as "nothing more than a well meaning baboon" and "the *original gorilla*."[62] Just as Lincoln placed the good of the country above his ego in terms of his cabinet selection, so he swallowed his pride when dealing with McClellan.

In one telling episode, the President, his personal secretary John Hay, and the secretary of State, William Seward, called on McClellan at his home. They had waited for some time. When the General finally arrived, he rebuffed his guests by refusing to acknowledge their presence. He then went upstairs to his bed chamber. After letting Lincoln wait for another half an hour, he sent his servant down with a note to inform the presidential entourage that he had retired for the evening. In his diary, Hay reported that, "I merely record this unparalleled insolence of epaulettes without comment. . . . Coming home I spoke to the President about the matter but he seemed not to have noticed it specially, saying it was better at this time not to be making points of etiquette and personal dignity."[63] On another occasion, "when the general failed to keep an appointment with the president. . . . After a long wait, Lincoln said: 'Never mind; I will hold McClellan's horse if he will only bring us success.'"[64] In sum, McClellan's arrogance, his incessant whining, his failure to take responsibility, his treachery in undermining the administration, and his smallness of soul in ridiculing the president, may be contrasted to Lincoln's magnanimity and his rare combination of both humility and greatness of soul.

What bearing did the virtue of humility have on the character of Lincoln's leadership? For one thing, Lincoln's humility enabled him to assess honestly his own strengths and weaknesses, allowing him to grow from mistakes. And it prevented the kind of arrogance that blinds a person to his own flaws and insufficiencies, as was the case with McClellan. Humility in politics is also opposed to self-righteousness. It eschews an ideological rigidity and a Manichean dualism that divides the world into competing camps of absolute good and absolute evil. As will be seen in the case of his Second Inaugural Address, Lincoln's humility prevented him from demonizing the South, thereby promoting national reconciliation.

In his discussion of the presidency in the *Federalist Papers*, Alexander Hamilton articulates a version of magnanimity that speaks to the unique tasks and challenges of the chief executive in a Democratic Republic. He maintains that the vitality and security of republican government requires an independent Executive. According to Hamilton, the "Executive should be in a situation to dare to act his own opinion with vigor and decision."

Hamilton capitalizes each letter of this term to emphasize its importance. The PUBLIC GOOD is not simply the will of the majority at any given moment. Such a simple equation would convert republican government into rule of the mob, a danger feared by Hamilton, and one that an independent and vigorous Executive is intended to counteract. In sum, Hamilton views the magnanimous man in a republic as one who defends the PUBLIC GOOD against the momentary impulses of the people. He reserves his highest praise for those statesmen who "saved the people from the very fatal consequences of their own mistakes"—that is, to those "who had the courage and magnanimity enough to serve them at the peril of their displeasure."[65]

As chief executive during this nation's greatest crisis, Lincoln epitomized Hamilton's description of magnanimity. Two related deeds in particular speak to Lincoln's greatness of soul in the face of intense political pressure to compromise his core principles: 1) his moral fortitude in sustaining the Emancipation Proclamation; and 2) his corresponding demand that the abolition of slavery serve as a precondition of peace and reunion with the seceded states.

The summer of 1864 was the lowest point of the war for the Lincoln administration. The Union army had stalled; Grant had suffered a string of humiliating defeats in his march to Richmond; casualties mounted—100,000 from April to August 1864. Antiwar Democrats fanned discontent over the battlefield carnage, the draft, the abridgement of civil liberties, the Emancipation, and the use of colored troops. They employed vitriolic rhetoric that pandered to the public's racial hatred and fears. The following remarks were typical of Copperhead newspapers: "In the name of freedom for Negroes [The Emancipation Proclamation] imperils the liberty of white men; to test an utopian theory of equality of races which Nature, History and Experience alike condemn as monstrous, it overturns the Constitution and Civil Laws and sets up Military Usurpation in their stead."[66] In a further effort to humiliate the Lincoln Administration, Copperheads published a pamphlet, ascribed to abolitionists, that defended the Emancipation as a means to miscegenation, or racial mixing—an idea particularly odious to the sensibilities of nineteenth century Americans.[67]

To make matters worse, Lincoln's Secretary of State, Salmon P. Chase, was scheming to replace him as presidential nominee for the Republican Party. The democrats nominated General George B. McClellan and the Copperhead, George Pendleton, as respective candidates for President and Vice President. To say the least, McClellan was hostile to black freedom. As General, he had criticized the president for issuing the Emancipation Proclamation, noting that it was illegal and warning that it would undermine the morale of the Union troops.[68] The election of McClellan and the democrats would have reversed many of the strides made toward black freedom, including the revocation of the Emancipation Proclamation.

The antiwar wing of the Democratic Party was prepared to trade victory for peace. The Copperheads reached the height of their influence during the summer of 1864.[69] As seen, they even succeeded in gaining the nomination of the Vice-President candidate, and in having one of their most notorious members, Clement Vallandigham, to write a "peace platform" for the Democratic Party.

Popular support for the Lincoln administration deteriorated to such an extent that Henry J. Raymond, the Chairman of the Republican Committee, informed the president that his chances of winning the election were poor for the following reasons: "The want of military success, and the impression in some minds, the fear and suspicion in others, that we are not to have peace in any event under this administration until Slavery is abandoned."[70]

Raymond's dire prediction reveals Lincoln's tenacity in demanding the end of slavery as a war aim and the intense public opposition to this policy at the time. Indeed, a year earlier in a letter to Republicans in Illinois, Lincoln magnanimously demanded a "peace worth the keeping"—namely, one that honored the principles of the Declaration and the promise of freedom to African-Americans. Like his understanding of the Union, Lincoln's vision of peace was qualified by "worthy" moral ends. In this same letter, Lincoln also displays a magnanimous contempt for those who "fall far from God's gifts." He has nothing but scorn for those northerners—particularly the Copperheads—whose bigotry blinded them to the heroic sacrifice of black troops for the Union cause:

> Peace does not appear so distant as it did. I hope it will come soon, and come to stay; and so come as to be worth the keeping in all future time. It will then have been proved that, among free men, there can be no successful appeal from the ballot to the bullet; and that they who take such appeal are sure to lose their case, and pay the cost. And then, there will be some black men who can remember that, with silent tongue, and clenched teeth, and steady eye, and well-poised bayonet, they have helped mankind on to this great consummation; while, I fear,

there will be some white ones, unable to forget that, with malignant heart, and deceitful speech, they have strove to hinder it.[71]

Despite Lincoln's plea for an honorable peace, the public was exhausted by war. It clamored for a return to the *status quo antebellum*, which would have restored slavery, and reversed the many strides towards black freedom. In the face of such intense political pressure, Lincoln momentarily considered, but ultimately decided against, revoking the Emancipation.

In a letter to Charles Robinson dated August 17, 1864, he reiterated his core conviction underlying his decision to uphold his policy:

> On this point, nearly a year ago, in a letter to Mr. Conkling, made public at once, I wrote as follows: "But negroes, like other people, act upon motives. Why should they do anything for us if we will do nothing for them? If they stake their lives for us they must be prompted by the strongest motive—even the promise of freedom. And the promise, being made, must be kept." I am sure you will not, on due reflection, say that the promise being made, must be *broken* at the first opportunity. I am sure you would not desire me to say, or to leave an inference, that I am ready, whenever convenient, to join in re-enslaving those who shall have served us in consideration of our promise. As matter of morals, could such treachery by any possibility, escape the curses of Heaven, or of any good man?[72]

Less than a week later on August 23, 1864, without revealing its contents, Lincoln circulated a blind memo to be signed by his cabinet. The letter, which was not to be opened until after the election, conceded defeat in the forthcoming race. Thus, Lincoln would rather suffer political defeat than commit the perfidious act of returning African-Americans to slavery, testifying to the fact that there were moral limits to his ambition. Fortuitously, Sherman's capture of Atlanta in late summer coupled with Sheridan's success in the Shenandoah turned the tide against the Democrats and ensured Lincoln's election by a landslide in the fall of 1864. By upholding "a peace worth the keeping" instead of "a peace at any price," Lincoln's statesmanship provides a fitting tribute to Hamilton's vision of magnanimity.

Lincoln's biblical magnanimity culminates in his *Second Inaugural Address*—what some have called his "greatest speech."[73] The circumstances of Lincoln's reelection are noteworthy. Lincoln had won a second term, a feat that had not been accomplished since Andrew Jackson. He had triumphed over his political opponents in the North and on the battlefield. After four years of carnage, the end of the war was near. With this context in mind, one would have expected a strong statement of personal vindication by Lincoln, rebuking his critics and proclaiming the righteousness of the Union's cause. Instead, his *Second Inaugural* shifted the entire drama of the war towards the inscrutable workings of God, the complicity of both sides, and the charitable admonition to bind up the nation's wounds. Noting the irony of each side invoking God's aid against the other, he states:

> Both read the same Bible, and pray to the same God; and each invokes His aid against the other. It may seem strange that any men should dare to ask a just God's assistance in wringing their bread from the sweat of other men's faces; but let us judge not that we be not judged. The prayers of both could not be answered; that of neither has been answered fully. The Almighty has His own purposes.[74]

Then, paraphrasing *Genesis* 3:18, Lincoln points to the manifest incompatibility between God's justice and slavery. Yet he consciously guards against self-righteousness in forbearing ultimate judgment upon the motives of the Southern people. Such judgment must be left to God.

Moreover, in what clearly shocked some in his audience, Lincoln humbly acknowledged the complicity of both North and South in the sin of "American Slavery." Neither side can claim perfect rectitude: the "prayers of both could not be answered."

> If we shall suppose that American Slavery is one of those offences which, in the providence of God, must needs come, but which, having continued through His appointed time, He now wills to remove, and that He gives to both North and South, this terrible war, as the woe due to those by whom the offence came, shall we discern therein any departure from those divine attributes which the believers in a Living God always ascribe to Him?[75]

The distinguished religious historian Mark Noll contrasts the humility and charity of Lincoln's above remarks with the self-righteousness and vindictiveness of northern clergy members. Around the same time as Lincoln's *Second Inaugural*, with the end of the war imminent, renowned preacher Henry Ward Beecher let loose the following anathema:

> I charge the whole guilt of this war upon the ambitious, educated, plotting, political leaders of the South. They have shed this ocean of blood. . . . A day will come when God will reveal judgment, and arraign at his bar these mighty miscreants. . . . Blood shall cry out for vengeance, and tears shall plead for justice. . . . And, then, the guiltiest and most remorseless traitors . . . these most accursed and detested of criminals, that have drenched in needless blood, and moved the foundations of their times with hideous crimes and cruelty, caught up in black clouds full of voices of vengeance and lurid with punishment, shall be whirled aloft and plunged downward forever and forever in an endless retribution; while God shall say, "Thus shall it be to all who betray their country"; and all in heaven and upon the earth will say, "Amen."[76]

Indeed, Lincoln's generous plan for Reconstruction may be contrasted to the more punitive plan proffered by the Radical Republicans. Recognizing that his message would not be popular with all, Lincoln defended his posture of reconciliation and humility in a letter to Thurlow Weed on March 15, 1865:

> Every one likes a compliment. Thank you for yours on my little notification speech, and on the recent Inaugural Address. I expect the latter to wear as well as—perhaps better than—any thing I have produced; but I believe it is not immediately popular. Men are not flattered by being shown that there has been a difference of purpose between the Almighty and them. To deny it, however, in this case, is to deny that there is a God governing the world. It is a truth which I thought needed to be told; and as whatever of humiliation there is in it, falls most directly on myself, I thought others might afford for me to tell it.[77]

Lincoln's letter to Weed illustrates the potential reconciliation between humility and magnanimity as understood by Aquinas. On the one hand, the Sixteenth President's scorn for those who self-righteously confuse their own will with the Divine will reflects the contempt that magnanimity has for those who are deficient in God's gifts. On the other hand, his affirmation of the ultimate inscrutability of the Divine will reflects a humility that acknowledges the distance between human deficiency and Divine perfection. Lincoln's courage to proclaim this message in the face of public outcry for vengeance against a defeated and prostrate South is yet further consistent with Hamilton's vision of magnanimity, which affirms the PUBLIC GOOD against the momentary passions of the people.

Further consonant with Aquinas's synthesis of magnanimity and Christianity, Lincoln ends his *Second Inaugural Address* with a plea for the Christian virtue of charity—perhaps the only force powerful enough to overcome hatred and revenge:

> With malice toward none; with charity for all; with firmness in the right, as God gives us to see the right, let us strive on to finish the work we are in; to bind up the nation's wounds; to care for him who shall have borne the battle, and for his widow, and his orphan—to do all which may achieve and cherish a just, and a lasting peace, among ourselves, and with all nations.[78]

In conclusion, the coexistence of both greatness and humility in the character of Abraham Lincoln reveals the potential compatibility between magnanimity and Christianity as described by Aquinas. Our admiration for Lincoln's greatness today, however, should not obscure us to the fact that he was denigrated by many in his own time. When it was revealed that *en route* to his inauguration he had entered Washington, D.C. in disguise to avoid an assassination plot, he was lampooned mercilessly by the press as a coward and a buffoon. For many, the uncouth, joke-telling, country bumpkin from Illinois paled in comparison to his Confederate counterpart—the dashing, polished, war hero Jefferson Davis. Indeed, many considered Davis to be the very embodiment of southern honor, of spirited, manly self-assertion. As a leader, however, Davis lacked both Lincoln's political skill and his humility.[79] Indeed, the presence of this latter virtue in Abraham Lincoln did not make him less of a man; it made him more of one.

NOTES

1. Larry Arnhart, "Statesmanship as Magnanimity: Classical, Christian and Modern," *Polity* 16, no. 2 (Winter 1983): 263–265; Kenneth L. Deutsch, "Thomas Aquinas on Magnanimous and Prudent Statesmanship," in *Tempered Strength: Studies in the Nature and Scope of Prudential Leadership*, ed. Ethan Fishman (Lanham: Lexington Books, 2002), 33–52; Carson Holloway "Christianity, Magnanimity, and Statesmanship, *The Review of Politics* 61, no. 4 (Fall 1999): 581–604.

2. Niccolo Machiavelli, *The Discourses*, trans. Leslie J. Walker, S. J. (New York: Penguin Books, 1987), 277–278, 139–150, 386.

3. Niccolo Machiavelli, *The Prince*, trans. Harvey C. Mansfield, Jr. (Chicago: University of Chicago Press, 1985), 88.

4. Jean-Jacques Rousseau, *Rousseau's Political Writings*, trans. Julia Conaway Bondanella (New York: Norton, 1988), 171.

5. Harvey C. Mansfield, *Manliness* (New Haven: Yale University Press, 2006), 1–21.

6. Mansfield, *Manliness*, 191.

7. The influence of Christianity in modifying pagan virile virtue has been deftly examined by the political philosopher Jean Bethke Elshtain in *Public Man, Private Woman* (Princeton, N.J.: Princeton University Press, 1981). Mansfield overlooks Elshtain's work on this subject.

8. Leo Strauss, *Spinoza's Critique of Religion* (New York: Schocken Books, 1965), 50.

9. Holloway, "Christianity, Magnanimity, and Statesmanship," 582.

10. Alexander Hamilton, James Madison, John Jay, *The Federalist Papers*, ed. Clinton Rossiter and Charles R. Kesler (New York: Mentor, 1999), *Federalist No. 69–72*: 383–408.

11. St. Thomas Aquinas, *Summa Theologica: Volume Three: II–II*, trans. Fathers of the English Dominican Province (Westminster, Md.: Christian Classics, 1981), II–II, q. 129, a. 1–8: 1721–1729.

12. Aquinas, *Summa*, II–II, q. 129, a. 2: 1723.

13. Roy P. Basler, ed., *The Collected Works of Abraham Lincoln*, 8 vols. (New Brunswick, N.J.: Rutgers University Press, 1955), 1: 8.

14. Quoted from Allen C. Guelzo, "A. Lincoln, Philosopher: Lincoln's Place in 19th Century Intellectual History," in *Lincoln's America*, ed. Joseph R. Fornieri and Sara Gabbard (Carbondale: Southern Illinois University Press, 2008) Forthcoming.

15. Ronald D. Rietveld, "Abraham Lincoln's George Washington" in *The Great Presidential Triumvirate at Home and Abroad: Washington, Jefferson, and Lincoln*, ed. William D. Pederson and Frank J. Williams (New York: Nova, 2006), 39–76.

16. Basler, *Collected Works*, 1: 9.

17. I am indebted to Professor Gabor Boritt for pointing this out.

18. Basler, *Collected Works*, 1: 108–115.

19. Basler, *Collected Works*, 1: 113–114. For a comparison between Washington's *Farewell Address* and Lincoln's *Lyceum Address* see: Joseph R. Fornieri, "Washington's Farewell Address and Lincoln's *Lyceum Address*" in *The Great Presidential Triumvirate at Home and Abroad: Washington, Jefferson, and Lincoln*, ed. William D. Pederson and Frank J. Williams (New York: Nova, 2006), 77–94.

20. Edmund Wilson, *Patriotic Gore: Studies in the Literature of the American Civil War* (New York: Oxford University Press, 1962), 108; George B. Forgie, "Lincoln's Tyrants," in *The Historian's Lincoln: Pseudohistory, Psychohistory, and History*, ed. Gabor S. Borritt and Norman O. Forness (Urbana:University of Illinois Press, 1988), 296.

21. Basler, *Collected Works*, 6: 392–393.

22. Basler, *Collected Works*, 2: 383.

23. Aquinas, *Summa*, II–II, q. 131, a. 2: 1732.

24. Aquinas, *Summa* II–II, q. 131, a. 1: 1731.

25. St. Augustine, *The City of God Against the Pagans*, trans. Philip Levine (Cambridge, Mass.: Harvard University Press), 15. 5.

26. *City of God* 5. 12.

27. John Patrick Diggins, *The Lost Soul of American Politics: Virtue, Self-Interest, and the Foundations of Liberalism* (New York: Basic Books, 1984); Ronald C. White, *Lincoln's Greatest Speech: The Second Inaugural Address* (New York: Simon and Schuster, 2002); Stewart Winger, *Lincoln, Religion, and Romantic Cultural Politics* (DeKalb: Northern Illinois University Press, 2002).

28. Thomas W. Smith, "The Glory and Tragedy of Politics," in *Augustine And Politics*, ed. John Doody, Kevin L. Hughes, Kim Paffenroth (Lanham, Md. Lexington, 2005), 187–216; R. W. Dyson, *St. Augustine of Hippo: The Christian Transformation of Political Philosophy* (London: Continuum, 2005).

29. *City of God* 5.19. John Von Heyking, *Augustine and the Politics of Longing in the World* (Columbia: University of Missouri Press, 2001).

30. Deutsch, "Thomas Aquinas on Magnanimous and Prudent Statesmanship," 41. See also chapter 4 of the present volume.

31. Aquinas, *Summa*, II–II, q. 161, a. 2: 1843.

32. Aquinas, *Summa*, II–II, q. 129, a. 3: 1724.

33. Aquinas, *Summa*, II–II, q. 161, a. 1: 1842.

34. Aquinas, *Summa*, II–II, q. 131, a. 1: 1731.

35. Deutsch, "Thomas Aquinas and Magnanimous Statesmanship," 41.

36. Aquinas, *Summa*, II–II, q. 133, a. 1–2: 1736–1738.

37. Aquinas, *Summa*, II–II, q. 133, a. 1–2: 1736–1738.

38. Deutsch, "Aquinas and Magnanimous Statesmanship," 40.

39. Aquinas, *Summa*, II–II, q. 129, a. 2: 1722.

40. This has been demonstrated by William Lee Miller in his outstanding book *Lincoln's Virtues: An Ethical Biography* (NewYork: Alfred A. Knopf, 2002).

41. Basler, *Collected Works*, 3: 334.

42. Basler, *Collected Works*, 3: 462, 2: 240, 454, 1: 112, 2: 243, 272, 3: 81.

43. Basler, *Collected Works*, 3: 511–512.

44. Basler, *Collected Works*, 2: 276.

45. Basler, *Collected Works*, 4: 151.

46. Basler, *Collected Works*, 240–241.

47. Joseph R. Fornieri, *Abraham Lincoln's Political Faith* (DeKalb: Northern Illinois University Press, 2003), 50–69; Lucas E. Morel, "Lincoln's Political Religion and Religious Politics," in *Lincoln Revisited*, ed. John Y. Simon, Harold Holzer, and Dawn Vogel (New York: Fordham University Press, 2007), 19–45; Allen C. Guelzo, *Abraham Lincoln: Redeemer President* (Grand Rapids, Mich.: William B. Eerdmans, 1999), 327; White, *Lincoln's Greatest Speech*, 128–148.

48. Basler, *Collected Works*, 1: 289.

49. Basler, *Collected Works*, 5: 478.

50. Basler, *Collected Works*, 7: 535.

51. Basler, *Collected Works*, 5: 403–4.

52. John G. Nicolay and John Hay, *Abraham Lincoln: A History*, 10 vol. (New York: Century 1890), 6: 340–42.

53. Fornieri, *Lincoln's Political Faith*, 50–69.

54. Reinhold Niebuhr "The Religion of Abraham Lincoln," in Kenneth L. Deutsch and Joseph R. Fornieri eds. *Lincoln's American Dream: Clashing Political Perspectives* (Washington, D.C.: Potomac Books, 2005), 378–392.

55. Basler, *Collected Works*, 4: 190–191.

56. Basler, *Collected Works*, 4: 441.

57. Douglas L. Wilson, *Lincoln's Sword: The Presidency and the Power of Words* (New York: Knopf, 2006), 100.

58. Jennifer L. Weber, *Copperheads: The Rise and Fall of Lincoln's Opponents in the North* (New York: Oxford University Press).

59. Basler, *Collected Works*, 4: 342.

60. David Herbert Donald, *Lincoln* (New York: Simon and Schuster, 1995), 333.

61. Doris Kearns Goodwin, *Team of Rivals: The Political Genius of Abraham Lincoln* (New York: Simon and Schuster, 2005).

62. Donald, *Lincoln*, 319.

63. Quoting from *Inside Lincoln's White House: The Complete Civil War Diary of John Hay*, ed. Michael Burlingame and John R. Turner Ettlinger (Carbondale and Edwardsville: Southern Illinois University Press, 1997, Paperback, 1999.)

64. (F. A. Mitchel to John Hay, E. Orange, N.J., 3 Jan. 1889, Nicolay-Hay MSS IHi.).

65. Hamilton, *Federalist No. 71*, 400.

66. Quoted from Weber, *Copperheads*, 64.

67. Weber, *Copperheads*, 160–161.

68. Allen Guelzo, *Lincoln's Emancipation: The End of Slavery in America* (New York: Simon and Schuster), 106–107.

69. Weber, *Copperheads*, 156–174.

70. Quoted from Weber, *Copperheads*, 158–159, 163–164.

71. Basler, *Collected Works*, 6: 406–410.

72. Basler, *Collected Works*, 7: 500–501.

73. White, *Lincoln's Greatest Speech*.

74. Basler, *Collected Works*, 8: 332–333.

75. Basler, *Collected Works*, 8: 332–333.

76. Mark A. Noll, "'Both . . . Pray to the Same God': The Singularity of Lincoln's Faith in the Civil War," *The Journal of the Abraham Lincoln Association*, 18 no. 1 (1997): 1–26.

77. Basler, *Collected Works*, 8: 356.

78. Basler, *Collected Works*, 8: 332–333.

79. Bruce Chadwick, *Two American Presidents: A Dual Biography of Abraham Lincoln and Jefferson Davis* (Secaucus N.J., Birch Lane Press, 1999); Brian R. Dirck, *Lincoln and Davis: Imagining America 1809–1865* (Lawrence, University Press of Kansas, 2001).

11

The Statesman as Great-Souled Man: Winston Churchill[1]

Will Morrisey

"In defeat, defiance; in war, resolution; in victory, magnanimity; in peace, goodwill": the ruling aphorism of Winston Churchill's *The Second World War* provides moral armature for the weakest virtue, prudence, the virtue that by itself can never dominate the passions but yet must dominate them, if human beings would survive and prosper. Churchill titles the first chapter of his memoir-history "The Follies of the Victors." At the close of the Great War "there was a deep conviction and almost universal hope that peace would reign in the world." It would have done, "easily," had "steadfastness in righteous convictions" and "reasonable common sense and prudence" prevailed. Statesmen did not lack the power to keep the peace. But they failed to use their power wisely.[2] Their wisdom failed because at the moment of victory they lacked the virtue that braces the architecture that wisdom designs—magnanimity.

Defiance, resolution, and goodwill also make prudence possible. In defeat, only defiance can prevent the soul from premature surrender. In the dark October of 1941 Churchill returned to his old school, Harrow, and told the boys, "surely from this period of ten months this is the lesson: never give in, never give in, *never, never, never, never*—in nothing, great or small, large or petty—never give in except to convictions of honour and good sense. Never yield to force; never yield to the apparently overwhelming might of the enemy."[3] Why not? Because Churchill knew from experience, shared by the British of his generation, that one does not know whether the apparent is real until the testing. "During the first four years of the last war the Allies experienced nothing but disaster and disappointment. That was our constant fear: one blow after another, terrible losses, frightful dangers. Everything miscarried." No one knew how to win the war, how it might be won, "until at the end, quite suddenly, quite unexpectedly, our terrible foe collapsed before us."[4] Without four years of defiance, prudent men then could not have exercised their prudence, but would have mistaken bad nerves for practical wisdom.[5] At the same time, defiance must not range without limits. Honor, a civilized refinement of the same spirited part of the soul from which defiance comes, and practical reason or "good sense," set limits to defiance. Defiance, honor, and reason intertwine, strengthening one another.

Resolution in war also gives prudence its chance. "Some people may be startled or momentarily depressed when, like your President, I speak of a long and hard war," Churchill told the assembled houses of the American Congress, a fortnight after Pearl Harbor. "But our peoples would rather know the truth, somber though it be." "As long as we have faith in our cause and an unconquerable willpower, salvation will not be denied us." It is true that Hitler also had faith and willpower; poised thus on the brink of the very continental nihilism he fought, Churchill immediately cited the Bible, very much staying in the Old Testament as he did so: "In the words of the Psalmist, 'He shall not be afraid of evil tidings; his heart is fixed, trusting in the Lord.'"[6] Resolution animated by trust in the cause of liberty and the strength of God gives statesmen and peoples alike the moral strength to see their real circumstances clearly and to act in the right measure.[7]

Goodwill makes prudence possible under the opposite condition, the condition of peace. This holds both for the peoples who win the war and for those who lose it, and not incidentally for their governing representatives as well. Although the victors in war should "enforce with tireless vigilance and authority the clauses of the [peace] treaty which forbid the revival of their late antagonist's military power," they should also "do all that is possible to reconcile the defeated nation to its lot by acts of benevolence designed to procure the greatest amount of prosperity in the beaten country, and labor by every means to create a basis of true friendship and of common interests, so that the incentive to appeal again to arms will be continually diminished."[8]

In ethics, circumstances matter. Prudence adjusts conduct to fit circumstances; moral actions do not consist in the rigid adherence to rules "no matter what." One writer takes Churchill's morality to resemble Machiavelli's: a prince must learn not to *be* good but rather to *use* the virtues (and the vices) for his security and well-being.[9] And Churchill does take Machiavelli's English disciple Thomas Hobbes as his guide with respect to one aspect of political life: "Integral communities," Churchill writes, "like living things, are dominated by the instinct of self-preservation," and their moral doctrines and beliefs derive from the interplay of this instinct with changing circumstances.[10] Nevertheless, the Hobbesian assessment of societies, and even of the majority of individuals within them, need not extend to all individuals. In fact

Churchill's account of defiance, resolution, goodwill, and especially of magnanimity inclines against such cynicism. Rather, the mood of defiance, the attitude of resolution, and the virtues of goodwill and magnanimity clearly come to light as ways for the human soul to *be*, not merely appearances put on in the struggle for survival and dominance. Circumstances call out each of these moral characteristics, bring each to the foreground of one's soul in its turn. The attempt to feign them or even to bring them to the foreground under the wrong circumstances (to make goodwill dominate in defeat, for example, or even in victory) will derange both war and peace.

MAGNANIMITY IN ABSENTIA: THE FAILURE OF VICTORY IN THE AFTERMATH OF THE GREAT WAR

Nowhere does Churchill illustrate this more clearly than in what may be his wisest book, *The Aftermath*, his account of the failure of the victors in the Great War to be magnanimous, and of the consequences of that failure for the ensuing peace.[11] The circumstances of the end of war brought supremacy and feebleness into tantalizing conjunction. England enjoyed "the highest position she has yet attained." "For the fourth time in four successive centuries she had headed and sustained the resistance of Europe to a military tyranny," defending the independence of the low countries on the Atlantic border of the continent from an empire-building land power. By the end of 1918 Germany and Russia could menace no one; Britain had France as an ally; the United States had reunited with its parent at least for purposes of geopolitics; the British Empire stood, more united than ever.[12] Yet "in no period of my official life . . . was public business so difficult as in those post-war years," with their turbulence and exhaustion. Beyond physical and material difficulties—great needs and opportunities without sufficient means to address them—souls wavered. "[I]t was not easy to adjust one's mind to the new dimensions. It was hard to realize that victory beyond the dreams of hope led to weakness, discontent, faction and disappointment; and that this was itself a process of regrowth."[13] At best, a new sense of war's reality prevailed; "stripped of glitter and glamour," war would no longer conjure images of conquering heroes, only of bureaucratically-managed mass slaughter.[14] Salutary as that disillusionment was, it also left the victorious peoples and statesmen morally unready to face the prospect of renewed war, and therefore in some degree helpless to prevent it.[15]

The political circumstances prevailing among the victors as their representatives met in Paris in 1919 diverged from those prevailing at the Congress of Vienna a century earlier. These political circumstances both reflected and influenced the new material and moral circumstances. The peacemakers of 1814 acted upon the shared principle of legitimacy, recognized as morally authoritative by regimes of kings and aristocrats. The peacemakers of 1919 represented the regime enemy of monarchy and aristocracy. Democracy's principle, national self-determination, had found expression in the writings of the German Romantic Johann Fichte and the Italian Mazzini long before Woodrow Wilson sought to write them into the Versailles Treaty. "During the nineteenth century the rise of Nationalism made it increasingly plain that all great Empires must reckon with this principle and increasingly conform to it, if they were to survive united and vital in the modern world. The almost complete exclusion of religion in all its forms from the political sphere had left Nationalism the most powerful molding instrument of mankind in temporal affairs."[16] The hereditary regimes of kings and aristocrats had found a moral affinity in the paternal rule of God and the fraternal rule of the churches. In Europe if not in the United States democracy found its animating moral principle in nationalism, not in the laws of nature and of nature's God. As aristocracy is to religion, democracy is to nationalism.[17]

Woodrow Wilson's Fourteen Points embodied this principle of national self-determination as the "one clear guiding principle" of international politics.[18] But how could that principle, embodied by those subordinate rules, actually rule a world in which the French wanted the coal-rich Saar district of Germany, and the Poles coveted Silesia? Was Wilson's plan "too good to be true?" Churchill asked. "Could it be a substitute for national armaments? Might it not turn out in the hour of need to be an illusion and those who had counted on it perish in some future earthquake?" Even with the exhaustion of Britain by the war, the United States might have taken on the function of "the great new balancing factor" with respect to the Continent, and so make Wilson's rules work, had Wilson not removed American forces from Germany, even before the Versailles Conference. "[N]o surge of liberal sentiment in the various countries could replace" such a military and geopolitical reality, but that reality depended upon American politics, not upon Wilson alone.[19]

David Lloyd George, Wilson, and Georges Clemenceau, "the three men at the head of Great Britain, the United States and France seemed to be the masters of the world." The elected representatives of the victorious democracies, their people "rejoic[ed] in victory and [were] inspired with gratitude and confidence for the chiefs who had led them there," and their armies and navies ranged unchallenged throughout the world. "There was nothing wise, right and necessary which they could not in unity decree." But for this they needed the virtue of the victor, magnanimity, seen in the motto of aristocratic Rome, "Spare the conquered and war down the proud."[20] Could democracies display that virtue? Could their statesmen?

Despite their many other virtues, none of the statesmen did. Wilson and Lloyd George succumbed to partisanship, Lloyd George and Clemenceau to revenge. Churchill does not much dwell upon the French prime minister, but he paints the portraits of the two English-speaking with some care.

Lloyd George by nature inclined to magnanimity. He had no vanity. His great soul did not shrink before the greatness of the task before him, this "new and perhaps more difficult phase of effort." With Churchill, he acknowledged "the great qualities of the German people," the "tremendous fight they had made against three-quarters of the world, and "the impossibility of rebuilding Europe except with their aid." When Churchill proposed immediate food relief for the Germans to prevent a bad regime change, a change toward communism, Lloyd George concurred. In the victorious "songs and cheers of the multitudes" no mass sentiments opposing such generosity could be heard.[21]

But with military victory the political unity of wartime dissolved. Political parties revived. Lloyd George's fellow Liberals resented conscription and the necessarily heavy hand with which the Prime Minister had sacked Party members who resisted his war measures. He lacked the magnanimity to include his main Party rival, Lord Asquith, in the peace delegation at Versailles, thus giving dissidents a champion who shared their disaffection. Worse, at election Lloyd George did not resist popular cries for vengeance against the Hun:

> He ought to have been more sure of himself at this time, and of the greatness of his work and situation. He could well have afforded, as it turned out, to speak words of sober restraint and magnanimous calm. . . . He tried his best. His speeches soon fell far behind the popular demand. On two occasions, one a great meeting of women, he was almost howled down.[22]

Newly enfranchised, enraged at the losses of husbands and sons at German hands, the women of England were the newest democrats. The masses of women and men alike now pulled against any display of the aristocratic virtues.

Lloyd George expected to dilute the popular passion for revenge by appointing, as he put it to Churchill, "the ablest men we can find, men not mixed up in politics or electioneering," to an Inter-Allied Commission assigned to settle the issue of war reparations. "[T]hey will examine the whole matter coolly and scientifically, and they will report to us what is feasible," thus giving democratic statesmen a plausible story to tell their constituents. That is, Lloyd George would have replaced the magnanimity of departed aristocrats with the expertise of technocrats. In practice this failed because the experts couldn't agree; their social science could not establish even "so elementary a point as the ability of the defeated nations to pay."[23] The new aristocracy of knowledge, more compatible with democracy than the old aristocracy of virtue and of birth, foundered on the waters of intellectual disputation.

More prudently, Lloyd George also saw a political solution. "What does it matter what is written in the Treaty about German payments? If it cannot be carried out, it will fall to the ground of its own weight." Meanwhile, the multitude will have their emotional satisfaction, and "we must let them all calm down."[24] In the event, they did, although what placated the English scarcely impressed the Germans as magnanimous, and that impression would contribute to a sour peace.

In response to British proposals for continued German political unity under a new, democratic regime, mild reparations, and an Anglo-American defense guarantee, Clemenceau "suggested that Lloyd George's magnanimity was achieved exclusively at the expense of France and the continental States, while England had received all the advantages and securities which were of interest to her."[25] The German population would double that of France in a generation. Mutual defense treaties had not protected Belgium; faith in progress and in democracy would prove a weak reed; without Russia as a threat to Germany on the east, Anglo-American guarantees (even if real) would fail; the League of Nations would prove useless, as would disarmament.[26] With such *Realpolitik* objections in hand, Clemenceau demanded a *Realpolitik* solution: French possession of the Rhineland. But such a territorial acquisition could not redirect German souls to peace, only to dreams of revenge. In the event, Clemenceau gave up on the Rhineland, but American rejection of the treaty ended the Anglo-American military guarantee and the French seizure of the Saar brought on German *revanchism* anyway, a few years later.[27]

Wilson lacked magnanimity altogether. He had served usefully during the war itself, "coming to the struggle fresh and cool," like "an impartial judge," "appear[ing] to the tortured and toiling combatants like a messenger from another planet sent to the rescue of freedom and justice here below." His Fourteen Points declaration "played an important part in holding the Western Democracies firmly and unitedly to the prosecution of the war, and also encouraged defeatist and subversive movements among the enemy populations" by appealing to pacifists and nationalists alike.[28] In war, defined narrowly as American military actions once they finally arrived in Europe and before the Armistice, Wilson did have resolution.

In victory, however, Wilson faltered. His proposal to abolish the right to conduct naval blockades during wartime and to end British naval superiority would have weakened the democracies' real capacity to enforce any peace settlement. More damagingly, he wrangled with his fellow-statesmen among the allies abroad and (as early as the mid-term elections of 1918) with his partisan enemies at home, in both cases assuming that he could appeal to public opinion over the heads of the representatives of the people. At the same time, he chose to participate in the peace conference along with (mere) prime ministers, putting himself on the level of men who were not heads of state. His lack of magnanimity, of the fine alloyage of elevation and helpfulness the great-souled man embodies, disabled him at the very summit of victory.[29] His "sense of personal superiority," whereby he supposed he understood 'what the people wanted,' made him a democrat of a decidedly odd sort, replacing the magnanimity of aristocratic *noblesse oblige*, which might animate an elected statesman, with the vanity of democratic partisan *leadership*, most particularly a leadership that claims to head not only the movements of a party but the very march of History itself.[30]

> His gaze was fixed with equal earnestness upon the destiny of mankind and the fortunes of his party candidates. Peace and goodwill among all nations abroad, but no truck with the Republican Party at home. That was his ticket and that was his ruin, and the ruin of much else as well. It is difficult for a man to do great things if he tries to combine a lambent charity embracing the whole world with the sharper forms of populist party strife.[31]

Democratic peoples, "though very resolute and persevering in war, knew nothing whatever about how to make a just and durable peace."[32] Wilson lost valuable time in negotiating over the peace treaty with his peers in his ill-conceived opinion-leadership efforts in Europe.[33] And, like Lloyd George, he did not bring opposition party senators with him to Versailles, despite the majority Republicans had in both houses of Congress. This small-souled omission cost him the chance of Senate ratification when he brought the peace treaty home.

Wilson in effect tried to go from the resolution of wartime (a resolution, Churchill knows all too well, that came rather late in the war) immediately to the goodwill of peacetime. The magnanimity needed in victory did not exist in the soul of the man whose spirit animated the conference and its treaty.[34]

Churchill's portraits of these statesmen of the Great War also portray, in their backgrounds, the relation of magnanimity to the regime problem. Magnanimity obviously finds a home in aristocratic regimes. It is less evidently at home in a democracy, but that is where prudence comes in. As a politician in a republic, Churchill distanced himself from the pretensions of conventional aristocrats. Campaigning for the House of Commons in 1909 he chaffed Lord Curzon for saying that all civilization has been the work of aristocracies. "Why, it would be much more true to say the upkeep of the aristocracy has been the hard work of all civilizations," he jibed, to the laughs and cheers of the crowd. But in the middle of his fun Churchill slipped another thought in: by aristocracy Curzon meant hereditary aristocracy, the rule of barons and earls, not "Nature's aristocracy, by which I mean the best and most gifted beings in each generation in each country, the wisest, the bravest, the most generous, the most skilful, the most beautiful, the strongest, and the most active."

That is "democracy properly understood"—"the association of all through the leadership of the best."[35] What Churchill means by democracy Aristotle would classify as a mixed regime consisting of aristocracy and democracy.

This notwithstanding, the contrast between the Conference of Vienna and the Conference of Versailles shows the superiority of the aristocratic regime in conditions of military victory. In 1814 the defeat of the politically tyrannical and socially democratic French regime left France exhausted; the aristocratic victors "had the physical power to impose their will." The 1919 victors, politically and socially democratic shared the weakness of the defeated. The diplomats of 1814, aristocrats "life-trained as statesmen or diplomatists, utterly wearied of war and hating change, met together in elegant and ceremonious privacy to reestablish and fortify, after twenty years of tumult, a well-understood conservative system of society." The statesmen of 1919, "orators and mass leaders," had "balanced themselves precariously upon the unsure shifting platform of retrenchment, and acted in conditions of publicity unknown since the ancient Greek polis. The democracy of 1919 substituted national fears and passions animating mass political parties for aristocratic deliberation and calm.[36]

Without proposing to abandon the democratic regime, Churchill insists that institutional safeguards, peopled by the relatively new quasi-aristocracy of businessmen, could moderate the democratic temper. He points to the British Munitions Council, responsible for demobilizing national industries after the war.

> The able business men among us, each the head of a large group of departments, had now been working for a year and a half in a kind of industrial cabinet. They were accustomed to unexpected changes enforced by the shifting fortunes of war. Four or five of them, representing the departments involving any project, would put their heads together in an intimate and helpful manner; and in a very few hours—or at most in a few days—orders would be given which worked smoothly downwards through innumerable ramifications.[37]

No scientific administration of technocrats, here, and no need for anything so grand as magnanimity. But this is the sort of institutional support that a statesmanship of magnanimity "at the summit" could put to use in order to secure victory.

The democratization or "massification" of warfare brought even more political democratization after the war. War veterans and women won the right to vote and in Britain the franchise expanded from eight to twenty millions. With the Liberal Party now split between the Lloyd George and Asquith segments, the Conservative Party saw its chance, and both sides appealed to the passions the war had fanned.

> Every cottage had its empty chair. Hatred of the beaten foe, thirst for his just punishment, rushed up from the heart of deeply injured millions. . . . In my own

constituency of Dundee, respectable, orthodox, life-long Liberals demanded the sternest punishment for the broken enemy. All over the country the most bitter were the women, of whom seven millions were for the first time to vote. In this uprush and turmoil state policy and national dignity were speedily engulfed.[38]

Such slogans as "Hang the Kaiser," "Abolish conscription," and "Make the Germans pay" (although the ruined Germans could not pay), appealing as they did to such popular passions, carried representatives far from the magnanimity victory requires.

Despite this, Churchill calls it "fatal" to "swerve" from popularly-elected government, "the only sure foundation for a State." The British Constitution remains "the most thorough and practical mechanism yet devised in the modern world for bringing the force of public opinion to bear upon the conduct of affairs." "This was a testing time, if ever there was one, for the renowned sagacity and political education of the British Democracy." The British people did better than most, but not well enough.[39]

Churchill illustrates what might have been done better by what he actually did as head of the War Ministry. Knowing that "the fighting man has a grim sense of justice, which it is dangerous to affront," Churchill proposed, as demobilization measures: a) that soldiers be released from service in accordance with length of service and age; b) that soldiers pay be more than doubled, so that those who remained in the ranks would not so sharply envy those who returned to civilian jobs; c) that the 80,000 new draftees continue in service. Churchill successfully defended these policies by appealing to a "democratic" and indeed "middle-class" passion, namely, the unwillingness to be cheated. "Unless we are to be defrauded of the fruits of victory and, without considering our Allies, to throw away all that we have won with so much cost and trouble, we must provide for a good many months to come Armies of Occupation for the enemy's territory."[40] These policies showed good results in "a very few days," and soldiers peacefully "resumed their civil status."[41] No military-populist English Bonaparte could arise to exploit resentment in the ranks or among the returning veterans. Years later, more than a year into the second Great War, Churchill could tell the American Congress, "I was brought up in my father's house to believe in democracy," and "have been in full harmony all my life with the tides which have flowed on both sides of the Atlantic against privilege and monopoly, and I have steered confidently towards the Gettysburg ideal of 'government of the people by the people for the people.'"[42] A politics of magnanimity can survive the regime change from the aristocracies of 1814 to the democracies of 1919 and 1941, against the militaristic monarchies of the first war and the tyrannies of the second. But the democracies won't have it easy.

Specifically, the statesmen of 1919 had before them a set of policies, animated by magnanimity yet consistent with the democratic regime. First, the

League of Nations rightly understood "not as a Super-State but as a Super-Function above all the valiant and healthful nations of the world." The League's "super-functions" would include exclusive control of air forces and of chemical weapons, with states retaining control of armies and navies. Airplanes and chemical weapons have no boundaries, so "a new instrument of human government would be created to wield them." The air squadrons would revive, in effect, "the old Orders of chivalry like the Knights Templar and the Knights of Malta to guard civilization against barbarism." They would give the League "the purpose of maintaining world peace against aggression." As for the fliers themselves, "let these be the new nobility," not the war profiteers.[43] The international character of the old warrior aristocracies, thus renewed, would give scope to magnanimity in the modern world.

The allied troops still under arms should have overthrown the Bolshevik regime in Russia, which did not "represent Russia." The Russian people themselves could then have elected a national assembly, embarking upon genuine democracy. The defeated German soldiers should have shared in this effort, with German civilians assisting in the economic and political rebuilding of Eastern Europe. This policy would have amounted to the truest "reparation," setting German souls on the course of economic and political freedom for themselves by making them think about how to obtain it for others. A similar enlargement of souls would have occurred in the Allied camp, if Britain and the United States had guaranteed the defense of France against any future German ambitions.[44] For "it is characteristic of a great-souled person to ask for help from no one, or only reluctantly, but to assist others eagerly, and to be highhanded toward those of high station or good fortune, but moderate toward those of a middle station."[45]

As for monetary reparations, the Allies should have calculated them on the basis of the principle of "equality of sacrifice" of blood, treasure, and territory, with territorial gains rated high in order to offset burdensome monetary payments. "Much has been destroyed that can never be repaired, but if we all stand together the burdens even on the vanquished need not be very great. We will have a world banknote on the double security of Victory and Reconciliation."[46] To insist on high monetary reparations fixed the souls of victors and vanquished alike on the lowest form of justice, sanctioning materialism not magnanimity.

Magnanimity in victory never emerged after the Great War. The minds of statesmen had concentrated on surviving and winning the war, and had little chance to consider the aftermath of war. Germany's sudden collapse made even rudimentary preparation for peace impossible. More subtly, while the necessary curtailment of ordinary democratic politics during the war elevated the wartime statesmen in the minds of their peoples, such elevation could not last long. "Wilson, Clemenceau and Lloyd George were soon to follow into retirement or adversity the Kings and Emperors they had dethroned. . . . The war of the giants has ended; the quarrels of the pygmies have begun."[47]

"To write this is not to blame peoples or their leading men," Churchill writes, magnanimously contradicting what he clearly suggests elsewhere. Both modern *states* as centralized, mass political societies and the *regime* of democracy as instituted, quite recently, in such societies had yet to achieve the necessary levels of prudence or of magnanimity required to be victorious well. "The American populace fell as far short of their Chief [Wilson] in disinterested generosity to the world, as the peoples of the Allied countries exceeded their own leaders in severity to the enemy." Insofar as the peoples thought and felt practically, they thought "of nothing so much as reunion, and building up again the home, the business, the old life." Insofar as they thought and felt more widely, they had nothing but "vague, general ideas, some harsh, some noble," none of them steady.[48] Democratic public opinion finds distraction in events themselves—always another crisis, real or imagined; in the "high ideals" statesmen like Wilson propose, hoping to take advantage of the propensity of the democratic mind for generality; and in the sheer busy-ness of the commercial-democratic way of life.[49] Characteristic of democracy, such traits also threaten it. "The Parliaments erected so hopefully by the nineteenth century were already, over a large part of Europe, being demolished in the twentieth. Democracy, for which the world was to be made safe by the greatest of struggles, incontinently lets slip or casts aside the instruments of freedom and progress fashioned for its protection by rugged ancestors," men of undemocratic regimes.[50] "Modern forces are so ponderous and individual leaders relatively so small, so precariously balanced, so frequently changed; the collective life moves forward so irresistibly, that too much vitality or perseverance or coherent policy should not be counted on from large communities."[51]

Thus the virtues of prudence and magnanimity require consideration of the regime question under conditions of modern statism and social egalitarianism, including the geopolitical conditions of modern Europe. "For four hundred years the foreign policy of England has been to oppose the strongest, most aggressive, most dominating Power on the Continent, and particularly to prevent the Low Countries falling into the hands of such a Power." To join with such a "military tyrant, whoever he was, whatever nation he led," must have been easy and tempting, but Britain under both aristocracy and democracy had preferred a regime of liberty, for themselves and for the continental nations as well.[52] To really settle the matter would require a lasting entente between France and Germany, and that would require regime change in Germany. In 1919 the Allied statesmen effected such change, but botched the job.

Wise policy would have crowned and fortified the Weimar Republic with a constitutional sovereign in the person of an infant grandson of the Kaiser, under a council of regency. Instead, a gaping void was opened in the national life of the German people. All the strong elements, military and feudal, which might have rallied to a constitutional monarchy and for its sake respected and sustained the new democratic and parliamentary processes, were for the time being unhinged. The Weimar Republic, with all its liberal trappings and blessings, was regarded as an imposition of the enemy. It could not hold the loyalties or the imagination of the German people.[53]

The regime problems facing the founders of German republicanism were straightforward. What to do with the aristocracy? How could the military elements of the regime, in particular, find institutional expression of their virtues, turn from vengefulness to patriotism and magnanimity? And what to do with the people, who had been "long brought up under paternal despotism, tempered by far-reaching customs of free speech and parliamentary opposition"? After the defeat, democracy brought liberty and with it the factionalism that is to liberty as air is to fire.[54]

Biennial parliamentary elections subjected these new democrats to "febrile political excitement and ceaseless electioneering." But the parliament was only a façade.

Behind the veneer of republican governments and democratic institutions, imposed by the victors and tainted with defeat, the real political power in Germany and the enduring structure in the post-war years had been the General Staff of the Reichswehr. They it was who made and unmade presidents and cabinets. They had found in Marshall Hindenburg [German head of state from 1925 to 1934] a symbol of their power and an agent of their will.[55]

They eventually chose Hitler as Hindenburg's successor. A hereditary monarch might have prevented this slide into tyranny by reversing the lines of respect and of authority—making it ascend upward from the military to the head of state rather than downward from the military to the head of state. Meanwhile, the German people, resentful of the reparations clauses imposed at Versailles, might have relented when the British and Americans quietly failed to enforce payments. But because "this apparently magnanimous process was still accompanied by the machine-made [that is, newspaper-inspired] howlings of the unhappy and embittered populations in the victorious countries, and the assurances of their statesmen that Germany would be made to pay 'to the uttermost farthing,' no gratitude or good will was to be expected or reaped."[56]

"If we could only weave Gaul and Teuton so closely together economically, socially, and morally as to prevent the occasion of new quarrels, and make old antagonisms die in the realization of mutual prosperity and interdependence, Europe would rise again."[57] Without magnanimity in victory, and therefore without prudence in the design of the peace settlement, Europe fell, instead, back into tyranny and another Great War.

MAGNANIMITY PREVAILING? THE AFTERMATH OF THE SECOND GREAT WAR

"How the great democracies triumphed, and so were able to resume the follies which had so nearly cost them their life": in calling attention to a failure of prudence the epigraph to the final volume of *The Second World War* more than suggests another failure of magnanimity, potentially more disastrous than the first.[58] In the event, the aftermath of the second battle in what Churchill often called the Thirty-Years' War between Germany and the Allies turned out much better than he expected. Churchill carefully prepared for such a result; his preparations had military, economic, and political dimensions.

In wartime, magnanimity should recede in favor of resolution. It should not disappear. In November 1942, Churchill rose in Parliament to praise German Field Marshall Erwin Rommel. "We have a very daring and skilful opponent against us, and, may I say across the havoc of war, a great general." Although some were offended, saying that no virtue in an enemy leader ought to be recognized, Churchill dismissed such complaints as a churlish "streak in human nature," one "contrary to the spirit in which a war is won or a lasting peace established."[59] More generally, the military end of unconditional surrender "in no way relieves the victorious Powers of their obligations to humanity, or of their duties as civilized and Christian nations." Churchill recalls the ancient Athenians who "overpowered a tribe in the Peloponnesus which had wrought them great injury by base, treacherous means" but nonetheless "forgave them and set them free," saying "This was not because they were men; it was done because of the nature of Man."[60] The great-souled man bears no grudges;[61] he can hold out genuine peace to a defeated rival, making surrender unconditional but neither disastrous nor even dishonorable.[62] The ancient Romans understood this, too. While "the moral principles of modern civilization seem to prescribe that the leaders of a nation defeated in war shall be put to death by the victors," this only "stir[s] them to fight to the bitter end in any future war"; "Julius Caesar followed the opposite principle, and his conquests were due almost as much to his clemency as to his prowess."[63]

Lack of magnanimity with respect to economic policies had helped to wreck the peace settlement of 1919, and Churchill moved to prevent a recurrence as early as the summer of 1941. In a radio broadcast from London, he rejected any postwar attempt "to ruin German trade"; "it is not in the interests of the world and of our two countries that any large nation should be unprosperous or shut out from the means of making a decent living for itself and its people by its industry and enterprise."[64] In the event, after more than three years of bitter warfare, Churchill wavered, at first opposing U. S. Treasury Secretary Henry Morgenthau's plan to restrict postwar the postwar German economy to agriculture, then agreeing to it at the second Quebec conference of Allied statesmen in September 1944.[65] A few months later he told the House of Commons that he endorsed the elimination *or control* of German *military*-industrial production, a position of more moderation and magnanimity. "Our policy is not revenge; it is to take such measures as may be necessary to secure the future peace and safety of the world."[66] He consistently opposed heavy postwar reparations, against the punitive instincts of Roosevelt and Stalin.[67]

Politically, Churchill insisted on the importance of *regimes* and of the "spiritual and moral ideas" that underlie them. In 1938 he told Americans, "People say we ought not to allow ourselves to be drawn into a theoretical antagonism between Nazidom and democracy; but the antagonism is here now."[68] After the war, pinpointing "no worse mistake in public leadership than to hold out false hopes soon to be swept away,"[69] he called for liberal-democratic regime change throughout the undemocratic nations of Europe but admitted—indeed insisted—that such nations often would require "authoritarian government" first, in order to prevent "anarchy."[70] Again realistically, he denied the feasibility of near-term democratization for nations with no experience at all in it: "I am a bit skeptical about universal suffrage for the Hottentots even if refined by proportional representation," he wrote to President Eisenhower, who had been sending him anticolonial literature.[71] But he did not restrict his support for republican self-government to the nations within Western civilization. He demanded "the revival and strengthening of democratic tendencies among the Japanese people," those tendencies including freedom of speech, of religion, of thought, and "respect for fundamental human rights"—all as part of the unconditional surrender of the military oligarchy to the Allies.[72] In politics magnanimity required not only military sternness blended with mercy in victory, and not only economic policies of generosity to the defeated, but also the founding of *enduring* republics in the nations of the enemy. These parts of Churchill's approach succeeded in the 1950s even as they had failed—never having been adequately implemented—in the aftermath of the previous war. However, the post-1945 settlement left the Russian regime untouched, and now the Soviet Union rivaled America and surpassed Britain. "Sombre indeed would be the fortunes of mankind if some awful schism arose between the western democracies and the Russian

Soviet Union," he told the House of Commons shortly after his meeting with Roosevelt and Stalin at Yalta in February 1945.[73] But magnanimity required of Churchill first of all that he not bend to pressures from his left at home and in the United States from those who wanted to pretend that the Soviets were democrats, too. Tyranny or "totalitarianism" amounts to nothing more than "a swindle democracy" based on "violence or terrorism" rather than "reason or fair play, on freedom, on respecting the rights of other people."[74]

At the Yalta Conference in February 1945, Churchill needed to exercise magnanimity in several ways, with respect to the regime question. He publicly overlooked persistent American suspicions that he wanted merely to establish monarchies not republics, and to maintain the British Empire above all else—that his endorsement of republicanism amounted to camouflage for Tory authoritarianism. More interestingly, he attempted to appeal to the tyrant Stalin as well as to the democrat Roosevelt, precisely in terms of magnanimity and democracy. At dinner on February 8 he reminded his peers that "Nations, comrades in arms, have in the past drifted apart within five or ten years of war. Thus the toiling millions"—the very ones in whose names both Stalin and Roosevelt made their claims to political authority—"have followed a vicious circle, falling into the pit, and then by their sacrifices raising themselves up again." Military conquest is "glorious, but there are greater conquests before us": the conquests of peace, conquests over "poverty, confusion chaos, and oppression."[75] Churchill, who had opposed Bolshevism from its beginning, knew very well that Stalin would not define "oppression" as he and Roosevelt did, but he could hope that Roosevelt and Americans generally might be brought round to seeing that more clearly.[76] To put the matter in Churchillian terms, even had Stalin accepted "magnanimity" as a moral category—which, as a Marxist-Leninist, he would not—in his mind the war continued. The real war, the war between the international social classes of capital and labor, had a long way to go. "Resolution," not magnanimity, remained for him the order of the day, and Stalin, like Hitler, had nothing if not resolution.[77] Knowing this, in response to a visit from former U.S. ambassador to the Soviet Union and arch-fellow traveler Joseph E. Davies, Churchill insisted:

> Except in so far as force is concerned, there is no equality between right and wrong. The great causes and principles for which Britain and the United States have suffered and triumphed are not mere matters of the balance of power. They in fact involve the salvation of the world.[78]

In the struggle for a world divided, as Tocqueville had foreseen, between "American" social equality under commercial republicanism and "Russian" social equality under tyranny,[79] the magnanimous man could find scope enough for his soul's work.

A STATESMANSHIP OF MAGNANIMITY

Democracy might save the world. But the regime of democracy also threatened itself, and therefore promised to fail to save the world. "[T]he structure and habits of democratic states"—their institutions and their ways of life—"unless they are welded into larger organisms, lack those elements of persistence and conviction which can alone give security to humble masses"; the structural and habitual elements of the democratic regime prevent their rulers (the third element of any regime) from pursuing any policy "for even ten or fifteen years at a time."[80] As seen in Churchill's account of the aftermath of the first Great War, democratic institutions and habits require statesmen to think not magnanimously, but in terms of petty calculations of electoral advantage.

Throughout his life, but especially prior to the second war, Churchill looked to a British empire of self-governing dominions as that entity which gave magnanimity its due, even in the service of modern democracy. "Only at the summit of a world power"—specifically, the "civilizing empire" of Great Britain—"can the truly great-souled man, that 'supreme combination of the King-Warrior-Statesman,' realize his full potential."[81] More than anyone, Churchill knew and felt the decline of the Empire. He also saw ways in which a great-souled statesman might still flourish, even without the Empire as it had been.

As in 1919, the end of the war ended "the sole bond of union" between communist Russia and the Western democracies, namely, "their common enemy." This called for a new geopolitical strategy: clear identification of the Soviet Union as "a mortal danger to the free world"; the establishment of "a new front" against its expansion, as far east as possible; the identification and control of Berlin, Czechoslovakia, and Austria as the crucial military and strategic chokepoints on the map of Europe; counter of communist Yugoslavia ambitions in Italy; "above all" settlement of "all major issues between the West and the East in Europe *before the armies of democracy melted* [with U. S. transfer of troops into the Asian theater of operations], or the Western allies yielded any part of the German territories they had conquered."[82] Churchill lacked nothing in realistic assessment of Soviet military and political power, bluntly offering Stalin wartime control of Rumania and Bulgaria, with equal great-power sway in Yugoslavia and Hungary at his one-on-one conference with Stalin in Moscow in October 1944.[83] Had this deal actually prevailed and continued into peacetime, the postwar Soviet empire would have been smaller. Had the atomic bomb not worked, the Soviet empire would have been larger yet.[84]

At Yalta Churchill temporized. Poland, at the center of northern Europe, then and later proved crucial to the geopolitical settlement. Churchill called for "a gesture of magnanimity" by the Soviets to this "much weaker power."[85] Counting his troop strength there, Stalin demurred. This time, not the victorious democracies but the victorious tyranny most signally failed the test of greatness. The following year, Churchill could then go to America itself, with full if tacit approval of the Truman Administration, and use the Soviet choice to dominate Poland (and indeed all of central and eastern Europe "from Stettin in the Baltic to Trieste in the Adriatic") as evidence of "totalitarian control" behind a geopolitical "Iron Curtain." The threat Stalin launched convinced Americans to keep troops in Europe and to agree to a "fraternal association of the English-speaking peoples," a "special relationship between the British Commonwealth and Empire and the United States," leading perhaps to "common citizenship" in the future. Such an association might save the Empire, providing continued institutional scope for a British statesmanship of magnanimity and give real weight to the proposed United Nations organization.[86] Although much of this proved unrealistic, America did stay in Europe and Poland, Czechoslovakia, and other Soviet dominions eventually punished Stalin's successors for his failure to be a great-souled man.

To hasten that punishment, Churchill made two complementary speeches in Europe. In September 1946 he addressed Zurich University, holding out the prospect of "a kind of United States of Europe" of "three or four hundred million people"—that is, with or without Russia. To do this, an act of magnanimity will be needed. "[T]here must be an end to retribution" and a reconciliation of nationalities. "The first step in the re-creation of the European family"—he meant the Europe "once united" as "the fountain of Christian faith and Christian ethics"—"must be a partnership between France and Germany. In this way only can France recover the moral leadership of Europe. There can be no revival of Europe without a spiritually great France and a spiritually great Germany" at the core of a federal system that would respect nationality while curbing nationalism. "Can the free peoples of Europe rise to the height of these resolves of the soul and instincts of the spirit of man?"[87]

The following May, in London, Churchill renewed this call. "This task of reconciliation requires on the part of France, which has suffered so cruelly, an act of faith, sublime in character; but it is by this act of faith and by this act of faith alone that France will regain her historic position in the leadership of Europe." Although Christianity had provided pre-nationalist Europe with faith and ethics, the Roman Empire had provided it with a political structure. "We hope to reach again a Europe purged of the slavery of ancient days in which men will be as proud to say 'I am a European' as once they were to say 'Civis Romanus sum.'" A United States of Europe would serve as "the urgent and indispensable step" towards the realization of "some effective World Super-Government," which, at this time, Churchill advocated as a restraint upon the lethal mixture of nationalism and nuclear weaponry.[88] Such a government would satisfy democrats' Hobbesian desire for self-preservation while giving scope of action for the statesman of magnanimous soul.

In the event, no World Super-Government or United States of Europe or formal reunion of Great Britain and the United States proved necessary to avoid nuclear war for the balance of Churchill's century, or to defend the regime of republicanism. The international institutions that Truman's men designed kept American troops and American investments in Europe, facing down the Soviet Union until its empire collapsed and its regime changed (if not much for the better). Crucially, the magnanimous statesmanship of de Gaulle of France and Konrad Adenauer of West Germany brought peace and prosperity to Western Europe. In acting as Churchill would have done with respect to one another they vindicated the life work of Winston Churchill.

NOTES

1. I am indebted to my colleague Robert Eden for his careful reading of this chapter.

2. Winston S. Churchill: *The Second World War* (Boston: The Houghton Mifflin Company, 1949–53), Vol. I: 3. Churchill first formulated this motto in 1919 for a French town that asked for an inscription for a war memorial. The townspeople rejected the motto, Martin Gilbert explains: "Magnanimity in victory was not a theme popular in France, or indeed in Britain, in 1919" (Martin S. Gilbert, "In Search of Churchill's Character," in *Statesmanship: Essays in Honor of Sir Winston Churchill,* ed. Harry V. Jaffa [Durham: Carolina Academic Press, 1981], 13). Democracy poses challenges even and perhaps especially to the magnanimous statesman.

3. Speech at Harrow, October 29, 1941, in *Never Give In! The Best of Winston Churchill's Speeches,* ed. Winston S. Churchill (New York: Hyperion, 2003), 307.

4. Speech in the House of Commons, June 18, 1940, in *Never Give In,* 228.

5. During the Second World War Churchill admired Charles de Gaulle, despite "his arrogant demeanor." "There he was—a refugee, an exile from his country under sentence of death, in a position entirely dependent upon the good will of the British Government, and also now of the United States. The Germans had conquered his country. He had no real foothold anywhere. Never mind; he defied all. Always, even when he was behaving worst, he seemed to express the personality of France—a great nation, with all its pride, authority, and ambition." (*The Second World War,* Vol. V: 682). And in the end de Gaulle proved right, taking the opportunity of victory and peace to refound French republicanism, to reconcile with a newly-republican German regime, and to make France again significant, if not quite great, in Europe and in the world.

6. Speech to the United States Congress, December 26, 1941, in *Never Give In,* 319. For the morally bracing effect of Churchill's resolution on the democrats who fought the war on the battlefield, see Isaiah Berlin, *Mr. Churchill in 1940* (Boston: Houghton Mifflin Company, 1949), 27–30. "This is the means by which dictators and

demagogues transform peaceful populations into marching armies," but "it was Mr. Churchill's unique and unforgettable achievement" to do so "within the framework of a free system without destroying or even twisting it."

7. As Manfred Weidhorn puts it, Churchill dealt prudently with "the adversary": "He knew the wisdom of Talleyrand's maxim. . . . 'Not too much zeal.' No matter how much his policy may whip up public sentiment against the enemy, a wise leader knows better. After all, he may have to negotiate peace some day with that same enemy."(Weidhorn, "A Contrarian's Approach to Peace," in *Statesmanship*, 34). This separates the statesman Churchill from the tyrant Hitler, whose resolution served his own *libido dominandi*.

8. *The Second World War*, Vol. I: 42–43. In the years after the Great War the victorious allies put their own disarmament, the dismantling of their powers of enforcing the disarmament of the vanquished, ahead of those acts of goodwill that might have brought the vanquished to reconciliation. This is goodwill mistimed and misplaced. Both unquestionable victory and reconciliation are indispensable.

9. See Weidhorn, in *Statesmanship*, 51. He has in mind Niccolo Machiavelli, *The Prince*, chapter 15.

10. Winston S. Churchill, *The Aftermath* (New York: Charles Scribner's Sons, 1929), 289–290.

11. For a fine and succinct account of *The Aftermath* see James W. Muller, "The Aftermath of the Great War," *Churchill as Peacemaker*, ed. James W. Muller (Cambridge: Cambridge University Press, 1997). Churchill first attempted to implement his principle, "In victory, magnanimity," while serving in the Colonial Office in the aftermath of the Boer War. British revenge on the Boers would only drive them to further resistance; better to "make it easy for the enemy to accept defeat" (Churchill quoted in Weidhorn, in *Statesmanship*, 27; see also 39).

12. *The Aftermath*, 1–2.

13. *The Aftermath*, viii. "The pageant of victory unrolled itself before the eyes of the British nation," but "too much blood had been spilt. Too much life essence had been consumed. The gaps in every home were too wide and empty. The shock of an awakening and the sense of disillusion followed swiftly upon the poor rejoicings with which hundreds of millions saluted the achievement of their hearts' desire" (3).

14. *The Aftermath*, 479.

15. See Berlin, *Mr. Churchill in 1940*, 7–9.

16. *The Aftermath*, 208–209.

17. Compare Alexis de Tocqueville, *Democracy in America*, trans. Harvey C. Mansfield and Delba Winthrop (Chicago: The University of Chicago Press, 2000), 519, on the need of democratic regimes to "preserve [religion] carefully as the most precious inheritance from aristocratic centuries."

18. *The Aftermath*, 209.

19. *The Aftermath*, 147–149.

20. *The Aftermath*, 5–6.

21. *The Aftermath*, 4–5.

22. *The Aftermath*, 37.

23. *The Aftermath*, 155.

24. *The Aftermath*, 157. See also Churchill's eulogy in the House of Commons, March 28, 1945, in Churchill, *Never Give In*, 378–381.

25. *The Aftermath*, 201.

26. *The Aftermath*, 222–223.

27. *The Aftermath*, 485.

28. *The Aftermath*, 98–99.

29. See Aristotle, *Nicomachean Ethics,* trans. Joe Sachs (Newburyport: Focus Publishing, 2002), 1124b.

30. *The Aftermath*, 112, 121, 142.

31. *The Aftermath*, 125.

32. *The Aftermath*, 125.

33. Nowhere did this loss of time tell so calamitously as in Russia. It took the Allied statesmen six months to arrive at a policy vis-à-vis the Bolshevik regime. Both Lloyd George and Wilson urged a peace treaty with the Bolsheviks but "the dominant elements of public opinion, both in Great Britain and in France" opposed this. By the time the statesmen settled on a course of action they were too late. See *The Aftermath*, 172 and 186.

34. In the great tyrant and repudiator of Versailles, V. I. Lenin, Churchill sees an equal lack of magnanimity and also a (consequent?) misreading of and vanity concerning public opinion. Unlike Wilson, the Soviet tyrant partook not of goodwill but of Clemenceau-like vengeance. Lenin combined the worst of Wilson and Clemenceau; like Wilson, he imagined that he and his party allies "could appeal by wireless telegraphy to the peoples of every warring state over the heads of their governments." *The Aftermath*, 64–65, 72. Both Wilson and Lenin conjured democracy in their own (very different) self-images, and their incantations equally failed.

35. "The Upkeep of the Aristocracy," speech at Burnley, December 17, 1909, in *Never Give In*, 38. Even as Lenin exhibited the danger of democratic tyranny, Hitler exhibited the danger of a sort of tyrannical pseudo-aristocratism. Hitler embodied the aristocratic warrior-principle gone mad, resolution unbridled by moderation, prudence, or honor, murderously attacking the foreign. See Churchill, *The Second World War*, Vol. I, 55–56.

36. *The Aftermath*, 116–117. The British corporate oligarchy had in fact emerged in part from the old landed aristocracy, and some of the "old" virtues remained; see Michael Mann, *The Sources of Social Power* (Cambridge: Cambridge University Press, 1993) II, 101–102.

37. Mann, *The Sources of Social* Power, 19.

38. Mann, *The Sources of Social Power,* 28–29.

39. Mann, *The Sources of Social Power*, 49–50. For an insightful discussion of Churchill and the regime question see Kirk Emmert, *Winston S. Churchill on Empire* (Durham: Carolina Academic Press, 1989), 45.

40. Emmert, *Winston S. Churchill on Empire*, 43–45. Churchill here followed the line of Benjamin Franklin, who taught that statesmen could guard normally-pacific commercial republican peoples against pacifism by appealing to the business man's fear of being cheated; see Will Morrisey: *A Political Approach to Pacifism* (Lewiston: The Edwin Mellen Press), Vol. 1: 7–9.

41. Emmert, *Churchill on Empire*, 53, 55.

42. Speech to the United States Congress, December 26, 1941, *Never Give In*, 317.

43. *The Aftermath*, 8, 11–12.

44. *The Aftermath*, 9–10.

45. *Nicomachean Ethics*, 1124b.

46. *The Aftermath*, 10.

47. *The Aftermath*, 13–17.

48. *The Aftermath*, 124–125. Compare Alexis de Tocqueville, *Democracy in America*, II, ii, chapter 3; by Churchill's time, Europe had begun to be "Americanized"— that is, democratized, with the *moeurs* of democratic life, including the penchant for general ideas.

49. *The Aftermath*, 390–391. Compare Tocqueville, *Democracy in America*, Volume II, part one, chapter 3.

50. *The Aftermath*, 484.

51. *The Aftermath*, 437.

52. Speech to the Conservative Backbench Foreign Affairs Committee, House of Commons, March 1936, in *Never Give In*, 125.

53. *The Second World War*, Vol. I: 11.

54. *The Second World War*, Vol. I: 26. See Publius, *The Federalist* No. 10 (Dubuque: Kent/Hunt Publishing Company, 1990), 44.

55. *The Second World War*, Vol. I: 58.

56. *The Second World War*, Vol. I: 9.

57. *The Second World War*, Vol. I: 28.

58. For a careful exegesis of the epigraph and of the sixth volume generally see Robert Eden, "History as Postwar Statecraft in Churchill's War Memoirs" (paper delivered at conference, "Churchill and the Postwar World," sponsored by The Woodrow Wilson Center and the International Churchill Society, at The Smithsonian Institution, Washington, D.C., May 1996).

59. *The Second World War*, Vol. IV: 67.

60. Speech in the House of Commons, January 18, 1945, in *Never Give In*, 370.

61. Aristotle, *Nicomachean Ethics*, 1125a.

62. Churchill, Speech in House of Commons, January 18, 1945, *Never Give In*, 371. With respect to allies, Churchill similarly pressed for the inclusion of the Free French forces in the advance into and occupation of Germany. See Warren F. Kimball, *Churchill and Roosevelt: The Complete Correspondence* (Princeton: Princeton University Press, 1984), 391.

63. *The Second World War*, Vol. VI: 631. Churchill acted in much the same way in fighting the Greek leftists who launched a civil war against British troops and rival Greek militias in Athens, after the Germans were defeated. Because "the establishment of law and order in and around Athens is essential to all future measures of magnanimity and consolation towards Greece," the "treacherous aggressors" must be crushed, even as the parties negotiated a political solution, brokered by the moderate Greek Orthodox Archbishop Damaskinos Papandreou. See *The Second World War*, Vol. VI: 288, 292, 297, 314–16.

64. Churchill, Radio Broadcast from London, August 24, 1941, in *Never Give In*, 301.

65. See *The Second World War*, Vol. VI: 156–157; Kimball, *Correspondence*, 316.

66. Speech to the House of Commons, February 27, 1945, *Never Give In*, 375.

67. See for example Kimball, *Correspondence*, 528.

68. "The Defense of Freedom and Peace: An Address to the People of the United States of America," October 16, 1938, in *Blood, Sweat and Tears* (New York: G. P. Putnam's Sons, 1941), 73.

69. *The Second World War*, Vol. IV: 61.

70. Churchill, Speech to the House of Commons, August 16, 1945, *Never Give In*, 409.

71. Letter to Dwight Eisenhower, August 8, 1954, in *The Churchill-Eisenhower Correspondence, 1953–1955*, ed. Peter C. Boyle (Chapel Hill: University of North Carolina Press, 1990), 167. Or, as Tocqueville puts it more positively: "The states where citizens have enjoyed their rights longest are those where they know best how to make use of them." *Democracy in America*, 229.

72. *The Second World War*, Vol. VI: 642–644.

73. Speech to the House of Commons, February 27, 1945, in *Never Give In*, 378.

74. Speech to the House of Commons, December 8, 1944, quoted in *The Second World War*, VI. 293–295. More than half a century later it is hard to recall the moral atmosphere of the 1930s and 1940s—which lasted among some democrats in the West for decades to come—which excused rough and even tyrannical practices by regimes of the "left"; this failure of memory makes it increasingly harder to see the moral and political courage it took for Churchill to say such things in Parliament and elsewhere at the time he said them.

75. *The Second World War*, Vol. VI: 362.

76. That Roosevelt did not see this clearly may be seen in his comment to his son in 1945: "Maybe the Russians will get strong in Europe. Whether that's bad depends on a whole lot of factors." Elliot Roosevelt, *As He Saw It* (New York: Duell, Sloan and Pearse, 1946), 185.

77. Even during the war itself, Churchill never lost sight of the distinction between resolution in wartime and magnanimity in victory. Christopher C. Harmon well remarks Churchill's resolution: "Once engaged in war . . . Churchill often sounded like Clausewitz, calling for the maximum use of force. He could be ruthless. He used, advocated, or at least considered fearsome weapons: gas, air bombing, the atomic bomb. When he believed a war was just, his strategy was to break the enemy will and produce complete and decisive victory. Christopher C. Harmon, "Wartime Questions to Postwar Answers: Riddles of War Termination," *Finest Hour: The Journal of Winston Churchill*, no. 129, (Summer 2005): 14.

Contrast this with the much-quoted exchange at the Tehran Conference of November 1943, when Stalin, "perhaps in mischief" (as Churchill recalls it), proposed the postwar execution of 50,000 German military officers and technicians. Roosevelt went along with the joke, if that is what it was, by recommending a "mere" 49,000. Churchill walked out in indignation: "I should rather be taken out into the garden here and now and be shot myself than sully my own and my country's honor by such infamy." *The Second World War*, Vol. V: 373–374. In mentioning honor he appealed to the same limitation he had commended to the boys at Harrow, as cited above. In battle, Churchill would not have hesitated to seek the destruction of every German officer, if that would hasten victory, but in victory itself magnanimity must replace such recourse to the terrible resolution of the swift sword. Churchill seems to have been especially disturbed at the president's son, Elliott, who went along with the patter; the next generation above all must eschew vengefulness.

78. *The Second World War*, Vol. VI: 579. See also 420–421. Churchill had begun to prepare public opinion for this eventuality as early as 1941; this time, unlike 1919, "the United States and Britain do not now assume that there will never be any more war again." Radio broadcast from London, August 24, 1941, *Never Give In*, 301.

79. Tocqueville, *Democracy in America*, 395–396.

80. *The Second World War*, Vol. I: 17–18. On the three elements of political regimes—the *politeia* or institutional structure, the *politeuma* or ruler(s), and the *bios ti* or way of life, habits of mind and heart, see Aristotle, *Politics* 1278b, 1295a.

81. Emmert, *Churchill on Empire*, 62.

82. *The Second World War*, Vol. VI: 456–457; italics in original. See also 569–570. At Yalta Roosevelt had already told Churchill *and Stalin* that the United States "would take all reasonable steps to preserve peace, but not at the expense of keeping a large army in Europe, three thousand miles away from home. The American occupation would therefore be limited to three years." *The Second World War*, Vol. VI: 353. See also Churchill's "Iron Curtain" telegram to President Truman in May 1945. *The Second World War*, Vol. VI: 573–574.

83. *The Second World War*, Vol. VI: 227–228. At the same conference Churchill also held out an honorable way for Stalin to turn back from expansion, recalling Stalin's declaration against regime change "by force or by Communist propaganda" in the Balkans, citing the dissolution of the Comintern as "a decision by the Soviet Government not to interfere in the internal political affairs of other countries," and, finally, an early version of what later writers would call "convergence theory"—that "viewed from afar and on a grand scale, the differences between our systems will tend to get smaller," anyway. *The Second World War*, Vol. VI: 232–233.

84. *The Second World War*, Vol. VI: 602; see also 639.

85. *The Second World War*, Vol. VI: 367.

86. "The Sinews of Peace," Fulton, Missouri, March 5, 1946, *Never Give In*, 418–419. The motto of this celebrated speech might have been, "In peace goodwill, but with sinews." For several excellent commentaries on the Fulton address see *Churchill's "Iron Curtain" Speech Fifty Years Later*, ed. James W. Muller (Columbia: University of Missouri Press, 1999). For an astute assessment of Churchill's dealings with Roosevelt, Truman, other leading Americans, as well as his writings addressed to the American people generally, see Eden, "History as Postwar Statecraft in Churchill's War Memoirs." Eden particularly notices what Churchill called "Roosevelt's great error" in failing to keep Vice-President Truman fully apprised of American foreign policies, military and civil, leaving President Truman initially unprepared to direct policy in a firm and timely way for several crucial months after Roosevelt's death. It might be added that this was a failure of magnanimity as well as of prudence—a new twist

on Lloyd George's failure to take Asquith into his confidence at the end of the first war, and on Wilson's somewhat more understandable failure to take his leading party rivals into his confidence in the aftermath of that war.

87. Churchill, Address at the University of Zurich, Zurich, Switzerland, September 19, 1946, *Never Give In*, 427–428.

88. Speech in London, May 14, 1947, *Never Give In*, 440–443.

Index

Abbey, Ruth, 124
Adenauer, Konrad, 214
Alexander of Macedon, 10, 172, 174–75
ambition, 10, 34–35, 39, 43, 46n12, 49,
  55, 94, 100, 102–03, 125, 148, 152,
  154, 161, 174–78, 180–81, 187,
  190–91, 206, 212, 214n5
Andronicus, 45n2
Appel, Frederick, 124
Aquinas, Thomas, 6, 24, 49–63, 87, 95,
  128n34, 133–34, 141, 149, 173,
  176–80, 185–86, 192; *Summa*
  Theologica, 58, 173
aristocracy, 4, 8, 58, 75, 95, 97, 172,
  200–01, 203–04, 207–08, 216n36
Aristotle, 1–2, 4–5, 7–8, 13–27, 29–32,
  35–39, 41–47, 49–50, 52, 54–55,
  59–60, 67, 69, 71, 81, 83–90, 93, 97,
  101–02, 107–08, 109–10, 112–16,
  120–23, 125, 125n1,126n4, 126n17,
  127n19, 127n24, 128n29, 128n34,
  133, 141, 147–53, 156, 161–62,
  164–65, 166n15, 167n20, 172–73,
  178, 204; *Eudemian Ethics*, 18;
  Nicomachean Ethics, 1, 5, 13–27, 29,
  41, 43, 45n2, 97, 107n2, 110, 112,
  114, 125n1, 147–49, 151–52, 165;

Poetics, 110; *Politics*, 18, 26, 43,
  45n2, 60, 114, 149
Arnhart, Larry, 46n12, 113
Arnold, Benedict, 154
Asquith, Herbert Henry, 201, 204,
  220n86
Athens, 22, 172, 209, 217n63
Atticus, 45
Augustine, 49, 51–52, 54, 59, 171, 175,
  177–78; *City of God*, 177–78

Beecher, Henry Ward, 191
Beschloss, Michael, 146
Bible, 30, 95–96, 159, 182–83, 191, 198
Bolt, Robert, 136
Brookhiser, Richard, 152, 163
Buchanan, James, 185

Caesar, Julius, 6, 10, 30, 34–35, 43, 61,
  120, 124, 147, 152, 154, 172,
  174–75, 209
Calvinism, 178
Carthage, 40
Catherine of Aragon, 135
Catholic Church, 135, 140
Cato the Younger, 152, 163
Celsus, 51

221

About the Editor and Contributors

Paul Carrese is professor of political science at the U.S. Air Force Academy and director of the Scholars Program, a Great Books honors program. He earned a doctorate at Boston College, and has been a Rhodes Scholar and a research fellow at Harvard University; in 2007–2008 he will be a Fulbright Scholar lecturing in political theory at the University of Delhi, India. He coedited John Marshall's *The Life of George Washington: Special Edition for Schools* (2001), and is author of *The Cloaking of Power: Montesquieu, Blackstone, and the Rise of Judicial Activism* (2003) and of articles on Montesquieu, Tocqueville, republicanism, constitutionalism, modern judicial power, and George Washington.

Jeffrey Church is a Ph.D. candidate in the Department of Political Science at the University of Notre Dame, where he is completing a dissertation on the concept of the individual in the thought of Hegel and Nietzsche. He recently published articles on Hume and the "Selfish System" in the *Journal of Politics* and Nietzsche and Socrates in the *History of Political Thought*.

Kenneth L. Deutsch is professor of political science at SUNY Geneseo. He has taught at Geneseo for thirty-five years. He has published numerous books on issues ranging from political obedience and resistance to the state, Indian and American political thought, constitutional rights and liberties, and three book projects assessing the political teachings and intellectual influence of Leo Strauss, one of the twentieth century's great political philosophers. He is an avid opera fan and collector. Over the past forty years he has collected thousands of records and CDs of live performances of opera and recorded vocal concerts. He reads books on religion and philosophy for fun.

James Fetter is a graduate student specializing in political theory in the University of Notre Dame's Department of Political Science. He is a Phi Beta Kappa graduate of Emory University where he majored in classics and political science and graduated with highest honors in classics. His work on the Cicero chapter in this volume is a part of his current thematic study of magnanimity in the thought of selected philosophers in the Western tradition.

Joseph R. Fornieri is associate professor of political science at The Rochester Institute of Technology. He is the author of *Abraham Lincoln's Political Faith* and several other works on Lincoln. He was the 2002 recipient of the Eisenhart Award for excellence in teaching. His most recent book, *An Invitation to Political Thought*, coedited with Kenneth L. Deutsch, is a textreader of the epic political philosophers in Western civilization and includes contributions from some of the most respected scholars in the field. Professor Fornieri lives in Fairport, New York, with his wife Pam and their two daughters, Isabella and Natalie.

Carson L. Holloway is assistant professor of political science at the University of Nebraska at Omaha. In 2005–2006 he was a William E. Simon Visiting Fellow in Religion and Public Life in Princeton University's James Madison Program in American Ideals and Institutions. His books include *All Shook Up: Music, Passion, and Politics* and *The Right Darwin? Evolution, Religion, and the Future of Democracy*. He is currently at work on a book on the thought of John Paul II and modern political philosophy. He lives in Omaha with his wife, Shari, and daughters Maria, Anna, Elizabeth, Catherine, and Jane.

Peter Augustine Lawler is Dana Professor of Government at Berry College. He is also executive editor of the scholarly quarterly *Perspectives on Political Science* and a member of the President's Council on Bioethics. His most recent book is *Homeless and at Home in America* (2007).

Will Morrisey is William and Patricia LaMothe Chair in the United States Constitution and associate professor of political science at Hillsdale College. He is the author of *Self-Government, The American Theme: Presidents of the Founding and Civil War*, as well as studies of Charles de Gaulle and Andre Malraux. He has served as an assistant editor of *Interpretation: A Journal of Political Philosophy* since 1979.

Walter Nicgorski is professor in the Program of Liberal Studies and concurrent professor in the Department of Political Science at the University of Notre Dame. His publications include essays on Cicero, liberal and character education, the American founding, Leo Strauss, and Allan Bloom. They have appeared in such journals as *Political Theory*, *Interpretation*, and *The Political Science Reviewer*, as well as in various thematic collections of essays. He is a contributor to and coeditor (with Ronald Weber) of *An Almost Chosen People: The Moral Aspirations of Americans* (1977) and (with Kenneth Deutsch) of *Leo Strauss: Political Philosopher and Jewish Thinker* (1994). He is former chief editor of *The Review of Politics* (1994–2004).

James R. Stoner Jr. is a professor in and the chair of the Department of Political Science at Louisiana State University. He is the author of *Common-Law Liberty: Rethinking American Constitutionalism* (2003) and *Common Law and Liberal Theory: Coke, Hobbes, and the Origins of American Constitutionalism* (1992), as well as numerous scholarly articles and essays. In 2002–2003 he was a visiting fellow in the James Madison Program in American Ideals and Institutions at Princeton University. He served from 2002 to 2006 on the National Council on the Humanities, to which he was appointed by President Bush.

Geoffrey M. Vaughan is associate professor of political science at the University of Maryland, Baltimore County (UMBC). Most of his scholarly efforts have focused on the philosophy of Thomas Hobbes, but he is currently working on two book-length projects on citizenship and political education. The first is a study of modern philosophy's turn to democracy; the second is a personal reflection on whether to become an American citizen.

Catherine H. Zuckert is a Nancy Reeves Dreux Professor of Political Science at the University of Notre Dame and editor in chief of the *Review of Politics*. Her previous writings include *Natural Right and the American Imagination: Political Philosophy in Novel Form* and *Postmodern Platos: Nietzsche, Heidegger, Gadamer, Strauss, Derrida*.